"Father Timothy M. Gallagher, O.M.V.'s highly useful and pellucidly written book—buttressed in an unobtrusive way with the best of Ignatian scholarship and years of pastoral experience—underscores why he is America's foremost interpreter and writer on Ignatian discernment and spiritual direction."

—**Harvey D. Egan, S.J.**
Emeritus Professor of Systematic and Mystical Theology,
Boston College

"Fr. Gallagher's writings and teaching on St. Ignatius' Rules for Discernment of Spirits over many years have strengthened the spiritual life of thousands, including my own. In his most recent book, *Setting Captives Free,* he enters even more deeply into these rules explaining them practically and with unparalleled spiritual insight. Here the refined wisdom of more than 30 years of experience as a teacher and spiritual director, the humble example of his personal attempts to live these rules, and his beautifully readable style, combine to produce another spiritual masterpiece. Even those who have not read his first seminal study on this topic will benefit from the spiritual wisdom contained here finding a sure path to deeper freedom in the love and service of God."

—In Christ,
The Most Reverend Andrew H. Cozzens, S.T.D.
Auxiliary Bishop, Archdiocese of St. Paul and Minneapolis

"*Setting Captives Free* is an apt name for this new reflection on Ignatius' Rules for Discernment by Fr. Timothy Gallagher. The freedom and insight that comes from delving ever more deeply into the wisdom of these rules liberates us for a more authentic relationship with God. The stories and examples that Fr. Tim shares, some very personal, put flesh around his careful teaching. We see through the light of his examples real experiences of spiritual seekers reflected in all their beauty and rejoice at the goodness of a God who wants this kind of freedom for us all.

—**Cathie Macaulay**, spiritual director, wife and mother, faculty of the Ignatian Centre, Montreal

"In this age when God invites Christian people—priests, religious, and lay—to maturity in the spiritual life, the rules for discernment of Saint Ignatius of Loyola are a treasure. Father Timothy Gallagher is the most thorough writer in English today on Ignatian discernment, and like his earlier works, *Setting Captives Free* offers discerning people an opportunity for a deepening of their practice. I think of Father Gallagher as a mystagogue in the classical sense of one who leads us deeper into the mystery of God, through reflection on the ways that God has been already active in our lives. I am thankful for his latest book."

—**Tim Muldoon**, author of *The Ignatian Workout* and *The Discerning Parent*

"Many have been led to a liberating encounter with the Rules for the Discernment of Spirits of St. Ignatius through the masterful writing and teaching of Father Timothy Gallagher. Now, Father Gallagher offers to the reader powerful insights gained through the years of his continued writing and teaching, illustrated with vivid examples from a wide variety of sources. I am confident that this new work will bring even greater freedom to all those desiring a deeper relationship with the God who desires to set us free."

—**Rev. Richard J. Gabuzda**, Executive Director,
The Institute for Priestly Formation

"Retreat directors often give St Ignatius's rules for the discernment of spirits to their retreatants. But consolations and desolations don't just come upon us during times of retreat! These rules are incredibly useful for making sense of daily life and for figuring out what we need to do—and to avoid doing! This book offers us the characteristic wit and wisdom of Father Timothy Gallagher."

—**Father Joseph Koterski, S.J.**, Fordham University

"Just when it seems everything has been said about discernment of spirits, Fr. Gallagher offers fresh new insights based on his extensive personal experience of teaching, spiritual direction, and applying Ignatius's rules in his own life. His book is the perfect resource for the prayerful discerner who desires to more deeply explore the nuances of St. Ignatius' rules."

—**Gregory Cleveland, OMV**, author of *Awakening Love,
An Ignatian Retreat with the Song of Songs*

"*Setting Captives Free* is both an accurate summary of the goal of the Rules for Discernment of the first week of the *Spiritual Exercises* and of the transformative effect of applying the rules in individual lives. Fr. Timothy Gallagher returns to the subject matter of his first book and fifteen years later has produced a further text, which reveals a maturity of spiritual reflection accumulated across those years. Readers familiar with his work will recognize both his 'trademark' of giving helpful examples drawn from daily life and his pedagogical style of reiteration for clarity and confirmation. In addition, within this work there is a generous sharing of his own personal experiences, sufferings and struggles and a hint of the sacrifices involved in such writing. At one point (118) in a reference that seems to resonate with personal experience he cites Elisabeth Leseur 'suffering is the great law of the spiritual world. We shall only know later the work accomplished by our suffering and our sacrifices. It all goes to the heart of God and there, joined to the redemptive treasure, it expands in souls in the form of grace'. It is to such grace that he directs the attention of his readers confidently encouraging them by means of the rules for discernment along the path to the heart of God."

—**Sr Gill K Goulding CJ STL PhD,** Professor of Systematic
Theology, Director of Advanced Ecclesiastical Degrees
Regis College

Setting
Captives
Free

Personal Reflections on
Ignatian Discernment of Spirits

TIMOTHY M. GALLAGHER, OMV

A Crossroad Book
The Crossroad Publishing Company
New York

The Crossroad Publishing Company www.CrossroadPublishing.com

In continuation of our 200-year tradition of independent publishing, The Crossroad Publishing Company proudly offers a variety of books with strong, original voices and diverse perspectives. The viewpoints expressed in our books are not necessarily those of The Crossroad Publishing Company, any of its imprints or of its employees, executives, owners. Although the author and publisher have made every effort to ensure that the information in this book was correct at press time, the author and publisher do not assume and hereby disclaim any liability to any party for any loss, damage, or disruption caused by errors or omissions, whether such errors or omissions result from negligence, accident, or any other cause. No claims are made or responsibility assumed for any health or other benefits.

Book design by Tim Holtz
Cover Design by George Forster

Library of Congress Cataloging-in-Publication Data
Names: Gallagher, Timothy M., author.
Title: Setting captives free : personal reflections on Ignatian discernment
  of spirits / Timothy M. Gallagher, OMV.
Description: New York : Crossroad Publishing Company, 2018.
Subjects: LCSH: Spiritual life—Catholic Church. | Ignatius, of Loyola,
  Saint, 1491–1556.
Classification: LCC BX2350.3 (ebook) | LCC BX2350.3 .G35 2018 (print) | DDC
  248.4/82--dc23
LC record available at https://lccn.loc.gov/2018007849

ISBN 978-0-8245-9907-2

Books published by The Crossroad Publishing Company may be purchased at special quantity discount rates for classes and institutional use. For information, please email sales@CrossroadPublishing.com.

Contents

Acknowledgments

I am deeply grateful to the many who have helped me in writing this book, in particular: to those who read and offered comments on the manuscript, Paul Empsall, James Gallagher, Elizabeth Koessler, Cathie Macaulay, and Richard McKinney; to Claire-Marie Hart, for her generosity in reading and editing the manuscript; to Carol McGinness, once again, for her invaluable aid with the practicalities of publication; to Sister Bernadette Reis, FSP, for her helpful counsel with technical issues regarding publication; to Roy M. Carlisle, whose encouragement and contributions as editor greatly benefitted this book; to Jean Blomquist, whose careful copyediting prepared the manuscript for printing; and to Gwendolin Herder, president, Christy Korrow, and all at Crossroad Publishing, who supported this book from its beginning to its publication, one more sign of a long-standing and fruitful relationship.

Finally, I thank the following for permission to reprint copyrighted material:

Excerpts from the *New American Bible, Revised Edition* © 2010, 1991, 1986, 1970 Confraternity of Christian Doctrine, Washington, D.C. and are used by permission of the copyright owner. All Rights Reserved. No part of the New American Bible may be reproduced in any form without permission in writing from the copyright owner.

Excerpts from the Catholic Edition of the Revised Standard Version of the Bible, copyright 1965, 1966 by the Division of Christian Education of the National Council of the Churches of Christ in the United States of America. Used by permission. All rights reserved.

Excerpts from *The Liturgy of the Hours,* © 1975, 1976 Catholic Book Publishing Co. Used by permission. All rights reserved.

Excerpts from *A Commentary on Saint Ignatius' Rules for the Discernment of Spirits: A Guide to the Principles and Practice* by Jules Toner, SJ. Used with permission. © 1982 The Institute of Jesuit Sources, Boston College, Chestnut Hill, MA. All rights reserved.

Excerpts from *The Spiritual Writings of Pierre Favre,* Edmond Murphy, SJ and John Padberg, SJ, eds. Used with permission. © 1996 The Institute of Jesuit Sources, Boston College, Chestnut Hill, MA. All rights reserved.

Excerpts from *101 Inspirational Stories of the Priesthood* by Patricia Proctor, OSC. Used with permission. © 2005 Franciscan Monastery of St. Clare. All rights reserved.

Introduction

Thirteen years ago, I wrote a book on Ignatian discernment of spirits, *The Discernment of Spirits: An Ignatian Guide to Everyday Living*.[1] In that book, I discussed Ignatius of Loyola's fourteen rules for discernment as applied to the everyday experience of Christians. These rules are practical guidelines for spiritual living. They instruct, and they supply tools for daily spiritual life.

Since writing that book, I have taught these rules repeatedly, year after year, in different settings with different groups. Each time I teach them, I study the material thoroughly. I review the entire presentation, reread Ignatius's text in the original, reflect on it, and explore how it applies to the specific group before me—laymen and women, priests, deacons, seminarians, or religious. Often, as I do this, new insights arise. I see new applications of the rules and new examples of them.

The same occurs when teaching the rules. As I teach them, I learn more about them. I learn also through questions raised by participants that open new channels of reflection. Sometimes months or years pass before I see the answers clearly. The privilege of accompanying others in spiritual direction and retreats, and witnessing the efficacy of the rules in these persons' experience, helps me comprehend the rules further. Conversations with persons who share their experiences of the rules widens my understanding as well. I also learn more about the rules from my own efforts to apply them in my own ordinary, daily spiritual living.

When new insights occur—as I study, teach, and interact with others as well as when I apply the rules in my own life—I note these insights on small sheets of paper that I keep on hand for this purpose. At this point, thirteen years after writing the first book, I have hundreds of these small sheets of paper.

In my earlier book, I offered a systematic presentation of the rules. Each rule was the subject of a chapter that explored, phrase by phrase, Ignatius's text. The application of the rule was clarified through relevant examples. That book sought to provide the reader with a structured and comprehensive grasp of each rule.

In this book, as in the last, I discuss all fourteen rules. This book, however, does not repeat the former systematic treatment. My purpose here is to share the further insights gained since writing the former book. In discussing each rule, I will first offer a summary of the structured treatment found in the earlier book. Thus, this new book may be read independently of the earlier. For a full, all-encompassing discussion of each rule, however, I refer the reader to the earlier book.

I view this new book as a conversation with the reader that explores additional understandings and applications of the rules.[2] It has arisen from the delight—and the labor—of learning, deepening, experiencing, and sharing the rules, witnessing the joy and new hope they have given to so many, and knowing, too, the difference they make in my own life. These Ignatian guidelines *set captives free*, free from the discouragement and sadness of spiritual desolation. They offer hope precisely where persons may have felt hope was not possible, and so release new energy for the spiritual journey.

This book, like the former, explores Ignatius's rules for discernment as applied to the ordinary, daily experience of those who love the Lord. As always, the focus is living the spiritual life—these rules are given in a book of spiritual *exercises*: they are concerned with what is to be done and how to respond to various spiritual situations. Though at times the rules will require careful thought and clear distinctions, the goal will always be their concrete application in daily life.

The years since writing the earlier book have only confirmed my conviction that the rules are most effectively presented through close attention to Ignatius's words and their illustration through real-life examples. I employ that method once again in this book, this time exploring further aspects of the text and supplying abundant new examples.

In this book, as in the last, I include quotations and examples from authors whom I find helpful in understanding the rules. This book, however, is more personal than the last. In it I share my own thoughts regarding the rules and my own experience of them. I will cite this experience as I have noted it in my journals.

I share it precisely because my experience of the rules is *ordinary*. My circumstances—religious and priest, engaged in specific ministries—are individual, as are my story and personality. But my experience of the rules is, I believe, like that of any person, in any circumstances—layman or woman, single or married, active in business or at home or in the Church, religious woman, deacon, or priest—who seeks to live the Christian life. I share it because I find that such examples aptly illustrate how the rules apply to common, everyday spiritual experience, and the difference the rules can make in such daily experience. Servant of God Dorothy Day affirmed that "you write about yourself because in the long run all man's problems are the same."[3]

I will describe experiences both of spiritual consolation and spiritual desolation. If the greater number of examples describes spiritual desolation, this does not mean that desolation has dominated in my life! I share such experiences because in these rules, Ignatius focuses above all on what is, for most of us, the major obstacle in the spiritual life: the discouragement of spiritual desolation. To illustrate Ignatius's counsels, therefore, the greater part of the examples must deal with spiritual desolation and the liberation from it that his rules supply.

In these journal entries I have occasionally changed external details to preserve an appropriate privacy. The entries are given according to the sequence of the rules—illustrations of each successive rule as I discuss it in its own chapter—rather than in chronological order. Since the journals cover thirty years, some entries reflect a younger and others a more mature experience. Within each chapter I have generally arranged the entries in chronological order.

My translation of Ignatius's text conserves as much as possible the wording and "flavor" of the original. Thus I have not removed redundancies in the rules—for example, "First Rule. The first rule: In persons . . ." I have also maintained Ignatius's use of "persons" (rules 1 and 2: "in persons who") and conformed my commentary to his vocabulary.[4] The same is true as regards the masculine pronouns in any text I cite. I reproduce this usage for the same purpose: to allow the reader direct access to the original. Obviously, however, I understand these texts to apply to all.

Readers will also note the extensive use of italics in this book. At times, I employ them in the ordinary way for emphasis; more often I adopt them as a pedagogical device—to highlight the particular element I wish the reader to see. I have used this approach in all my Ignatian writing and find that it assists clarity in discussing discernment.

When *Spiritual Exercises* is given in italics, the title indicates Ignatius's written work (as does the italicized abbreviation *SpirEx*). When Spiritual Exercises is given in roman type, the title indicates the lived experience of the Ignatian retreat.

In my own life, these fourteen rules have become a treasure. They set me free to accept God's loving grace in time of spiritual consolation, and they supply indispensable wisdom in the struggle of spiritual desolation. In their light, I know what to do and what not to do in such times. I have been blessed, in these years, to receive similar sharings from many others who find in these rules a like freedom.

The title of this book, *Setting Captives Free*, expresses its basic message. Jesus did not come that we might be captive to spiritual desolation and its attendant discouragement; he came to *set captives free* (Lk 4:18), free *from* deception, and free *to* love and serve the God whom Jesus revealed to us as Love. Ignatius's fourteen rules provide practical guidelines that foster such freedom in daily living. Their wisdom gives light to increasing numbers today. May this fresh exploration of these rules offer new hope on our spiritual journey.

Text of the Rules

Rules for becoming aware and understanding to some extent the different movements which are caused in the soul, the good, to receive them, and the bad to reject them. And these rules are more proper for the first week. (313)

First Rule. The first rule: In persons who are going from mortal sin to mortal sin, the enemy is ordinarily accustomed to propose apparent pleasures to them, leading them to imagine sensual delights and pleasures in order to hold them more and make them grow in their vices and sins. In these persons the good spirit uses a contrary method, stinging and biting their consciences through their rational power of moral judgment. (314)

Second Rule. The second: In persons who are going on intensely purifying their sins and rising from good to better in the service of God our Lord, the method is contrary to that in the first rule. For then it is proper to the evil spirit to bite, sadden, and place obstacles, disquieting with false reasons, so that the person may not go forward. And it is proper to the good spirit to give courage and strength, consolations, tears, inspirations and quiet, easing and taking away all obstacles, so that the person may go forward in doing good. (315)

Third Rule. The third is of spiritual consolation. I call it consolation when some interior movement is caused in the soul, through which the soul comes to be inflamed with love of its Creator and Lord, and, consequently when it can love no created thing on the face of the earth in itself, but only in the Creator of them all. Likewise when it sheds tears that move to love of its Lord, whether out of sorrow for one's sins, or for the passion of Christ our Lord, or because of other things directly ordered to his service and praise. Finally, I call consolation every increase of hope, faith, and charity, and all interior joy that calls and attracts to heavenly things and to the salvation of one's soul, quieting it and giving it peace in its Creator and Lord. (316)

Fourth Rule. The fourth is of spiritual desolation. I call desolation all the contrary of the third rule, such as darkness of soul, disturbance in it, movement to low and earthly things, disquiet from various agitations and temptations, moving to lack of confidence, without hope, without love, finding oneself totally slothful, tepid, sad and, as if separated from one's Creator and Lord. For just as consolation is contrary to desolation, in the same way the thoughts that come from consolation are contrary to the thoughts that come from desolation. (317)

Fifth Rule. The fifth: In time of desolation never make a change, but be firm and constant in the proposals and determination in which one was the day preceding such desolation, or in the determination in which one was in the preceding consolation. Because, as in consolation the good spirit guides and counsels us more, so in desolation the bad spirit, with whose counsels we cannot find the way to a right decision. (318)

Sixth Rule. The sixth: Although in desolation we should not change our first proposals, it is very advantageous to change

ourselves intensely against the desolation itself, as by insisting more upon prayer, meditation, upon much examination,
and upon extending ourselves in some suitable way of doing
penance. (319)

Seventh Rule. The seventh: Let one who is in desolation consider how the Lord has left him in trial in his natural powers,
so that he may resist the various agitations and temptations
of the enemy; since he can resist with the divine help, which
always remains with him, though he does not clearly feel it;
for the Lord has taken away from him his great fervor, abundant love and intense grace, leaving him, however, sufficient
grace for eternal salvation. (320)

Eighth Rule. The eighth: Let one who is in desolation work
to be in patience, which is contrary to the vexations which
come to him, and let him think that he will soon be consoled,
diligently using the means against such desolation, as is said
in the sixth rule. (321)

Ninth Rule. The ninth: There are three principal causes for
which we find ourselves desolate. The first is because we are
tepid, slothful or negligent in our spiritual exercises, and so
through our faults spiritual consolation withdraws from us.
The second, to try us and see how much we are and how
much we extend ourselves in his service and praise without
so much payment of consolations and increased graces. The
third, to give us true recognition and understanding so that
we may interiorly feel that it is not ours to attain or maintain
increased devotion, intense love, tears or any other spiritual
consolation, but that all is the gift and grace of God our Lord,
and so that we may not build a nest in something belonging to another, raising our mind in some pride or vainglory,

attributing to ourselves the devotion or the other parts of the spiritual consolation. (322)

Tenth Rule. The tenth: Let the one who is in consolation think how he will conduct himself in the desolation which will come after, taking new strength for that time. (323)

Eleventh Rule. The eleventh: Let one who is consoled seek to humble himself and lower himself as much as he can, thinking of how little he is capable in the time of desolation without such grace or consolation. On the contrary, let one who is in desolation think that he can do much with God's sufficient grace to resist all his enemies, taking strength in his Creator and Lord. (324)

Twelfth Rule. The twelfth: The enemy acts like a woman in being weak when faced with strength and strong when faced with weakness. For, as it is proper to a woman, when she is fighting with some man, to lose heart and to flee when the man confronts her firmly, and, on the contrary, if the man begins to flee, losing heart, the anger, vengeance and ferocity of the woman grow greatly and know no bounds, in the same way, it is proper to the enemy to weaken and lose heart, fleeing and ceasing his temptations when the person who is exercising himself in spiritual things confronts the temptations of the enemy firmly, doing what is diametrically opposed to them; and, on the contrary, if the person who is exercising himself begins to be afraid and lose heart in suffering the temptations, there is no beast so fierce on the face of the earth as the enemy of human nature in following out his damnable intention with such growing malice. (325)

Thirteenth Rule. The thirteenth: Likewise he conducts himself as a false lover in wishing to remain secret and not be revealed. For a dissolute man who, speaking with evil intention, makes dishonorable advances to a daughter of a good father or a wife of a good husband, wishes his words and persuasions to be secret, and the contrary displeases him very much, when the daughter reveals to her father or the wife to her husband his false words and depraved intention, because he easily perceives that he will not be able to succeed with the undertaking begun. In the same way, when the enemy of human nature brings his wiles and persuasions to the just soul, he wishes and desires that they be received and kept in secret; but when one reveals them to one's good confessor or to another spiritual person, who knows his deceits and malicious designs, it weighs on him very much, because he perceives that he will not be able to succeed with the malicious undertaking he has begun, since his manifest deceits have been revealed. (326)

Fourteenth Rule. The fourteenth: Likewise he conducts himself as a leader, intent upon conquering and robbing what he desires. For, just as a captain and leader of an army in the field, pitching his camp and exploring the fortifications and defenses of a stronghold, attacks it at the weakest point, in the same way the enemy of human nature, roving about, looks in turn at all our theological, cardinal and moral virtues; and where he finds us weakest and most in need for our eternal salvation, there he attacks us and attempts to take us. (327)

Prologue

Be Aware, Understand, Take Action

*Return to your heart! . . . Christ dwells
in the inner self; in the inner self you
will be renewed in the image of God.*
—St. Augustine

For whom is this teaching on discernment? That Jesuits and others explicitly associated with Ignatian spirituality feel interest in Ignatian discernment is evident. At times, however, I present the rules to several hundred people, and there is no Jesuit in the room. A question then arises: Why are so many people—many of them laypeople engaged in the world—desirous of learning Ignatian discernment? None of them—including the presenter!—are Jesuits. Is this a teaching essentially for Jesuits and those who adopt Ignatian spirituality? Or does it apply more broadly in the Church?

On the practical level, the question is answered by the wide and growing interest in Ignatian discernment among people of all vocations: lay, religious, and clergy. This interest is real, and it is deep. I have witnessed it now for many years. In fact, it was through the eyes of such persons that I first understood the power of Ignatian discernment. Their perception of how greatly Ignatius's rules helped them in daily life revealed to me, more than any study, the treasure these rules contain.

A historical pattern of the Spirit's working in the Church underlies this interest. St. Francis of Assisi, for example, with his love of evangelical poverty and simplicity of life, assists not only his Franciscans but also all in the Church who seek the poverty in spirit that gives entrance to the Kingdom (Mt 5:3). Likewise, the teachings of SS. John of the Cross and Teresa of Avila on the higher states of prayer guide not only Carmelites but also all in the Church who seek to understand mystical prayer. Again, St. Benedict's love for the liturgy blesses not only his Benedictines but also, through them, strengthens the liturgical life of the entire Church. In the same way, St. Ignatius of Loyola's teaching on discernment offers wisdom not only for Jesuits but also for all in the Church who seek to discern.

None of these spiritual paths is exclusive. One may seek poverty in spirit without reference to Francis, deeper contemplation without John and Teresa, more nourishing liturgy without Benedict, or discernment without Ignatius. In each case, however, these figures stand in a special way as resources for the entire Church. They do so because so many over the centuries have found them helpful in their respective spiritual competencies. The clarity, practicality, and usability of Ignatius's teaching on discernment is a gift offered to all who love Christ.

Background to a Conversion

Ignatius's awareness of discernment began the day of his conversion. The chronicler of Ignatius's early life draws a discreet veil over the waywardness of those years: "Until the age of twenty-six, he was a man given to the vanities of the world."[1] Ignatius never doubted his Christian faith, but like his father and all his brothers, he cared more for feats of arms, romantic exploits, deeds of chivalry, and glory and renown in the world. In the years before his conversion, he was something of a young Augustine.

Some anecdotes will illustrate the point. When Ignatius was twenty-four, he returned to his native town of Azpeitia in northwestern Spain. One night, together with one of his brothers, he committed what the court records describe as "premeditated and enormous . . . crimes."[2] When these were discovered, Ignatius fled Azpeitia "in a great hurry," only to be arrested and imprisoned in Pamplona.[3]

We possess documents chronicling how, for three years, Ignatius requested permission to carry a sword in public and to be accompanied by two attendants. He explained that a man was utterly determined to take his life; in fact, this man took concrete steps toward that goal, on one occasion wounding Ignatius. We do not know what Ignatius did to so anger this man, but knowing the way he was living in these years, it is not difficult at least to guess.[4]

Finally, when Ignatius was in Pamplona, a group of young men one day approached him on the street. They pushed Ignatius against a wall; he unsheathed his sword and ran after them down the street. A witness recounts, "If someone had not stopped him, he would have killed one of them, or one of them would have killed him."[5] This was Ignatius until the age of thirty: "a man given to the vanities of the world."

Then the French sent an overwhelming army south of the border to take Pamplona. The city, recognizing the impossibility of defense, surrendered—all but the castle. And the castle did not surrender because Ignatius was there, Ignatius who considered that simple surrender in any circumstances was unworthy of an honorable soldier. His energy inspired what all knew would be an unsuccessful defense.

When the French learned that the castle would not surrender, they brought their cannons to bear and began a bombardment of its walls. In the bombardment, a cannon ball
passed between Ignatius's legs, damaging the left and completely shattering the right. With his fall, the defenders immediately surrendered.

Ignatius tells us that the French treated this thirty-year-
old Spaniard with respect, and themselves carried him on
a stretcher for a journey of several days back to his native
town of Azpeitia.[6] Once there, the doctors examined Ignatius's leg. They found that the bones—whether because the
leg was set badly on the battlefield or because the bones
were jostled out of place during the journey home—did not
lie properly, and that the leg would not heal unless it were
rebroken and reset. The doctors performed this "butchery,"
as Ignatius describes it—there was no anesthesia in those
days—adding that he underwent it "without saying a word,
nor showing any other sign of pain other than the tight
clenching of his fists."[7]

After the surgery, Ignatius reached the point of death
. . . and then began to recover. When he was well enough
to examine his legs, he found that beneath the knee on the
right leg, one bone lay on top of another, creating an ugly
protrusion. His biographer, Pedro de Ribadeneira, SJ, who
knew Ignatius in later years, tells us that the protuberance
would have prevented Ignatius from wearing the "smart and
close-fitting boots" that he liked to wear. Ribadeneira adds
that Ignatius would not tolerate this since "he was a lively
and trim young man who liked court dress and good living."[8]
When I view portraits of refined male dress in Ignatius's
time—paintings, for example, of Charles V, king of Spain at
this time—with their tight stocking-like clothing up to above

the knee, I wonder, too, if this may have moved Ignatius to detest the protruding bone.

Ignatius, so conscious of his appearance, refused to go through life this way and insisted that the doctors cut away the offending bone. They hesitated to do it because the leg had now healed and the surgery would not be quick. But Ignatius—never easy to resist—prevailed and underwent this third surgery, again with only the tight clenching of his fists.

At times, as I read this account, I reflect on the ways of God's providence. The doctors must have performed the earlier surgery very poorly if one bone remained so visibly upon another. Their professional failure, a humanly unfortunate occurrence—today we would have a lawsuit!—opened a space in which God could intervene in Ignatius's life. Had the surgery been successful, in all likelihood the conversion story would end here: Ignatius, as he so desired, would simply have returned to his earlier life, the life his father and all his brothers were living, and Ignatian spirituality might never have been.

After this third surgery, the doctors applied ointments and instruments to try to stretch the leg. In fact, Ignatius would limp a little for the rest of his life. Eventually, a time came when he was healthy in every way except that he could not use his leg. To pass the time, Ignatius asked for reading. He desired the novels of knights and romance he was accustomed to reading—the writing parodied, for example, in *Don Quixote*. But his sister-in-law, the lady of the house, gave him the only two books she had: a life of Christ and a volume with lives of the saints. Somewhat unwillingly, but to pass the time, Ignatius began to read.[9] The stage was now set for the moment that would change his life.

Delight and Discontent

As he lay on his convalescent bed, Ignatius spent hours, day after day, thinking of how he would win the heart of a woman whom he does not name. She was of high rank, "not of the lower nobility, nor a countess nor a duchess, but of higher station than any of these."[10] The scholars have pondered the identity of this woman; in regard to this, Ignatius "maintained an absolute reserve."[11]

One real possibility is that this was Catherine, the younger sister of King Charles V of Spain.[12] Ignatius may have seen her on a few occasions when he was a page in the household of the royal treasurer. A note of unreality, however, accompanied these hours of pondering what Ignatius called "the worldly deeds he desired to achieve"[13]: in the aristocratically stratified culture of his day, Ignatius, who was indeed a member of nobility, but of very minor and local nobility, would never have social access to a woman who belonged to the highest ranks of society, most likely royalty.

If, in fact, this was Catherine, a lovely historical postscript followed. Thirty-two years later, Catherine, now queen of Portugal, made the Ignatian Spiritual Exercises.[14] Her director, Jesuit Father Diego Miró, wrote to Ignatius in Rome, telling him of how he planned to guide her Exercises.[15] I have often wondered what it must have meant for Ignatius to receive that letter and realize that, by following God's plan for his life, he served his lady in a way he could never have guessed so many years before.

But grace was also at work. As Ignatius read the lives of the saints, questions arose in his heart: "What if I should do what St. Francis did? What if I should do what St. Dominic did?"[16] Striking questions! For the first time, most likely, in his life, Ignatius discovered another kind of heroism, and his first thought was this: *If these saints did such heroic things for God, why should I do less?* Ignatius continues, "His whole thought was to say to himself, 'Saint Dominic did this, therefore I have to do it. Saint Francis did this, therefore I have to do it.'"[17]

Such literal imitation of the saints betrays an as-yet rudimentary level of spiritual formation. What emerges clearly, however, is the immediate thought of heroic service of God. In that space of generosity, God's grace could work. When I share this with people, at times I feel a silence come over the hall: Yes, in our respective vocations, why should we be less heroic?

Eventually, the *discontent* that consistently followed the delight of pondering these "worldly deeds"—that is, the pursuit of the unattainable woman—and the *happiness* that consistently followed the delight of pondering these "deeds of God"—that is, life in imitation of the saints—led Ignatius to realize that the first was not God's plan for his life and the second was. As he states so simply, "One time his eyes were opened a little,"[18] and he perceived these patterns in his heart relative to two diverse projects of life. Once Ignatius understood this, he abandoned the worldly project and energetically pursued the project of holiness. The results we know.

Strikingly, Ignatius's conversion occurred precisely *in the context of discernment*: attention to the movements of his heart relative to different sets of thoughts. Through awareness of this interior experience, understanding what was and what was not of God in it, and actively embracing what was of God and rejecting what was not, Ignatius's life was changed. From the very beginning, discernment of spirits characterized his spiritual journey. Ignatius would later codify these three steps in the title statement to his rules: "Rules for *becoming aware* and *understanding* . . . the different movements caused in the soul, the *good* to *receive* them, and the *bad* to *reject* them" (*SpirEx* 313).[19]

When I share Ignatius's conversion experience, at this point I ask the group, "What if, that day, Ignatius's eyes had not been 'opened a little'? What if he had never become aware of, understood, and taken action in response to this interior spiritual experience? What would have been different in his life?" "Most probably," I answer, "he would have continued to live as before, as his father and his brothers were living. What would have been different," I further ask, "in the life of his university companion, the future St. Francis Xavier, and the Church in Asia? In the life of another university companion, the future St. Pierre Favre? In the life of Jesuit St. Edmund Campion and the Church in England? In the life of Jesuit St. Peter Claver and the Church in Latin America? In the lives of countless laypeople, priests, and religious who have benefited from Ignatian spirituality through the centuries?" These questions immediately reveal the immense fruitfulness of living with such spiritual awareness, understanding, and action.

I then add that among the many things that would have been different, our group would not be gathered at this moment to learn Ignatian discernment. Had Ignatius's eyes not been opened to discernment that day, I know, too, that my own life would be radically different. The ripples of grace that have gone out into the Church and the world because one man's eyes were "opened a little" to become aware of, understand, and take action in response to the spiritual movements in his heart relative to different sets of thoughts, continue to expand and bless the Church and the world.

I ask a second question as well: "What will be different in our lives if we can begin to live with our spiritual eyes 'opened a little,' enough to notice the spiritual experience in our hearts and thoughts, to work with it until we understand what in it is of God and what is not, and to take action accordingly, faithfully accepting what is of God and firmly rejecting what is not?" I answer, "The same two things that happened in Ignatius's life will happen also in ours: a grace-filled step of personal transformation toward God, and, like Ignatius in his time, we will become agents of renewal in the Church—or as the Church says today, of a new evangelization. Living the discerning life matters."

Ignatius was the first captive set free by the discernment he would later formulate in the rules we will explore.[20] These rules have guided many to that same freedom.

"To Some Extent"

In his title statement to the rules, Ignatius writes that these are "rules for becoming aware and understanding *to some extent* the different movements that are caused in the soul" (*SpirEx* 313). From the outset, Ignatius advises us that his rules will not say all that might be said about discernment of spirits.

We find something similar in the final words of this title statement: "These rules are *more proper* for the first week." Ignatius informs us of the setting in which these rules are most likely to operate: the "first week" of the Spiritual Exercises, that is, the stage of the spiritual journey in which we seek growing freedom from sinfulness and greater readiness to love and serve God—the stage in which many of us are likely to find ourselves.[21] These fourteen rules, then, pertain *more* properly to the spiritual experience typical of this spiritual situation. Having said this, Ignatius does not address further questions that might arise: If these rules apply more properly but not exclusively to this "first week" experience, might they also apply outside this experience? If so, to what experience? And how would they assist in that experience? Ignatius gives no answers.

Again, in the fifth rule Ignatius affirms that "in consolation the good spirit guides and counsels us *more.*" More than what? Ignatius does not specify.[22] In the ninth rule, he tells us that "there are three principal causes for which we find ourselves desolate," and describes these three. If these are the principal causes, obviously there may be others, less significant but also real. Which might these be? Once more, Ignatius feels no need to address the question.

Behind such limits lies an important pedagogical principle. In these rules, Ignatius does not attempt to say all that could be said about discernment of spirits. The rules help us become aware of and understand *to some extent* the different movements experienced in our hearts and thoughts.[23] Precisely because they illuminate this experience without attempting to explore it exhaustively, they are usable in practice—and that is Ignatius's goal in writing them.

We may have had the experience of needing help with a computer function. We approach a person skilled in computers and present our question. The expert answers the question, and we understand how to perform the function. But if the expert continues to explain and overwhelms us with information on variations of the function or problems we may face at some point, very likely our initial clarity will weaken, submerged in a wealth of related information. All that the expert says is true, and it answers real questions.

Explained in other settings when such questions have arisen, it will benefit the hearer. Said, however, to this person, at this time, with this need, it confuses rather than helps.

I think of these fourteen rules as a lighted path through a dark forest. There is light only for the path itself; it does not light up the depths of the forest. Travelers on the path, as they walk, encounter many side paths leading into the wide spaces of the forest. Exploration of these side paths would be of interest and could lead to a fuller understanding of the forest. But it would also take the travelers off the path. In that case, the travelers would arrive only later or not at all, should they lose their way. Yet the goal of the path is to arrive. Ignatius stays firmly on the path, and that is why his rules are clear and usable.

I have learned, over the years, to follow Ignatius's pedagogical choices in presenting the rules: to explain his text without exploring further issues that he feels no need to explore. When I do so, the rules become clear and applicable for the hearers. I have never forgotten a man who, when I explained this approach, exclaimed, "Why, that's usable!" He was right. Such precisely was Ignatius's intention in writing these rules.

"His Eyes Were Opened"

Discernment began for Ignatius when he first noticed his interior spiritual experience. The first step in discernment is to *be aware*: "Rules for *becoming aware* and understanding to some extent the different movements that are caused in the soul."

When I present this first step to groups, we always explore this question: Why is it so hard for us to stop, to be, as

Augustine says, "within,"[24] and notice what is happening in our hearts and thoughts? I long wondered about this, sensing this reluctance in myself, in others, and in the culture around us. Obviously, this question matters because the subsequent steps in discernment—understanding and action—will never occur unless we first *become aware* of this interior spiritual experience.

This reluctance in the human heart needs to be recognized, and, I would say, even reverenced. There is a reason for it. Nonetheless, the heart that desires the discerning life cannot surrender to this reluctance, but must be warmly invited to an awareness that can lift sometimes long-standing burdens.

First, however, this reluctance to be "within" and aware of interior experience must be recognized. Of it, John Henry Newman writes, "We are busy in the world, and what leisure time we have we readily devote to a less severe and wearisome employment."[25] With greater vigor, Simone Weil affirms that "something in our soul has a far more violent repugnance for true attention than the flesh has for bodily fatigue," and concludes that "a quarter of an hour of attention is better than a great many good works."[26] Thomas Merton speaks of such awareness as an "interior asceticism" through which we review the stirrings of our hearts and their related thoughts: Where are they from? Where are they going? Toward God? Away from God? Merton describes this attention as a discipline, an asceticism of our thoughts.[27]

Once, when I discussed this with university students, a young woman said, "I had thoughts, but I never thought about my thoughts." It was a great summary, a moment of insight. A door had opened for her; if she would pass through it, a new life of discernment awaited.

Why are we reluctant to be "within" and aware of our spiritual experience? Why does this awareness require courage? Many answers, all of them valid, may be given:

- the need for instruction to help us understand the spiritual experience of our hearts and thoughts

- a culture that marginalizes faith and so doubts the existence of spiritual experience

- the accessibility of exterior things that we can see and hear and touch, and the greater effort needed to grasp interior experience

- the difficulty in disciplining our attention to focus "within"— an increasing issue in the digital age

- the multiplicity and rapid shifts of our emotions and thoughts

- human sinfulness that burdens such awareness

- the deceptions of the enemy who, obviously, does not wish our eyes to be "opened a little" with the wonderful growth this offers

- something within us that both desires and resists intimacy

- the fear of entering a realm that we cannot control

- the pressure of a society that imposes busyness, rendering interior awareness yet more elusive[28]

Who of us does not experience some, if not many, of these factors?

This is an impressive array of answers! All are valid, and all contribute to resistance to spiritual awareness. I believe, however, that underlying them all and adding to their weight is another factor, best described by the seventeenth-century

philosopher Blaise Pascal in his discussion of *diversion*—
that is, the flight from our own limitations. These limitations are real: to be "within" is to be aware of our mortality,
our moral inadequacies, our spiritual shortcomings, and
any unhealed emotional pain. Any one of these may be difficult to face; taken together, courage may be required if we
are to be "within" and aware. Because it is difficult to face
such limitations, we find it easier, Pascal says, though ulti-
mately unsatisfying, to *divert* our awareness "without"—to
keep sufficiently occupied that we need not be aware of these
limitations.[29]

In a famous passage, Pascal writes, "Sometimes when I set
myself to consider the various agitations of men, and the dan-
gers and pains to which they expose themselves at Court, or
in wars that give rise to so many quarrels, passions, bold and
often wicked enterprises, and the like, I have often said that
all of man's unhappiness arises from one thing, that . . . "[30]
When I share this quote with groups, I pause before completing Pascal's sentence, and say, "You and I have just finished
reading, listening to, or watching the daily news. In our hearts
is a vague sense of trouble at all the wars, the fighting, and
the sad and violent events to which we have been exposed. If
we were asked to name the single, deepest cause of all these
troubles, how might we answer?" After a moment for reflection, I complete the quotation with Pascal's answer: "I have
often said that all of man's unhappiness arises from one thing,
that he *does not know how to stay quietly in his room.*"[31] A
powerful answer, and one that merits consideration for our
lives in general and for the spiritual life specifically. We do
not know how to stay quietly in our rooms, Pascal explains,
because we are afraid of our own limitations, and so we flee
them, diverting our attention outward.

Though the roots of diversion lie in a person's heart, cultural factors may increase the tendency to diversion. When an entire culture shapes itself on this flight from what is "within," it creates a busyness that further pressures individuals to be "without." Is this not true today? Why are we so busy? Why do we so seldom have time simply to stop and be "within"? We have more time-saving devices than ever before in history: dishwashers, microwaves, vacuum cleaners, cars, computers, and the like. Why then are we so much busier than the people of preceding generations?[32]

I believe that in the First World, in the measure in which faith declines, the culture will grow busier. Faith in a loving God, a Savior, gives us the courage to be "within." It tells us that to be "within," far more than to face our limitations, is to encounter the infinite, personal, warm, and eternal love of the Savior: it is to know the light that shines in the darkness and which the darkness has not overcome (Jn 1:5). To the degree this faith is marginalized, our culture will flee—divert its focus—to its strength: efficiency and productivity. Finally, we become busy because we need to be busy, because we are afraid not to be busy. To be aware, then, we need the faith that supplies courage for such awareness.

We need also the necessary skills—the requisite contemplative capacity. When I see people sitting peacefully before a fire in the hearth; gazing at the beauty of the mountains, the sea, or the stars; absorbed in reading; quietly studying; listening to beautiful music; or attentive to the persons around them, my heart lifts. A *natural* contemplative capacity is growing, the necessary support for the spiritual capacity to be within.[33] A faithful life of prayer develops the specifically *spiritual* capacity for this awareness: time spent regularly in communion with God.[34]

"Love Casts Out Fear"

Such considerations indicate that discernment is never the first thing in the spiritual life. The spiritual life does not begin with discernment but with something that precedes it and makes it possible.

"There is no fear in love" (1 Jn 4:18).[35] If we stand before the door of a house and know that beyond the door is one who loves us, it is not hard to open the door and enter the house. When the human heart discovers that to be within is above all to encounter the love of the Redeemer, then love casts out fear, and we can be within and aware.

Evangelization, then—simply to know that there is a Redeemer who loves us, a Trinity that dwells in our hearts, a Lord who loves us infinitely—must always precede discernment. Evangelization is then followed by catechesis, the deeper penetration into the mysteries of our faith. A heart that has welcomed the Savior, opened itself to growth in faith, and that now lives that faith daily, is ready for discernment. In the thirty-five years that I have taught Ignatius's rules, I have seen clearly that the only presupposition for grasping these rules is personal faith in Christ, with some sincere effort to live that faith. Persons who live thus always understand Ignatius's rules: the rules only put words to what they have already experienced.

I see in the encounter of Mary Magdalene with the risen Jesus an image of the courage to be spiritually aware (Jn 20:11–18). After Peter and the other disciple leave the tomb, Mary remains there alone. She cannot leave this last link to the one she loves; she is also afraid of the emptiness of the tomb, the sign that her Lord has been taken from her. Mary does, therefore, what we often do when our hearts are similarly torn: she stands frozen, unable to move, and her tears express her pain.

Then this wonderful woman of God has the courage *to look into the darkness* of the tomb. She finds that it is not as empty as she feared, and a process begins that leads to that deeply personal encounter with Jesus expressed in the exchange of names. Her heart lifts, knowing that she will never be alone again, that the Lord who has conquered death will never cease to pronounce her name with love.

The courage to look within, to be aware of the spiritual experience in our hearts and thoughts, opens the door to a new and rich encounter with the Lord we love. This awareness is the gateway to the discerning life. It is to live like Mary of Nazareth, alive to God's action in her life, pondering it and keeping it in her heart (Lk 2:19, 51).

"The Good, to Receive Them"

To receive: this is our primary stance before God, the God who endlessly pours out gifts of love upon us.[36] As the years pass, I come to appreciate more deeply Ignatius's emphasis on receiving the gifts that God continually offers us. This is our primary "task" in the spiritual life: to let God love us and share with us his grace and blessings. Ignatius expresses God's delight in giving by affirming that "we will sooner tire of receiving his gifts than he of giving them."[37] A remarkable sentence and one that merits reflection!

Ignatius will dedicate most of his rules to helping us reject the enemy's desolations and temptations. He does so because this is where most of us especially need help. That need, however, can never obscure the truth that the primary call in discernment is to *receive* (*recibir*) the love and gifts that God ceaselessly offers us. When we open our hearts to God's consolations and graces, we live the most important part of the discerning life, and we grow richly toward God.

Christian Anthropology Made Practical

One reason for the power of Ignatius's rules today is, I believe, that they take Christian anthropology seriously and render it practical. Our secularized culture generally consigns the movements of the heart and their related thoughts to psychology. When a tragedy occurs in a school, for example, psychologists and counselors are called to help deal with the consequent emotional pain. Certainly their help can be of great value.

Almost invariably, however, these professionals operate from a purely natural anthropology, one that does not recognize that only Christ "fully reveals man to man himself."[38] They offer, therefore, a valuable help toward healing and growth but not all the help that could be offered. A whole dimension of the human person with the richest resources for growth remains untapped: God's presence and love, his grace operative in the human heart, and the avenues by which this grace flows to the person: prayer, Scripture, the sacraments, spiritual direction, and the like. Similarly, no light is shed on the discouraging lies of the enemy who willingly works in such emotional vulnerabilities.

Persons, consequently, are left defenseless on the spiritual level and without resources to respond to their spiritual stirrings and thoughts. This is the deepest level of their being, with the most potent resources for healing and growth. When the human person is understood in the light of Christ, writes psychiatrist Karl Stern, "the whole of anthropology as conceived by philosophers and psychologists is at once deepened in a very peculiar way. It is as if a great, but albeit two-dimensional, picture received a third dimension and came to life."[39]

Five hundred years ago, Ignatius entered the realm of the heart and crafted a set of guidelines for responding to interior experience, both joyful (spiritual consolation) and discouraging (spiritual desolation), on the spiritual level. These guidelines, when well explained, equip hearers to be *aware* of, *understand* the significance of, and *take action* in response to their spiritual experience. Said differently, they take Christian anthropology—the fact that only in Christ can the human person be understood fully—seriously, and render it operative. When one applies these guidelines, the full Christian understanding of the human person ceases to remain a theological construct and is rendered concretely applicable in daily living. For over three decades, I have seen many apply these guidelines with much fruit.

This does not deny the great help offered by sound psychology. I recognize that help with deep gratitude for its teaching and for the professionals who apply it. This does say, however, that more help is available than is generally offered. When both means of help, the psychological and the spiritual, are supplied simultaneously, marvelous growth results, each strengthening the other: the eagle flies with two wings. Ignatius's rules for discernment provide a uniquely effective tool for awareness, understanding, and appropriate response to affective and cognitive spiritual experience, and so for integral healing and growth.

Chapter 1

Sensual Delights and
a Stinging Conscience

Don't you feel Him in your heart,
weighing you down, worrying you,
never letting you be, and drawing you
on at the same time, enticing you with a
hope of tranquility and joy?
—Alessandro Manzoni, *The Betrothed*

The first two rules, like the third and fourth (spiritual consolation—spiritual desolation) and the fifth and sixth (harmful changes in desolation—helpful changes in desolation), form a pair. In them, Ignatius explains how the good spirit and the enemy work in persons in two contrasting situations: those moving decisively away from God and into serious sin (rule 1), and those moving decisively toward God in increasing freedom from sin and growing service of God (rule 2).

These rules are the following:

First Rule. The first rule: In *persons who are going from mortal sin to mortal sin*, the *enemy* is ordinarily accustomed to propose apparent pleasures to them, leading them to imagine sensual delights and pleasures in order to hold them more and make them grow in their vices and sins. In these persons the *good spirit* uses a contrary

1

method, stinging and biting their consciences through their rational power of moral judgment.

Second Rule. The second: In *persons who are going on intensely purifying their sins and rising from good to better in the service of God our Lord*, the method is contrary to that in the first rule. For then it is proper to the *evil spirit* to bite, sadden, and place obstacles, disquieting with false reasons, so that the person may not go forward. And it is proper to the *good spirit* to give courage and strength, consolations, tears, inspirations and quiet, easing and taking away all obstacles, so that the person may go forward in doing good.[1]

Manuscript evidence suggests that Ignatius added these two rules at a later time, after the rules that now follow them. In the Spanish *Autograph*, the most authoritative manuscript, the numbers of the subsequent rules are changed twice to accommodate the two new rules.[2] Ignatian scholarship generally recognizes in these changes a confirmation that the present first two rules were composed later than the rules that follow.[3] Why then did Ignatius add these two rules and place them at the beginning of the series?

Time and experience most likely revealed to Ignatius the need to clarify from the outset that the actions of the good spirit and of the enemy change according to the subjective disposition of the persons in whom they act—that is, the direction these persons have chosen and are pursuing in their spiritual lives.[4] It is critically important to grasp this fact if we are to apply the rules correctly. A failure to do so will cause serious errors in understanding which spirit is at work in a person's experience, with consequent harm to the person.

If persons are moving decisively *away from God and into serious sin* (rule 1), the *enemy,*[5] Ignatius says, will induce complacency and even delight in this way of life (first half of rule 1). The goal of the enemy, obviously, is to keep these persons on this path. The *good spirit,*[6] on the contrary, will trouble these persons, never leaving them in peace (second half of rule 1). The goal of the good spirit, again obviously, is to move these persons away from this sinful life and toward God, their only true source of happiness.

If persons are moving decisively *away from sin and toward God* (rule 2), the tactics of the two spirits reverse. Now the *enemy* will attempt to trouble these persons so that they will desist from their progress toward God (first half of rule 2); the *good spirit,* on the other hand, will bring them joy to encourage their continued growth toward God (second half of rule 2).

Such teachings indicate that to apply the rules correctly to a person's experience, we must first verify the subjective disposition of the person—the direction this person has chosen and is pursuing in the spiritual life: Is this person moving *away from God* and living a life of serious sin? Or is this person striving to overcome sin and grow *toward God* in love and service?

If the person is moving *away from God* and living a life of serious sin, then the action that induces complacency and even delight is of the *enemy.* In this situation, the action that troubles and disturbs the person is of the *good spirit.*

If, however, the person is moving away from sin and *toward God,* then it is the *enemy* who will trouble and disturb the person. The *good spirit,* on the contrary, will bring joy and peace to the person.

As regards the first situation, an important point is touched here. We say—and rightly—that our God is a God of peace.

But our God is above all a God who loves his children too much ever simply to let them go (Mt 18:12–14), and who is willing *to trouble the hearts* of those who stray in the hope of leading them back to him, the only true source of their joy.[7]

To understand, then, the peace-inducing or troubling action a person may experience in the spiritual life, we must first ask: Is this person heading *away* from God or *toward* God? When we have verified this, we will know which spirit is at work in this person's experience.

How did Ignatius come to understand the working of the two spirits in these two contrasting situations? In all likelihood, he first learned this through Spirit-guided reflection on his own experience. In the years preceding his conversion at age thirty, Ignatius lived the experience of the first rule—the person moving away from God and into a life of serious sin; after his conversion, he lived that of the second rule—the person moving away from sin and toward God. Remarkably, once Ignatius gave his heart to God, those years of sin became a source of grace for generations: his understanding of how the spirits worked in him at that time has helped many to understand their own experience. I find in this a powerful reflection on God's mercy: when we give our hearts to God, there is nothing in our lives—no matter where we have been or what we have done—that God cannot turn to good.

"From Mortal Sin to Mortal Sin"

To whom does the first rule apply? Who specifically are these "persons who are going from mortal sin to mortal sin" in whom the enemy and good spirit work in the way described? The answer is less evident than may appear, because Ignatius uses the term "mortal sin" in two different senses.[8]

Often in his *Spiritual Exercises*, Ignatius employs the phrase "mortal sin" in the sense common today, as *grave* sin in contrast with venial sin. Thus, for example, in the *Exercises* persons pray for "a sense of shame and confusion, seeing how many have been condemned eternally for a single mortal sin" (*SpirEx* 48), whereas God's mercy has spared them from a similar fate. Ignatius speaks likewise of the person who "will not consent to any mortal sin or venial sin or even to what has any likeness to a deliberate sin" (*SpirEx* 349). In these cases and in many others, Ignatius uses the phrase "mortal sin" as we do today with the meaning of grave sin in contrast to lighter or venial sin.[9]

At other times, however, Ignatius employs the phrase "mortal sin" in the sense of "capital sin," that is, the seven capital (root) tendencies toward sin that we experience as a legacy of original sin.[10] Thus, at one point in the *Exercises*, Ignatius invites persons to examine themselves on "the ten commandments and the seven mortal sins" (*SpirEx* 238). And again, "In order to know better his faults against the mortal sins, let him look at their opposites; and so to avoid them better, let the person propose and seek with holy exercises to acquire and retain the seven virtues contrary to them" (*SpirEx* 245).[11] In such texts, Ignatius uses "mortal sin" not as *grave* sin but as *capital* sin—these seven root tendencies—thereby extending the range of "mortal sin" beyond grave sin alone.

The question thus arises: Who is this person who is "going from mortal sin to mortal sin"? Does Ignatius intend here those like the young Augustine before his conversion, that is, persons who are far from God and living confirmed lives of grave sin? Are these the only persons to whom rule 1 applies? Or might these be persons who love the Lord but at some point sin venially or commit even lesser faults with respect to one or another capital sin—persons who, for example, slip into slight movements of pride, anger, envy, jealousy, or any of the capital sins? Depending on how we answer, rule 1 may apply to very different persons.

With respect to the text alone, both interpretations are possible, and various commentators have favored one or the other.[12] On this basis, one may adopt either the stricter interpretation ("mortal sin" means grave sin) or the broader ("mortal sin" means the seven capital sinful tendencies). The latter widens the range of rule 1 to include even small areas of regression in otherwise progressing Christians.[13] In such areas of regression—lighter or venial sins, negligence in prayer, diminishment of apostolic zeal, and so forth— the enemy, this interpretation says, induces contentment of heart and the good spirit induces trouble of heart. Such areas of regression obviously exist, and in this interpretation, Ignatius intended rule 1 to clarify how the spirits work in them.

Though the broader interpretation is textually possible, I incline to the first interpretation, that when Ignatius speaks of a person "going from mortal sin to mortal sin," he intends the phrase "mortal sin" as grave sin. I hold this position for several reasons.

First, this is *rule 1*, the rule in which, together with rule 2, Ignatius lays the most basic groundwork for discernment of spirits. From a pedagogical perspective, I find it almost impossible to believe that Ignatius would intend to intro- duce from the outset the refined applications of the broader interpretation. Long experience in teaching the rules has shown me that listeners would be confused were I to present rule 1 in this broader light. As Ignatian author Jules Toner, SJ, writes, "In Rules I:1–2 [the first two rules], Ignatius, as

a good pedagogue, has stated pure cases in order to com-
municate an initial understanding that is unconfused by
complexities."[14]

Second, in persons "going from mortal sin to mortal sin,"
Ignatius says, the enemy "is ordinarily accustomed to propose
apparent pleasures to them, leading them to imagine *sensual
delights and pleasures*." That the enemy would ordinarily
propose sensual delights and pleasures to persons far from
God and confirmed in grave sin is not difficult to imagine.[15] It
is harder to see why Ignatius would mention only this tactic
of the enemy were rule 1 to apply to progressing Christians
who may slip lightly in some aspect of their spiritual lives.
Why not include an inducement to anger, pride, envy, sloth,
or jealousy? Experience confirms that Christians in this situation experience such tactics of the enemy.

Third, the parallel with rule 2 also suggests that "mortal
sin" here means grave sin. The persons of rule 2 are persons "going on *intensely purifying their sins* and *rising from
good to better* in the service of God our Lord." These persons are not simply drifting in the spiritual life or progressing
slightly but are progressing with intensity, spiritually rising
from good to better. The energy and decisiveness of such persons in their movement toward God suggest a like energy and
decisiveness in those "going from mortal sin to mortal sin"
in the parallel rule 1.[16] If this is so, then the stricter interpretation of the rule is more likely to be accurate: "mortal sin"
signifies grave sin.[17]

What then of failures such as venial sin, slight faults, or
imperfections? How do the good spirit and enemy work in
persons who love God—progressing Christians—who may
regress in some limited area of their spiritual lives? If the
stricter interpretation of rule 1—that "mortal sin" signifies

grave sin rather than capital sin—is true, does Ignatius treat of such lesser regressions elsewhere in the rules?

Our earlier caution against viewing these rules as a treatment of any spiritual situation that may arise applies once again. Nonetheless, in a later rule Ignatius explicitly mentions times when "we are tepid, slothful, or negligent in our spiritual exercises" (rule 9), and explains how discernment applies in such situations. In persons who love God but, at some point, grow "tepid, slothful, or negligent" in some aspect of their spiritual lives, God will withdraw consolation, Ignatius says, and will permit the enemy to bring spiritual desolation (rule 9). In God's intention, Ignatius explains, the discomfort of such desolation will alert them to the area of negligence and so lead them to eliminate that negligence.

In rule 9, as in rule 1, the action of the good spirit is unsettling: permitting the discomfort of spiritual desolation (rule 9) and stinging and biting in the conscience (rule 1). In both, the goal is the same: if the person is open to the action of the good spirit, that unsettling action will lead the person to a spiritually healthy change. The unsettling action, however, of rule 9 (spiritual desolation) is less stark than that of rule 1 (stinging and biting in the conscience). We would expect this to be so, since the faults of rule 9 (negligence, sloth, or tepidity in spiritual exercises) are lesser than those of rule 1 (grave sins). I believe that rule 9, more than rule 1, reveals Ignatius's thought on discernment regarding lesser faults.[18]

"Through the Synderesis of Reason"

In persons going from mortal sin to mortal sin, Ignatius writes, the good spirit works by "stinging and biting their consciences through their rational power of moral judgment." A more literal translation would read: "stinging and biting their consciences through *the synderesis of reason* [*por el sindérese de la razón*]."[19] What is *synderesis*, and why does Ignatius employ this term in rule 1?

In my earlier book, I avoided this term for the sake of clarity. In the present setting, we may explore this term and see what it adds to our understanding of rule 1.

Synderesis is, writes theologian Servais Pinckaers, OP, the intuitive knowledge or "the primordial perception of the good proper to man."[20] Joseph Cardinal Ratzinger describes synderesis as "an inner sense, a capacity to recall, so that the one whom it addresses, if he is not turned in on himself, hears its echo from within. He sees: 'That's it! That is what my nature points to and seeks.'"[21] In classic scholastic theology, synderesis is the "natural or innate habit of the mind to know the first principles of the practical or moral order without recourse to a process of discursive reasoning."[22]

What does this mean? *Synderesis* describes the deep, innate sense in the human person of the basic principles on which all right action must be based. Every human person possesses this sense of these basic principles: it is the "primordial perception" of which Pinckaers writes, and the inner awareness that exclaims, as Ratzinger affirms, "That's it! That is what my nature points to and seeks." In scholastic terminology, it is the "habit of the mind" that knows "the first principles of the practical or moral order." The most basic of these principles, St. Thomas writes, is that good is to be done and evil avoided.[23]

No human persons, wherever they have been in life, whatever they may have done, whatever they may be doing at present, no matter how far they may be from God, can ever escape or deny this innate awareness—this synderesis that tells them that good is to be done and evil avoided. This deep, connatural, and inescapable synderesis, Ignatius says, is the human space in which the good spirit will work in persons "going from mortal sin to mortal sin."[24]

The profound message is this: that God—in Francis Thompson's lovely image, the relentless Hound of Heaven— will *not* give up the effort to call the human person back to himself (Lk 15:3–32) and to the only life that can bring happiness, here and in eternity. When persons are "going from mortal sin to mortal sin," and all other motivations—love of God, the desire to live uprightly, the hope of bringing others to Christ, the effort to live one's vocation well, zeal for the spread of the Gospel, and so forth—fail, the good spirit will work in the one space that remains: the *synderesis* deeply inscribed in their hearts. These persons may strive to ignore this synderesis, and the enemy may assist this effort; yet no matter how they try, they cannot escape it. Precisely here, therefore, is where the good spirit will work.

Those who may have gone "from mortal sin to mortal sin" at some point in their lives will recognize—now with gratitude—this "stinging and biting" of the good spirit in their consciences "through the synderesis of reason," and how it led them back to God. Below, I will supply examples from a variety of written sources.

"The Enemy"

When I teach the rules, I note that Ignatius often employs the word "enemy" to describe our foe in the spiritual life. In these fourteen rules, Ignatius uses the phrase "bad spirit" twice; in these same rules, he uses the word "enemy" seven times.[25] At one point, he adopts the plural, "all his enemies" (rule 11), and in the last three rules, he expands the title to "the enemy of human nature." In his classic letter to Sister Teresa Rejadell on discernment, Ignatius employs the word "enemy" thirteen times.[26]

The term "enemy" includes the *personal angelic being*, the evil one, who is biblically described as the adversary, the tempter, and the father of lies.[27] It likewise includes the remaining two elements of the classic triad,[28] that is, the *flesh* or "concupiscence," the weakness of our humanity as a legacy of original sin, and the *world*, that is, influences around us that, unless resisted, will move us away from God.

Over the years, I have learned the value of the term "enemy" in presenting the rules. When explained as we have here, listeners perceive it as clear and solidly rooted in our spiritual tradition. The term "enemy" also avoids the pitfalls of either dismissing or overemphasizing our adversary.[29] The word permits a fruitful discussion of this agency in the spiritual life without, however, assigning it a greater role or power than it has.

When I present this, I always emphasize that the enemy and good spirit are not equal parts. Both are real, and both have influence in the spiritual life. This influence must be recognized. The enemy, however, is no more than a fallen creature—yes, of a higher ontological order than we as a purely spiritual being, and therefore not to be taken lightly—yet still no more than a fallen creature. The good spirit, on the other hand, is the omnipotent and infinite God, Creator, Redeemer, and Sanctifier, who loves us with an eternal, personal, warm, and faithful love.[30] Consequently, we live the discerning life with a fundamental sense of hope. This hope suffuses everything in Ignatius's rules: they express a spirituality of grace and redemption.

"Leading Them to Imagine Sensual Delights and Pleasures"

Ignatius tells us that in persons "going from mortal sin to mortal sin, the enemy is ordinarily accustomed to propose apparent pleasures to them, leading them to imagine sensual delights and pleasures." Antoinio Denis, SJ, asks the following: "Why are sins of the flesh alone mentioned here, when other sins are much more grave, such as impiety, unbelief, blasphemy, murder, and the like?"[31] Denis offers a threefold reply: first, among those "going from mortal sin to mortal sin," sins of the flesh are more widespread than other sins; second, this kind of sin, by contrast with others, can be repeated frequently and become a constant preoccupation; finally, from this kind of sin the passage to other sins easily takes place.[32]

I often wondered about the question Denis raises and have found no other author who seeks to answer it. Most probably, Ignatius formulated this rule as he did the others from his own experience—recalling his life before his conversion—and the experience of the many who sought his spiritual help. Such experience led him to describe this particular tactic as the one the enemy is "ordinarily accustomed" to adopt in those "going from mortal sin to mortal sin."[33]

"Stinging and Biting Their Consciences": Some Examples

Examples of the action of the good spirit in those "going from mortal sin to mortal sin" abound in life and literature. In such persons, Ignatius writes, the good spirit acts by "*stinging and biting* their consciences through the synderesis

of reason." This troubling action of the good spirit, stinging (*punzando*) and biting (*remordiendo*) their consciences, is
intended, if they receive it, to bring them back to God. With a
lovely metaphor, Pascal writes that "it is like an infant whom
his mother snatches from the hands of thieves, and who must
love, in the pain he suffers, the loving and legitimate violence
of her who procures his freedom."[34] The following examples
illustrate this loving "violence" of the good spirit in those
"going from mortal sin to mortal sin."

"Stinging Anointings of Healthful Sorrows"

Remembering the years when he was "going from mortal sin
to mortal sin," St. Augustine turns to the Lord and says, "It
was pleasing in your sight to reform my deformities, and you
disturbed me by inward goads to make me dissatisfied until
you were revealed to my inward sight. Thus by the secret
hand of your remedy my swelling was reduced, and the disordered and bedimmed sight of my mind was made whole from
day to day by the stinging anointings of healthful sorrows."[35]

With his customary literary skill, Augustine perfectly iden-
tifies the stinging action of the good spirit in one far from
God: the good spirit troubles him with "inward goads" and
"stinging anointings," whose purpose is to make him "dissatisfied" with his present spiritual state and to experience
"healthful sorrows." By this action, his spiritual "swelling"
is reduced, and his spiritually "disordered and bedimmed"
vision is made whole. Augustine finally opens his heart to this
stinging action of the good spirit, and conversion follows.

"My Soul Desired Escape and Liberation"

In his *Seven Storey Mountain*, Thomas Merton recounts a
night in Rome in the years before his conversion. Merton gives

us to understand that at this time he was far from God. He was in his room that night with the light on, when suddenly he felt a vivid awareness of his father, deceased a year earlier. Merton describes the experience: "The whole thing passed in a flash, but in that flash, instantly, I was overwhelmed with a sudden and profound insight into the misery and corruption of my own soul, and I was pierced deeply with a light that made me realize something of the condition I was in, and I was filled with horror at what I saw, and my whole being rose up in revolt against what was within me, and my soul desired escape and liberation and freedom from all this with an intensity and an urgency unlike anything I had ever known before."[36]

The pain of this experience bears fruit in Merton: "And now I think for the first time in my whole life I really began to pray—praying not with my lips and with my intellect and my imagination, but praying out of the very roots of my life and of my being . . . to help me get free of the thousand terrible things that held my will in their slavery. There were a lot of tears connected with this, and they did me good."[37] The good spirit stings and bites, piercing Merton with a relentless light; his whole being rises up in revolt against his spiritual condition, and an intense desire for "escape and liberation and freedom" awakens in his heart. Real prayer and tears follow, and Merton has moved toward conversion.

"The Growing and Growing of a Weight"

In Alessandro Manzoni's magnificent novel, *The Betrothed*, a character steeped in evil begins to be troubled by his crimes. This man, whom Manzoni calls the "Unnamed," now feels "not exactly a remorse, but a certain discomfort at his crimes. These, accumulating in his memory if not in his conscience, rose up before him again in all their number and ugliness every time he committed a new one; it was like the growing and growing of a weight that was already uncomfortable."[38] This weight increases to an intolerable burden, above all in the silence of tormented nights.

Unable to endure this, the Unnamed goes to meet the holy Cardinal Frederick Borromeo. He is deeply moved by the affection with which the cardinal receives him. The cardinal asks the Unnamed if he has good news to share. The Unnamed replies, "*I* have good news, I? I whose heart is a hell; how can I have good news for you? Tell me, if you know it, what is this good news you are expecting from a man like me?" Manzoni gives the cardinal's response, "'That God has touched your heart, and wants to make you His,' replied the cardinal placidly." The Unnamed cries out, "God! God! God! If only I could see Him! If only I could feel Him! Where is this God?"

The cardinal answers, "You ask me that? You? And who is nearer to Him than you? Don't you feel him in your heart, weighing you down, worrying you, never letting you be, and drawing you on at the same time, tempting you with a hope of tranquility and joy, a joy that will be full, immense, as soon as you recognize Him, acknowledge Him, implore Him?"[39] The Unnamed's conversion soon follows, and his life changes completely.

Don't you feel him in your heart, weighing you down, worrying you, never letting you be: with these expressions, Manzoni aptly describes the "stinging and biting" action of the good spirit in one "going from mortal sin to mortal sin." *And who is nearer to Him than you?*—beautiful words that powerfully describe the unshakable love of a God who will not abandon those far from him, and whose stinging and biting is directed toward healing.

"Those Thoughts Kept Haunting Me"

Noel Morales was raised Catholic and practiced his faith through college. When he finished his studies, Noel found a job with an airline and began working. Harmful influences led him to abandon the Church and engage in immoral behavior. With a new "friend," Noel "hung out even more than usual after work until I was completely hooked on that sinful lifestyle. I was without a right direction and was totally lost. I found I couldn't quit living that way because I was enslaved by it."[40] Noel continues, "It was too late for me to stop; I was helpless and had no strength. My bank account went down to a zero balance, and I ran out of money. It was the darkest hour of my life."

At this point, Noel writes, "One day I came to my senses and thought to myself, 'After all these years with my life in dissipation and consumed with worldly pleasures, something is still lacking in my life.' I finally realized that those temporary satisfactions and pleasures could not fill what my heart was yearning for. I asked myself once, then twice, then three times, 'Why? What am I living for? Who am I?' Those thoughts kept haunting and troubling me. 'Who can I turn to?' I wondered."

The pain of this "darkest hour" leads to a change: "That evening, I found myself on my knees in prayer with tears rolling down my face as I begged God for help. That silent conversation with him was a sort of relief and alleviation of the excruciating pains I was experiencing. It made me believe that I already had the strength I needed finally to release the burdens I carried inside myself." This was the beginning of a conversion that would completely change Noel's life, healing him and bringing him back to God.

Once again the stinging and biting action of the good spirit in one "going from mortal sin to mortal sin" is evident.

Noel experiences thoughts that keep "haunting and troubling him." The "excruciating pains" he feels bring him to his knees in ardent prayer for release. Because Noel is open to this stinging and biting action, he returns to God and finds new peace. In this account as in the preceding, the relentless, heartfelt love of God for those far from him appears—this God *who will not let these persons go*, but who ceaselessly troubles their hearts in the hope of leading them to the one true joy the human heart can know.

Such is the teaching of Ignatius's rule 1. What now will happen when the person *does* turn away from sinfulness and toward God? How will the good spirit and enemy then act? Ignatius will address this in rule 2.

Chapter 2

Placing and Removing Obstacles

I felt myself renewed to my very depths
by Him, ready for a new life, for duty,
for the work intended by His providence.
I gave myself without reserve, and I
gave Him the future.
—Servant of God Élisabeth Leseur

Ignatius's second rule is the following:

Second Rule. The second: In *persons who are going on*
intensely purifying their sins and rising from good to
better in the service of God our Lord, the method is
contrary to that in the first rule. For then it is proper to
the *evil spirit* to bite, sadden, and place obstacles, disquieting with false reasons, so that the person may not
go forward. And it is proper to the *good spirit* to give
courage and strength, consolations, tears, inspirations
and quiet, easing and taking away all obstacles, so that
the person may go forward in doing good.

In this rule, Ignatius turns to the spiritual situation contrary to that of persons "going from mortal sin to mortal sin."
He describes this situation according to two complementary
qualities: such persons are "going on intensely purifying their
sins" and simultaneously "rising from good to better in the

service of God our Lord." In this second and happier spiritual situation, persons are energetically—"intensely"—seeking growing freedom from sin and concurrently "rising from good to better" in God's service: they are actively pursuing new steps to love and serve God more fully.

In this blessed spiritual situation, charged with energy and growth, how will the enemy and the good spirit act? This is the question Ignatius addresses in rule 2. Some examples will concretize the spiritual profile he intends in this rule.

Peter's Experience

Peter is a fifty-three-year-old married man and the father of three children. He was raised Catholic and, apart from a few years in college, has always practiced his faith. For him, this means attending Sunday Mass, seeing that his children receive the sacraments, and praying on occasion.

One Sunday, as Mass was ending, the pastor announced a forthcoming parish retreat and warmly invited his parishioners to consider attending. The retreat would be held in a local retreat house during the coming Lent. Peter had never made a retreat, and something about the thought of a weekend away—with talks on the faith, times of prayer, and space for quiet—appealed to him. That evening he spoke with his wife, who encouraged him to attend. Peter registered for the retreat and looked forward to the experience.

When the weekend arrived, Peter found the talks engaging and the times of prayer fruitful. On Saturday evening, a penance service was held with preparation in common and individual confession after. Peter decided to receive the sacrament and approached one of the priests, who received him with goodness and understanding. Peter generally went to confession before Christmas and Easter, but this was different. The talks, the quiet, and the prayer had prepared him for a deeper experience of this sacrament.

Peter shared with the priest his new insight into habits that were not spiritually good for him: ways of using the Internet and television that diminished his spiritual energy; kinds of conversation into which he had drifted and that he now saw were harmful; practices at work that skirted moral boundaries regarding honesty; a slowness to assist his wife and children when this conflicted with his own interests.

Peter spoke openly of all this to the priest and found the priest's response helpful. His words lifted Peter's heart and helped him experience God's love, mercy, and forgiveness. As he left the confessional, Peter felt a deep peace, a peace he had long sought.

That evening Peter walked on the grounds of the retreat house. His heart was filled with a quiet joy. He found himself desiring to begin a new spiritual journey. Peter resolved that he would go to confession regularly, and after the retreat did so. He changed his use of the Internet and television, eliminating the harmful practices. Unobtrusively, Peter distanced himself from the damaging conversations and questionable business practices. He also sought to overcome the self-centeredness that limited his love for his wife and children. In Ignatius's terms, Peter is now a person who, with humble trust in God and diligent effort, is *going on intensely purifying his sins.*

As Peter did this, something else happened. He grew more patient with his children and more present to his wife when she needed him. He was more cheerful at work and more ready to assist his fellow workers, who appreciated his new attentiveness to them.

During the retreat, Peter had learned of a men's group in the parish that met before work on Wednesday mornings. He joined the group and enjoyed the sharing and the talks. Some of the men went to daily Mass, and a few months later Peter also began attending Mass occasionally during the week. As the weeks passed, this practice grew more frequent. Peter's new interest in his faith encouraged similar steps in his wife, and a new spirit of faith and harmony gradually developed in their home. In Ignatius's terms, Peter is now a person who is *rising from good to better in the service of God our Lord.*

The Profile of Rule 2

In a different vocation, something similar might be said of the priest who has dinner with a priest-friend and is struck by the new spiritual depth he sees in his friend. The conversation awakens new spiritual desires in him, and he, too, begins to remove unhelpful practices from his life, simultaneously growing in love and service of his parishioners. Further examples might include the married woman who takes new steps to remove spiritual obstacles and to grow in prayer and service of the Lord as she lives her family life; the young man who begins seminary life with energetic desire to grow in God's love and service; the woman who enters religious life and is now actively seeking new closeness to the Lord and more faithful service. In each case, the profile of rule 2 is present: these are persons growing in freedom from sinfulness and rising in God's love and service.

Rule 2, like rule 1, most likely arose in significant part from Ignatius's reflection on his own experience. His life *prior* to his conversion amply fits the profile of rule 1; his life *after* that conversion displays all the spiritual energy presumed in rule 2. Both rules provide an exact description of his spiritual state in these successive situations. A grace-given insight permitted him to describe the workings of the enemy and good spirit in both situations, an insight further confirmed through the experience of those who sought his spiritual guidance.

In rule 2, Ignatius outlines *four basic tactics* of the *enemy* when seeking to *hinder* these persons' spiritual growth; he likewise names the *five basic tactics* of the *good spirit* in seeking to *facilitate* these persons' growth. Over the years, I have come to see this rule as fundamental. If persons who love the Lord assimilate it well, they will find that they understand much of their spiritual experience and so know how to respond to it. We will examine first the tactics of the enemy and then those of the good spirit.

The Tactics of the Enemy: Hindering the Growth

Ignatius names four tactics by which the enemy seeks to hinder growth. The enemy, he says, will *"bite, sadden, and place obstacles, disquieting with false reasons."*

Biting

The enemy will attempt, Ignatius says, to *bite*, that is, to gnaw at the peace and joy progressing persons experience as they grow. Ignatius's word, the Spanish *morder*, expresses exactly this: a biting, gnawing action. In this way the enemy seeks to weaken these persons' energy for growth, leading them to desist from further efforts.

I believe that this tactic of the enemy is very common. I see it often in my own experience, and I see it in others. It may present itself thus, for example: "Yes, that (your prayer, your service of the Lord, your living of your vocation, your love of others, and so forth) went well, but . . . " The "but" may be followed by various forms of gnawing: "Yes, that went well, but why did it take you so long? Yes, that went well, but you pushed too hard. Yes, you have grown in this area, but why didn't you address this before? Yes, that went well, but you could have done more . . . " and many similar accusations. Such gnawing is not an incitement to sin but simply an attempt to diminish our spiritual energy. If we are not aware of this action of the enemy, it will burden us; if we are aware of it, name it for the biting of the enemy that it is, and reject it, our energy for spiritual growth will continue undiminished.

In a letter of spiritual direction, Ignatius writes that if the enemy "sees that . . . a person avoids not only all mortal sin and all venial sin (as much as the latter is possible, for we cannot avoid them all) but even tries to keep from himself the very appearance of slight sin, imperfection, and defect, he tries to darken and confuse that good conscience by suggesting sin where there is none, changing perfection into defect, his only purpose being to *harass and make one uneasy and miserable*. When, as frequently happens, he cannot induce one to sin, or even hope to do so, he tries at least *to vex him*."[1] *Harass*, make one who is growing *uneasy and miserable*, and, when he cannot induce this person to sin, at least to *vex* him: this perfectly describes the enemy's tactic of *biting*.

As is generally true with these rules, Ignatius writes from experience. After his conversion, Ignatius spent three days at the Benedictine abbey of Santa Maria de Montserrat, preparing and making a life-changing confession. Some months later, in a time of great spiritual growth, a thought began to trouble him regarding that confession. Ignatius recounts of himself: "Even though the general confession he had made in Montserrat had been made with great diligence and completely in writing, as has been said, nonetheless it seemed to him at times that he had not confessed some things, and this caused him much affliction."[2] In a time when Ignatius is "going on intensely purifying his sins" and "rising from good to better" in God's service, the enemy does not attempt immediately to lead him into sin but simply *bites* and gnaws at the peace Ignatius would otherwise feel in God.

Are we aware of this tactic of the enemy in our own experience? Do we name it and reject it?

Saddening

The enemy will also, Ignatius affirms, attempt to *sadden* the person who is rising spiritually. Peter, for example, experiences a quiet joy at the spiritual newness that has entered his life with new freedom from sinfulness, a more lively faith, and increased energy to love at home and in the workplace. A day comes, however, when he notes a diminishment of that joy. Now a film of sadness overlays his prayer, his involvement in the parish, and his efforts to love. Now his spiritual energy is dampened, and he no longer feels "any interior taste or relish" for the things of God.[3] Questions, perhaps imperfectly articulated but very much felt, may arise: "Why continue with all this when there is no longer much joy in it? What is the value of all this?"

If Peter is not aware of this tactic of the enemy and does not reject it, the sadness he feels may lead him to relinquish his efforts to "rise from good to better"—and such is the enemy's purpose. All who are growing in the Lord may well experience this tactic of the enemy.

Placing Obstacles

As Peter pursues spiritual growth, the enemy will attempt to *place obstacles* in his path. The same will be true of all who seek to progress in God's love and service.

When Augustine pursues freedom from his former life of sin, he tells us that "I was held back by mere trifles, the most paltry inanities, all my old attachments. They plucked at my garment of flesh and whispered, 'Are you going to dismiss us? From this moment we shall never be with you again, for ever and ever. From this moment you will never be allowed to do this thing or that, for evermore.'"[4] Lightly behind these whisperings are questions like these: "You want to change? You want freedom from your sinfulness? How many times have you tried? How long has it ever lasted? What makes you think it will be any different this time? You know yourself. You know you are too weak. You know you cannot live without this."

Such is the enemy's tactic in persons seeking to rise spiritually: *obstacles, obstacles, obstacles.* These persons, too, will hear the enemy's whisperings: "You are too weak. You cannot do it. Why get your hopes up? Why make efforts that will go nowhere?" May I ask, Have any of us heard such whisperings when we have desired to grow spiritually?

Nekhlyudov, the principal character in Tolstoy's novel *Resurrection*, desires at this point to rise from the moral depths into which he has fallen. As he considers this step, he, too, experiences the enemy's obstacle-placing action: "'Haven't you tried before to improve and be better, and nothing came of it?' whispered the voice of the tempter within. 'So what is the use of trying anymore? You are not the only one—everyone's the same—life is like that,' whispered the voice.'"[5]

Gerald is a forty-one-year-old married man who, after twenty years away from the Church, has recently returned to the sacraments. For six months now he has faithfully attended Sunday Mass with his family and is making sincere efforts to overcome earlier patterns of sinfulness. He rejoices at the new peace he experiences and the new harmony in his family and at work.

Today Gerald is attending Sunday Mass. The Gospel is Luke 11:1–13, "Lord, teach us to pray."[6] The priest gives a simple but heartfelt homily on prayer, and invites his parishioners to consider spending ten minutes a day in prayer with the readings of the Mass for that day. As Gerald listens, he feels God's closeness, and his heart is warmed with gratitude to God for the goodness of what is happening in his life. A thought comes to him: "If simply praying once a week at Sunday Mass is already making this difference, what would happen if I did what Father is suggesting and prayed daily?" Further thoughts arise: "I could certainly arrange my morning to set aside ten minutes each day. And, actually, all I have to do is ask my wife for help because she has been doing this for some years. She will be happy to show me how to find the readings and get started." Gerald resolves that he will speak with his wife that evening when the children are in bed and will begin this practice the next morning.

The day continues with its various activities. At supper, a tension arises between Gerald and his teenage son and does not resolve well. This tension burdens Gerald's heart as the evening unfolds. Now the children are asleep, and Gerald is in his study, preparing for work the next morning. He remembers that he had planned to speak at this time with his wife about the ten minutes each day with Scripture.

But now the thoughts are different: "Who are you kidding? You've been away from the Church for twenty years, and look at the way you've lived. You've never even read Scripture. What makes you think you'll understand anything written there? Why approach your wife about a practice that is bound to fail? You'll just embarrass yourself and her. You had a nice experience at Mass this morning, but that doesn't change anything, and it is not going to last." *Obstacles, obstacles, obstacles . . .* in the way of one who is seeking to rise from good to better in God's service.

We readily perceive that what happens next matters. If Gerald succumbs to the enemy's obstacle-placing action and does not speak with his wife that evening, what will his prayer look like a week later? A month? A year? Five years? But if, with courage and spiritual awareness, Gerald rejects this action of the enemy, holds firm to the grace of the Mass that morning, speaks with his wife, and begins the ten minutes the following morning, what will his prayer now look like a week, a month, a year, and five years later? *Right here*, in the silence of this evening, a key decision is being made regarding spiritual growth. And *right here* is where Ignatius wants to help us. Most of the spiritual life consists of precisely such situations and decisions—quiet, generally unseen, "small" decisions that shape our spiritual journey. The wisdom of the Ignatian rules—living the discerning life—can make all the difference.

Disquieting with False Reasons

As the enemy places obstacles in Gerald's path that evening, he may attempt a further tactic as well. The enemy may seek to *disquiet* Gerald with *false reasons*. He may suggest *reasons* to desist from praying the ten minutes daily; in accord with his nature as the liar (Jn 8:44), these will be *false* reasons, and they will have a debilitating resonance in Gerald's heart, they will *disquiet* him, diminishing his affective energy for growth.

The enemy may bring "reasons" such as these: "You want to begin daily prayer with Scripture? You know what this is really about? You've been getting nice feedback on your new spiritual journey, and you like the compliments. You want more of them. And you know what else is at work in this desire? You won't admit it, but you are competing with your wife. You want to be as spiritual as she is. And if you are really honest, you'll admit that you'd like the children to see you as even a little more spiritual than she." All these and similar "reasons" are false. None of this was present that Sunday morning at Mass, but only a happy sense of God's closeness and of gratitude, with a desire to grow in the spiritual life. Yet if Gerald is not aware of this tactic of the enemy, these false reasons may well disquiet him and weaken his resolve to go forward.

I have seen this tactic of the enemy take a number of forms. When persons grow in the spiritual life and in living their vocations, the enemy may whisper the following: "See, you were never authentic before." If the person believes this lie, the joy of growth is changed into disquiet of heart.

In times of spiritual progress, of newness in prayer, understanding, and service, this question may arise: "Why weren't you praying like this before? Why didn't you see this before? Why didn't you give yourself in service like this before? There is something wrong with you. You're so slow to take these steps." The truth is exactly the contrary: blessed and fruitful growth is occurring in these persons' lives. Again, if these persons believe these false reasonings, their hearts will indeed be disquieted.

When the journey of growth involves struggle, a voice may be heard: "It's too late. Look at what you've done! Look at the way you've lived! You've marred things, and it can't be undone. You've failed in your efforts to love God, and now it's too late. It can't ever really change." Or, a slight variation of the same: "Look at you struggling. You're going backward in your spiritual life. It's all going to end badly."

In yet another way, the enemy may attempt to disquiet with false reasons. When persons who love the Lord find thoughts and desires contrary to that love arise involuntarily in their hearts, they may be troubled: "See, look at you! You feel such desires. You think such thoughts. You are unworthy of closeness with God. You are a failure in your spiritual life. And you will never change."

John of the Cross speaks of *voluntary* thoughts and desires that *do* hinder spiritual growth, and then, turning to the *involuntary* thoughts and desires that *do not*, continues:

> I am not writing here of the other natural desires that are not voluntary, and of thoughts that go not beyond the first movement, and other temptations to which the soul is not consenting; for these produce in the soul none of the evils aforementioned. For, although a person who suffers from them may think that the passion and disturbance that they then produce in him are defiling and blinding him, this is not the case; rather they are bringing him the opposite advantages. For, in so far as he resists them, he gains fortitude, purity, light, and consolation, and many blessings, even as Our Lord said to Saint Paul: That virtue was made perfect in weakness.[7]

Natural desires that are not voluntary . . . thoughts that go not beyond the first movement, and other temptations to which the soul is not consenting: to know that such are not sinful and that, on the contrary, *we grow* through resisting them, closes the door to many false reasonings of the enemy that seek to disquiet us. To banish the enemy's false accusations from such sensitive places of the heart awakens hope and energy for the journey.

The Hindering Tactics of the Enemy: Some Examples

I quote the following from my journals over the years. I offer them as representative, in one person's experience, of how these tactics of the enemy may present themselves in daily life.

"Three Ways of Biting in My Prayer"

From notes on a meeting of spiritual direction with Father Ed, my spiritual director for many years:

> Today Ed helped me to see three different ways in which the enemy "bites" at my peace when in prayer. With his help, I saw the following:
>
> When I feel drawn to spend quiet time in prayer, just with the Lord and without much mental activity, and find this nourishing and joyful, there is the voice that says, "You're not really praying. You should be doing more, reflecting on a scriptural passage, using the time better." This voice awakens a small sense of uneasiness that weighs on my prayer. It is not clamorous; it just saps the joy. Because it is not clamorous, I don't easily see it.
>
> When I want to share "small" things with the Lord, ask help in daily matters, or share daily concerns about work, relationships, projects, small tensions, and similar things, there is a voice that says, "With all the real problems in the world, people in the midst of wars and hunger, deep physical suffering, and lives torn apart, you should be ashamed to bring such small concerns to the Lord. With such great needs in the world, you are asking for help with these small burdens?" Ed quoted Jesus's words that even the hairs on our head are counted, that

not a single sparrow falls to the ground without our Father knowing it (Lk 12:6–7). Everything in my life matters to God, and this hesitation that weighs on my freedom to share these things in prayer because they are so small is the enemy's biting. I should reject it.

Sometimes I remember the writings of spiritual figures like John of the Cross who say that many come to the threshold of deeper prayer, stop short, and never go further. When my prayer seems dry or difficult, after all these years, at times I think of those writings and wonder if I am not among these persons. This, too, awakens a quiet sense of burden, just a thread, not loud or in the forefront, yet it causes doubt and a little uneasiness. This, too, Ed says, is the enemy's biting and is to be rejected.

In such ways, we may experience this "biting" action of the enemy, quietly weakening the joy of the spiritual journey. It is blessed to see it and find freedom from it.

"You Could Have Done More"

I noted the following after some weeks of writing, when I was about to leave the parish that had hosted me and return to my community residence. The parish was near my family home, and I was staying there so that, while writing, I could also assist my mother. At that time, she was alone, in questionable health, and needed the family. The days, divided among parish, writing, and family, were intense and fruitful. I was to leave the next day:

I feel no energy to work today, and I must. There is packing to do and the car to get ready. Everything has

to be in place so that I can leave tomorrow morning. I
don't really know what I want. Probably it is to have
my own work and life again. Maybe part of it is just the
transition. It has not been easy to be here, and I miss my
own setting.

There is some sense of guilt, since I haven't worked
on the writing these past few days. Ed counseled against
it, and I have found it helpful to take things more lightly.
I have some energy back now. The decisions the family
faces have taken so much energy.

I think there may be some plain spiritual desolation
in this. In reality, things have gone well with the writing,
and I've been able to help the family in important ways.
The voice that accuses is harsh: both words, "accuse"
and "harsh," tell me something about which spirit is at
work. The thoughts are: "You should have done more.
You should have worked harder. You are not doing as
much as others you know. You tell everyone that you've
done a lot, but you know you could have done more."

The signs of the enemy are here: the accusations and
the harshness. The truth is that I didn't work on the
writing this past week because, though I tried, family
issues took all my time and energy. Ed confirmed this
when we spoke. Had I tried to write regardless in these
circumstances, I would have finished this time utterly
exhausted.

I think this is really what is bothering me: the enemy is
at work in these accusations. I need simply to let them go.

I believe that when I wrote these words I was seeing clearly
how the enemy, working in vulnerable spaces in my heart, was
"biting" with regard to a time that had been rich relationally

and fruitful in respect to writing. Describing this in the journal helped me see it more clearly.

"I'll Slide into the End"

This next entry was written on the fifth day of a six-day preached retreat. Each day I gave two talks and met individually with retreatants. I can still see the room and desk at which I sat when writing in my journal. Objectively, the retreat was going well, and the people were receptive. The vulnerable space here was the tiredness that developed over the days and the sense of aloneness as I wrote:

> I can see various tactics of the enemy at this point in the retreat. The feeling that, with three talks to go, "I'm tired of this," with a heaviness of heart. When there were two talks left, I felt a sense that "It's over," again with heaviness and lack of desire to give the remaining talks. From this same heavy space came the thought, "I don't want to 'pump out' another talk. It's gone well thus far; now I'll just slide into the end."

In such ways, I see the enemy's saddening action. Certainly, after five intense days of guiding a retreat, some physical and emotional weariness was natural. But the spiritually heavy and sad feelings regarding the retreat were not objective and, unless rejected, would only diminish my dedication and joy in this service.

"This Will Be a Long and Hard Road"

One way that I experience the enemy's obstacle-placing action is the sense that a new step I hope to take in the spiritual life will be possible, yes, but only after many years of hard effort. The effect is to eliminate any hope of taking this new step in the present or near future. I suspect that I am not alone in this!

This next entry summarizes Ed's advice after a meeting with him:

> In everything, whatever burdens you carry, turn quickly to the Persons of the Trinity, to Mary, and ask for help. Reject the sense that "I can't do it, it will be unbearable, the future will go badly . . . " Turn to the Trinity and ask for help. They are eager to be with you and help you. Move from a stance in which you feel that you must make things happen, and open your heart to receive the grace and strength the Lord wants to give you as you do these things.
>
> This is not hard to do. It is simple, easy. The enemy will place obstacles, make it seem that this is a huge shift, major, slow, hard. That this move from pushing to receiving requires a long and hard road. No, it is easy. You only have to ask and to receive. It can be done now.

"A Quiet, Soft Source of Worry"

The following is also from the weeks in the parish mentioned above, when I was writing and helping my mother. The arrangement with the pastor was that I would say a daily Mass and otherwise be free for these further responsibilities. They were fruitful weeks, and I was grateful for them. One day I noted troubling thoughts and the response to them:

> Where there is fruitfulness, it seems that there will be an attack. The enemy's accusations are still there: "You rise earlier than the other priests. You are proud, competing with the pastor who also rises early. You are trying to impress the other priests." No, I'm just working at the rhythm that works best for me in periods of writing.

Again, "You are working hard, driving yourself, wearing yourself out. This is not what God wants. It's coming from you." No, after some weeks of writing, I feel good, am happy in the work, look forward to it, and am maintaining a healthy pace in general. Yes, I could take breaks sooner at times, but this is very different from the enemy's lies. His way is to take a small thing and make a quiet, soft source of worry out of it.

Finally, "You aren't helping very much with Masses, when there is so much that could be done in the parish." This can lead me to live the days with an uneasy feeling. Again, the arrangement was clear, why I am here, and where my time should be spent.

I need this attention to the enemy's soft lies, low-key, quietly spoken, which can cause tribulation in the soul, lessening of peace, agitation that is not dramatic, just a touch of agitation.

All of this was, I believe, the enemy's attempt to disquiet with false reasons. The contrast of these disquieting thoughts with the richness of what was in fact happening was striking.

The Truth Will Set You Free

The pleasures the enemy proposes, Ignatius writes, are *apparent* (rule 1), and his reasons *false* (rule 2). Everything the enemy suggests will be either an outright lie or the truth twisted in some way. People who love God and seek spiritual progress tell me how life changing it is to realize that the voice that bites, saddens, places obstacles, and disquiets with false reasons, *is not God's voice* but rather that of the enemy. This realization sets captives free.

When those who are *growing toward God* (rule 2) confuse the biting, saddening, obstacle-placing, and disquieting
action of the *enemy* with the stinging action of the *good spirit*
in those *heading away from God* (rule 1)—a situation utterly
different than their own—great pain results. When, that is,
with good will but without the necessary spiritual formation,
they believe that this troubling action of the enemy is actually
the good spirit speaking the truth about their spiritual situation, discouragement follows. On the contrary, when they
understand that this troubling action of the enemy is all a lie,
that it is not God's word to them, that it does not define their
spiritual identity, *captives are set free.* Then they know that
this troubling action is to be rejected for the lie it is. I do not
overstate the power of this realization when I say that it can
be life changing.

Persons have told me that when they felt this biting and
disquieting action of the enemy they thought it meant that
they were bad. To know that they are not the authors of this
experience, that it arises from another agent, and that this is
a normal part of the spiritual journey, brings great freedom.
Then they know that they can take action to reject these tactics of the enemy.

The Tactics of the Good Spirit: Facilitating the Growth

We turn now to the work of grace in those who love God
and are striving to "rise from good to better" in God's service. For Ignatius, the final word is always grace and redemption. I have always loved this dimension of these rules: they
are a spirituality of redemption, with a profound and happy
awareness of God's "sufficient grace" (rule 7) that helps us

"resist all our enemies" (rule 11) on the spiritual journey. If the enemy is at work in those growing toward God (rule 2, first part), God's grace is much more at work, strengthening them in this growth (rule 2, second part).

Ignatius names several ways in which the good spirit aids those who seek to rise spiritually. In such persons, he says, the good spirit will "give *courage and strength, consolations, tears, inspirations, and quiet, easing and taking away all obstacles.*" As with the first part of rule 2, we will examine and exemplify these tactics.

"Courage and Strength"

When one making the Ignatian retreat is desolate and struggling with temptation, Ignatius writes, his director should not be severe with him but gentle, "giving him *courage and strength* to go forward" (*SpirEx* 7). Ignatius employs precisely the same vocabulary here to describe the work of the good spirit in those growing toward God. In such persons, he affirms, it is proper to the good spirit "to give *courage and strength.*"[8]

When Augustine feels helpless to break his attachment to sin, the good spirit, portrayed as the virtue of Continence personified, "smiled at me to give me courage."[9] This loving and encouraging action of the good spirit assists Augustine finally to break the "chain" that bound him to sin.

A woman who loves the Lord rises one morning and walks down the corridor to put on coffee and begin the day. This afternoon she will meet with the doctor to get the results of the biopsy, and, understandably, she is afraid. As she walks down the corridor, her eye catches a placard she has placed on the wall with the parable of the "Footprints in the Sand."[10] Just for a moment, as she passes, the meaning of the parable speaks to her heart: in our times of burden, God is close, carrying us safely through the trial. Her heart lifts, and she knows that the Lord will be with her this day in all that may happen. The good spirit, in a thousand creative ways, gives courage and strength to those who love the Lord.

A woman, active in the Church in her own country, immigrated to a new nation. She joined the local parish and sought her customary involvement in it. Parish life there, however, was so culturally different that she found this increasingly difficult. Finally, at Mass one Sunday, she could bear it no longer. As the readings were beginning, she rose, walked down the aisle, and started down the front steps of the church: she was leaving and was never returning. At that moment, in God's providence, a woman who had arrived late for Mass walked up the steps. As they passed, the woman entering smiled at the woman leaving. The woman leaving stopped, turned around, and went back into the church. When she shared this story, she had been a leader in that parish for forty years. Again, in endlessly creative ways, the good spirit gives courage and strength to those who love and seek God.

A man sincerely seeking God and engaged in a journey of conversion found himself struggling spiritually. He was living in New York City at the time, and describes what followed: "Evening after evening I went to St. Patrick's Roman Catholic Cathedral on Fifth Avenue and spent an hour there praying to God for help and guidance. I liked it there. It was as if the cathedral spoke to me in a quiet, unfaltering voice. It seemed to say: 'Be patient. God will lead you. There are dark nights in every soul—dark nights that precede the dawn. Persevere—don't give up. Stay close to God in doubt and darkness. He will bring you through it.' It was in this assurance that I got through the summer."[11] Here, too, the good spirit gives "courage and strength" to one pursuing growth toward God.

What of our own stories? How have we experienced this encouraging and strengthening action of the good spirit when we so needed it to grow in our spiritual lives?

"Consolations and Tears"

At times, the good spirit stirs in such persons' hearts a lively awareness of God's closeness and love. Then their hearts grow warm with God's love, and the joy of this experience engenders new spiritual energy. Ignatius calls such experiences *consolation*. The consolation felt in the heart may also be expressed through physical *tears*. Ignatius will return to both consolation and tears in rule 3. Consequently, we will explore these in the following chapter.

"Inspirations, and Quiet"

The enemy brings *false reasons* to the mind that *disquiet* the heart; the good spirit brings *inspirations* to the mind and *quiet*—that is, peace, to the heart. Here Ignatius highlights a cognitive dimension in the good spirit's action: such *inspirations* bring clarity to the person and reveal the steps to be taken. Likewise, the good spirit instills a warm *quiet* of heart—the rest, as Augustine writes, that our restless hearts seek.

Earlier, for example, we spoke of Gerald at Sunday Mass and the homily on Luke 11:1–13, "Lord, teach us to pray." When the priest invites his parishioners to pray for ten minutes with the daily readings from Mass, the good spirit brings inspirations to Gerald: "If praying once a week at Sunday Mass is already making so great a difference, what would happen if I prayed daily? I could certainly arrange my morning to set aside ten minutes each day. And all I have to do is ask my wife for help since she already does this daily. I will speak with her this evening and begin this practice tomorrow." The good spirit gives clarity—inspirations—to Gerald regarding the next steps to be taken.

As we review our spiritual journeys, all of us will recognize this action of the good spirit. Through the words or example of a friend or spouse or spiritual guide, through a sermon, through prayer with Scripture or before the Blessed Sacrament, and in many other ways, the good spirit has shown us the way, so that we "may go forward in doing good."

"Easing and Taking Away All Obstacles"

In those rising toward God, the enemy *places obstacles*; in such persons, the good spirit *eases and takes away all obstacles*. The word "all" expresses Ignatius's confidence that, with the aid of the good spirit, *every* obstacle on this path toward growth can be overcome.

We may return once more to Gerald's experience, now later on that same Sunday after the grace-filled Mass. The conversation at supper with his teenage son does not resolve well, and Gerald is somewhat discouraged as the evening unfolds. Now his thoughts about beginning the daily prayer are different: "You've been away from the Church for twenty years. You've never even read Scripture. What makes you think you'll understand anything written there? Why speak to your wife about a practice that is bound to fail? You'll just embarrass yourself and her." The enemy *places obstacles* in the way of one who is seeking to rise from good to better in God's service.

Burdened by these obstacles, Gerald is on the point of relinquishing this new step when his eight-year-old daughter comes into his study to say good night. She hugs him and says, "I love you." Gerald returns her hug and says, "I love you, too." Something in Gerald's heart lifts, and when she leaves the room, he finds himself resolving, "I will speak this evening with my wife as I planned this morning, and I will begin the prayer tomorrow." Through the love of his daughter, the good spirit has *eased and taken away all obstacles*, so that Gerald "may go forward in doing good."

The Strengthening Tactics of the Good Spirit: Some Examples

I take these examples, like those given earlier in this chapter, from my journals. They describe ways in which I have experienced the encouraging action of the good spirit.

"This Brings Peace and Hope"

I wrote the following in a time of physical difficulty that required me to cancel most of my ministry. This page describes the conclusions of my examen prayer[12] one evening:

> I see two different approaches to my situation. One approach says, "It's over. You won't do any more ministry. And it's your fault." This voice brings fear, depression, and desolation.
>
> The other approach says, "God's love is at work in all of this, giving you time to rest, to pray, to make progress on your writing, keeping you from the danger of trying to do too much. The future is in God's hands, and he loves you. The Father gives good things to those who ask (Mt 7:11)." This brings peace and hope.
>
> The first approach is the lie of the enemy. The second is the good spirit.

I was struck that evening by the contrariety of two different perceptions of the same experience: the discouraging lies of the enemy and the action of the good spirit giving "courage and strength." I knew that I would bring this to spiritual direction in my next meeting.

"I Find an Uplift of Heart"

The Virgin Mary has often been the "instrument" of the good spirit in giving me courage and strength. On one day of struggle:

> Again, Mary, you lift my heart, and I experience consolation in the midst of tiredness, feeling too alone, and concern for the writing I am doing. I ask for your help with all of this, and I find an uplift of heart. You are a space of the good spirit for me.

And after finishing an eight-day Ignatian retreat:

> Mary is the answer to the insinuations of the enemy that the newness of the retreat will fade, that things will go back as they were before, that this grace will be lost. When I turn to you, Mary, I feel that this is just beginning, that it will grow. I feel "courage and strength."

"Why Would God Ever Not Want You to Go to Mass?"

I share the following with the permission of the narrator:

> I was raised Catholic and had a good education in the faith, but I had been away from the Church for years. Then I met my future wife. On our first date, we walked together around a lake. As we were parting, I asked, "Will I see you again?" She answered, "You can come

to Mass with me this Sunday." I didn't know how to answer, and I said that I would get back to her.

That night I struggled until 2:00 a.m., unable to sleep, going back and forth, not knowing what to do. I felt that I couldn't go to Mass. Finally, at 2:00 a.m., the thought came to me, "Why don't you pray?" I got down on my knees and tried to pray.

A thought came to me: "You are just using Mass for a date. You can't do that." Then another thought came to me: "Why would God ever *not* want you to go to Mass, whatever the reason?" That was my answer. I went back to bed, fell asleep, and went with her to Mass that Sunday. It was the beginning of my return to the Church.

The *inspirations* of the good spirit in one considering—however hesitantly—new steps toward God are evident in this account. The first was the invitation to pray; the second, the question "Why would God ever *not* want you to go to Mass, whatever the reason?" When the young man acts on both inspirations, he does indeed "go forward in doing good."

"I Don't Know Why I'm So Moved"

This was one of those airplane conversations, and I have never forgotten it. The woman seated next to me told me that she was about to go to Mass for the first time in ten years. She explained that she was raised Catholic but had not been to church for years. She said that she had almost finished her studies in medical school, that she had always been successful, but for the first time, she was facing failure. I sensed the heaviness in her heart as she asked, "Yet how can I return to God? For years, when all was well, I ignored him. Now just because I need something, I'm planning to go back to Mass.

How can I go to God this way?" (Such considerations are classic instances of the enemy's obstacle-placing action in one seeking to move toward God.)

I asked her if she knew the parable of the prodigal son, and she said, no, she did not know it. I explained that when the son returns, his motive is centered on his own need, but that is all the father needs. Then the father runs, overcomes the distance between them, embraces his son, kisses him, and celebrates his return with joy. This parable brought tears to her eyes, and I could see the light and hope it awakened in her. She said, "I don't know why I'm so moved."

I felt that I did know why. Through the power of the Scriptures, the good spirit *eased and took away all obstacles* so that she might go forward on her new journey toward God.

Such is Ignatius's second rule. In rules 3 and 4, Ignatius will introduce two fundamental spiritual experiences: spiritual consolation (rule 3) and spiritual desolation (rule 4). We turn now to the first of these.

Chapter 3

When the Soul Is
Inflamed with Love

*Suddenly I felt a very sweet touch that
warmed my whole being and stirred me
to feelings of deep and moving gratitude
to the Beloved.*

—Georges Vanier

Ignatius provides a series of examples to clarify what he
understands by *spiritual consolation*. I have italicized each:

Third Rule. The third is of spiritual consolation. I call it
consolation when some interior movement is caused in
the soul, through which the *soul comes to be inflamed
with love of its Creator and Lord*, and, consequently
when it *can love no created thing on the face of the
earth in itself, but only in the Creator* of them all. Likewise when it sheds *tears* that move to love of its Lord,
whether out of sorrow for one's sins, or for the passion
of Christ our Lord, or because of other things directly
ordered to his service and praise. Finally, I call consolation *every increase of hope, faith, and charity*, and *all
interior joy* that calls and attracts to heavenly things and
to the salvation of one's soul, quieting it and giving it
peace in its Creator and Lord.

In rule 7, Ignatius describes spiritual consolation as "great fervor, abundant love, and intense grace," and in rule 9 as "increased devotion, intense love, tears, or any other spiritual consolation." In rule 3, as in these later and briefer descriptions, the warm, encouraging quality of *spiritual consolation* emerges: an affectively uplifting experience (and so "consolation") on the level of the spiritual life, of faith, of our relationship with God (and so "spiritual").

Only in rules 3 and 4 does Ignatius employ the first person singular: "*I* call it consolation when . . . " and "*I* call desolation all the contrary . . . " Elsewhere in the rules, Ignatius adopts the first person plural as well.[1]

Spiritual and Nonspiritual Consolation

The issues surrounding the distinction between spiritual and nonspiritual consolation are much discussed by the commentators and are subject to varying opinions. Because of this, I will explore this matter with care. Clarity on this distinction matters greatly, since the rules can only be applied accurately when spiritual consolation is understood well.

The Distinction Between Spiritual and Nonspiritual Consolation

Let us note that Ignatius speaks not only of *consolation* but also specifically of *spiritual* consolation. Elsewhere he employs parallel adjectives: "*divine* consolation" and "*interior* consolation," in which "interior" is synonymous with "divine" and "spiritual."[2] Ignatius's use of such adjectives indicates that in rule 3 he intends only those consolations (uplifting movements of the heart: joy, hope, gratitude, love, peace, and the like) that can be described specifically as *spiritual*, and does not intend those consolations to which this adjective, in the sense he uses it here, does not apply. For Ignatius, as mentioned, *spiritual* denotes the level of faith, of the spiritual life, of our relationship with God. Such consolation, as he will say in rule 9, is "the gift and grace of God our Lord." "Spiritual," therefore, as Ignatius intends it, denotes a *supernatural* consolation, something that our human nature alone cannot produce, a consolation that is a gift of *God's grace*. In rule 3, Ignatius provides many examples of such spiritual consolation, and we will examine them below.

Ignatius repeats the adjective "spiritual" twice again in rule 9: "or any other *spiritual* consolation," "or the other parts of the *spiritual* consolation." Having clarified in rule 3, however, that he intends a specifically spiritual consolation, Ignatius does not repeat the adjective each time he employs the term "consolation." To do so would uselessly burden the text and would contradict Ignatius's consistent practice of avoiding any superfluous words.

From the philosophical perspective, "spiritual" may be used in two senses: to denote *the supernatural level* (God's grace) and to denote *the higher level of human nature* (the soul with its intellect and will). In this second sense, any consolation involving the intellect and will, even if not specifically on the supernatural level, is spiritual.

Ignatius, however, is not concerned with such philosophical issues. When he speaks of *spiritual* consolation, he intends "spiritual" in the first sense, that is, a consolation that human nature alone cannot produce and that is a gift of God's grace. Ignatius composed these rules for his *Spiritual Exercises*, that is, for the *practice* of the spiritual life, and his single concern is that we recognize spiritual consolation on the supernatural level. I find that when the rules are explained well, hearers

readily understand that by "spiritual" Ignatius intends "supernatural," that is, a joy, a peace, a sense of being loved by God,
and similar movements that do not arise from our human
nature alone but that are the work of God's grace in us.[3]

What, then, shall we say of uplifting movements of the
heart (and so "consolations") that *do* arise from our unaided
human nature? Examples abound: the enjoyment of an out-
ing with friends, the goodness of sharing a meal with family,
the uplift of heart while listening to cheerful music, the joy
of love between spouses and between parents and children,
the blessing of friendship, the delight of contemplating the
beauties of nature, the renewal of energy arising from healthy
exercise, the satisfaction of a job well done, and many similar
experiences.[4] From the perspective of discernment, what shall
we call these?

Such experiences are clearly consolations: they involve
uplifting movements of the heart. But if they are not *spiritual*
consolations, in the supernatural sense just explained, what
kind of consolations are they? What adjective must precede
the word "consolation" to describe these? Ignatius does not
himself supply such an adjective.

The fact that he does not has occasionally been seen as
an indication that Ignatius made no distinction between two
kinds of consolation, those that are spiritual (supernatural)
and those that are not. Apart from the serious difficulties
inherent in this position—we will examine these shortly—
the fact that Ignatius does employ the adjectives "spiritual,"
"interior," and "divine" when speaking of consolation specifies his understanding of it in these rules. Adjectives *modify* and *limit* the nouns they precede. Ignatius wants us to
understand that the consolation he envisages in rule 3 must
be such that these adjectives can apply to it, that is, it must be

"spiritual" and *"divine,"* on the *supernatural* level, a gift of God's *grace*. Any consolation to which these adjectives could not apply would exceed the consolation Ignatius intends in rule 3 and throughout the rules.

What then shall we call those consolations to which the adjective "spiritual," as Ignatius employs it here, does not apply? Various possibilities may be proposed: we may speak of "natural consolation," "human consolation," "psychological consolation," "emotional consolation," or similar terms. Any of these adjectives might be appropriately used. I have chosen the adjective "nonspiritual" as synonymous with these and as the closest to Ignatius's own adjective, "spiritual." I first encountered this term in Jules Toner's *Commentary* on these rules.[5] I have retained it because it harmonizes with my approach to the rules, that is, to expound them by examining attentively what Ignatius writes in his text. Of the various words suggested, "nonspiritual" is the most like Ignatius's own choice of the word "spiritual."

In each of the examples given, the person experiences an uplift of heart (and so "consolation") on the natural level (and so "nonspiritual"). To feel an uplift of heart, for example, as one contemplates a beautiful sunrise, is to experience a *nonspiritual consolation*. It is important to note that nonspiritual does not necessarily mean "bad." In each of the examples given, the person experiences a naturally good and healthy nonspiritual consolation.

A page in the writings of the Servant of God Dorothy Day illustrates both spiritual and nonspiritual consolation. Day describes the influence in her early years of a friend, Mary Harrington, and how after one conversation "my small heart was enlarged. I could feel it swelling with love and gratitude to such a good God for such a friendship as Mary's. . . . And the thrill of joy that stirred my heart when I came across spiritual truth and beauty never abated, never left me as I grew older." Day comments, "Natural goodness, natural beauty, brings joy and a lifting of the spirit, but it is not enough, it is not the same. The special emotions I am speaking of came only at hearing the word of God. It was as though each time I heard our Lord spoken of, a warm feeling of joy filled me. It was hearing of someone you love and who loves you."[6]

Day experiences *spiritual* consolation: she feels her heart "swelling with *love* and *gratitude* to such *a good God*," and feels a *"thrill of joy* that stirred my heart when I came across *spiritual truth and beauty."* When she hears others speak of God, "a *warm feeling of joy"* fills her because it was "hearing of *someone you love and who loves you."* The specifically *spiritual* nature of Day's *consolation* ("love and gratitude," "thrill of joy," "warm feeling of joy") is evident: it is entirely related to her faith, her spiritual life, and her relationship with God.

Day further describes the difference she notes between this spiritual consolation and *nonspiritual* consolation: *"Natural goodness, natural beauty,* brings *joy and a lifting of the spirit,* but it is not enough, it is not the same. The special emotions I am speaking of came only at hearing the word of God." The *consolation* ("joy and a lifting of the spirit") Day experiences when she encounters goodness and beauty in nature are experiences of *nonspiritual* consolation: they are good experiences, but Day clearly perceives the difference with respect to spiritual consolation.

Spiritual and Nonspiritual Consolation in Combination

Two points must be noted. First, the *distinction* between spiritual and nonspiritual consolation must be made. If not, grave misapplications of Ignatian discernment may follow with serious consequences.

A married man, for example, finds himself attracted to another woman and knows that the attraction is reciprocal. When they converse, he finds his heart energized and uplifted. A priest finds himself drawn to a woman of the parish and also experiences an uplift of heart when speaking with her. Both, evidently, experience consolation: the uplift of heart that a man and woman feel when mutually attracted.

If the married man or the priest, however, were to identify this consolation as the spiritual consolation of which Ignatius speaks in rule 3, and were to understand it as an indication of where God is leading, disastrous consequences would obviously ensue. Neither is experiencing *spiritual consolation*; both, rather, are experiencing *nonspiritual consolation*, the natural uplift of heart that a man and woman feel when placed together and mutually attracted. This nonspiritual consolation is not an indication of where God is leading: it is simply a natural response to a natural situation. Such cases and many others like them indicate why the distinction between spiritual and nonspiritual consolation must always be observed in discernment.[7]

The failure to make this distinction at times brings Ignatian discernment into discredit, for obvious reasons. The problem is not with Ignatius's teaching but rather that those applying it have not labored seriously enough to understand it, and so misapply it.

Second, the *balance* between spiritual and nonspiritual consolation must also be maintained. While the distinction must not be omitted, neither should it be overemphasized. In God's providence, very often *healthy nonspiritual consolation* is the space into which God infuses the further gift of *spiritual consolation*.

A mother gazes at her infant daughter in repose and delights in her beauty (nonspiritual consolation). As she gazes, a warm stirring of gratitude to God arises in her heart, as her delight in this moment tells her of God's goodness to her throughout her life (spiritual consolation). A man finishes a demanding project at work, knows that it is done well, and feels good about the project (nonspiritual consolation). As he reflects on this, he finds himself filled with joyful confidence that the Lord will accompany him in all the difficulties of his life (spiritual consolation). A woman listens to stirringly beautiful music and finds her heart uplifted (nonspiritual consolation). As she listens, her heart grows warm with the awareness of God's beauty and closeness to her (spiritual consolation). In these and in many other examples we might give, healthy nonspiritual consolation has become the space into which God has infused the grace of spiritual consolation.[8]

In summary, the distinction between spiritual and non-spiritual consolation is key for any accurate application of these rules in discernment. We must always keep it before our eyes. At the same time, we must recognize that often the two will be found together: healthy nonspiritual consolation as the space into which God infuses the grace of spiritual consolation. The combination of this distinction and this balance permits us to apply the rules well.

A Theology of Spiritual Consolation

Spiritual consolation is, as Ignatius affirms, an experience of God's *grace*. Can we specify more precisely the nature of this grace?

Grace may be either a stable condition of the soul or a help given in a particular moment for a particular need. The first is habitual grace; the second is actual grace. The Church explains: "*Habitual grace*, the permanent disposition to live and act in keeping with God's call, is distinguished from *actual graces*, which refer to God's interventions, whether at the beginning of conversion or in the course of the work of sanctification."[9] One classic text further defines actual grace as "a supernatural, transient help given us by our Lord to enlighten our mind and strengthen our will in the performance of a supernatural act."[10] Actual grace, thus, is an intervention or help given by God in a specific moment to assist us in the work of our sanctification at that time. These are, another author writes, "passing aids" through which "the person's power to do good is increased."[11]

One author comments, "Theologically speaking, we may say that consolation is an *actual grace*, by which a person experiences psychologically the spiritually strengthening effects of the attraction of God for his creature and of his action in the creature."[12] Spiritual consolation, thus, is an actual grace, a gift given by God in a determined moment, by which we experience psychologically the uplifting effects of God's work in us, strengthening us at that time for spiritual growth. Another classic texts explains, "This consolation . . . is not a stable condition of the soul. It is rather a supernaturally bestowed spiritual experience of such a nature that when it is present acts of virtue are performed easily, even with delight, relish, and ardor."[13] The examples Ignatius gives in rule 3 will clarify the nature of this "delight, relish, and ardor."

Spiritual consolation is always a gift and grace of God. At times, God may simply give spiritual consolation freely; at other times, God may give it when our hearts are disposed to receive it through faithful prayer and sincere efforts to live according to his word.[14] Our part, therefore, is to live in such a way that we are prepared to receive this grace should God choose to grant it.

Rule 3 is the one rule centered on spiritual consolation in itself. Its purpose, like all the other rules, is practical, in this case to acquaint us with spiritual consolation so that we will recognize it in our experience and know how to respond to it. Nonetheless, its single focus on spiritual consolation in itself gives it a particular beauty, and I have come to love this rule and to welcome the opportunity to teach it. In the transmitting and receiving of its content something uplifting always occurs. Rule 3 continues to bless us today.

Experiences of Spiritual Consolation

Ignatius lists these experiences of spiritual consolation under five headings. We will review them and offer examples of each.

"Inflamed with Love of Its Creator and Lord"

A woman prays daily with Scripture, and today her text is the healing of the woman with the hemorrhage (Mk 5:25–34). She reads through the text attentively a first time, but nothing strikes her in any particular way. She rereads the text slowly. She notes how this woman hopes for healing but only as an anonymous brush of a finger in a crowd. The woman does touch Jesus's garments and is healed. But now Jesus asks who touched him. The disciples make the obvious answer about the press of the crowd, but Jesus knows, and the woman knows.

As the woman prays with this scene, she sees this woman, now healed, come with great courage, fall down before Jesus, and tell him the whole truth. As she prays, she hears Jesus's first word of response, "Daughter," which tells the woman that she is much more in his heart than an anonymous brush of a finger in a crowd, but that a deep and beautiful relationship is established between them. As the woman praying perceives Jesus's response, her heart is warmed with an awareness that Jesus says the same to her, "Daughter," and that he loves her, too, with all the richness this word signifies. Her heart is, in Ignatius's words, "inflamed with love of her Creator and Lord." She is experiencing a gentle and rich spiritual consolation.

All of us can name experiences of this kind, perhaps at Mass, when reading Scripture, in times of quiet prayer, in times when we perceive God's loving action in our lives, or in many other circumstances. The enkindling of the heart may, as here, be gentle. At other times, it may be stronger or even very strong, so that our hearts are truly "inflamed" with love of our God. These are beautiful experiences of spiritual consolation, and we are rightly grateful for them.

"Love of Created Things in Their Creator"

A priest faces a decision in his ministry and struggles to be open to what he perceives the Lord wills. He is making a retreat to seek the Lord's light and strength in this matter. Today he prays with the annunciation of the angel Gabriel to Mary (Lk 1:26–38). He describes his experience of prayer:

> I prayed with the annunciation to Mary and the incarnation of Jesus. I focused simply on Mary. Very strong consolation, with tears. Love for Mary, with a sense of her deep beauty, a great sense of reverence, of hope, of melting of barriers to do God's will in this matter of how I am facing my ministry.

A sense of Mary's total openness, totally flexible, with no resistance, no "my way of programming things": simple openness, with beauty, depth, and love. As I see this in Mary, something in my own encrusted adherence to "my way" seems to give way.[15]

The first experience of spiritual consolation is evident here. As he prays, this priest's heart is inflamed with love of God: "Very strong consolation, with tears." In the warmth of this love, something else happens. The struggle he has been experiencing between where the Lord is leading and other attachments in ministry now disappears, and he is totally open to God: "a great sense of . . . melting of barriers to do God's will in this matter of how I am facing my ministry. . . . As I see this in Mary, something in my own encrusted adherence to 'my way' seems to give way." Again, the richness and beauty of this grace are evident.

Such availability to God is a second experience of spiritual consolation that may be given when the first is present. When "the soul is inflamed with love of its Creator and Lord," Ignatius writes, a further grace may be given: "and *consequently* when it can love no created thing on the face of the earth in itself, *but only in the Creator of them all.*" In this second experience of spiritual consolation, persons do not love created things—places, occupations, relationships, material things, and the like—less, but all the more because they love them with the truest and happiest love: in the Creator of them all. In the example just cited, the priest is now free to love the place, persons, and occupations of ministry in the truest sense—in God. Because of this grace, the earlier tension between love for "created things" and God's leading in his life dissolves, and the priest is free to love them in the richest and most fruitful way—as Ignatius says, "in the Creator of them all."

"Tears for the Love of the Lord"

The body, too, may share the experience of spiritual consolation. Tears may "manifest, accompany, and complete" the heart's experience of God's love.[16] We are not simply spirits, but incarnate spirits: through tears, the whole person may share in the spiritual consolation.[17]

A man rises and goes to church this morning. He arrives thirty minutes before Mass and dedicates the time, according to his habitual practice, to praying with the day's Gospel. He is tired and discouraged because of problems that have arisen at work. The church is large and cold, and only a few others fill its emptiness at this hour.

This day's Gospel is the encounter of Jesus with the disciples on the way to Emmaus (Lk 24:13–35). As the man reads this text, he sees these two disciples, whose hearts are sad and who have lost hope, quietly leave the community. He sees how Jesus approaches them, listens to them, and speaks with them. He watches their "slow" hearts become "burning" hearts (Lk 24:25, 32). Then he reaches the moment when they arrive at the village, and Jesus appears to be traveling further. He hears the prayer of these two disciples, a prayer this man, too, has often made to the Lord, "Stay with us! Darkness is falling" (see Lk 24:29). The man sees how Jesus welcomes that prayer, goes in with them, and their lives are changed. As he reads this, the beginning of a tear comes to his eye: "Lord, you are with me, too, in my tiredness and discouragement. You hear my prayer when I call out to you."

This, too, is a beautiful experience of spiritual consolation, of "tears that move to love of his Lord." I know as I write this that all of us will recognize such tears in our own spiritual experience, and we rightly treasure these times of grace.

The woman who enters the Pharisee's house never says a word but expresses everything with her tears (Lk 7:36–50). Her tears are tears of spiritual consolation, "out of sorrow for one's sins," as Ignatius writes in rule 3. These are blessed and healing tears that express her heart's awareness that, perhaps for the first time in her life, she is welcomed, respected, understood, loved, and set free for a new life.

In a letter to his spiritual director, St. Pius of Pietrelcina writes, "Although I hope in the divine mercy of Jesus, dear Father, I tremble very much indeed. For this have I wept silently, for this have I shed *tears of sorrow* that were at the same time a source *of great happiness to me.*"[18] *Tears of sorrow* that were *a source of great happiness*: again, these are blessed tears of spiritual consolation. We, too, may have experienced such tears of joy when we have known God's forgiveness in our lives.

I have never forgotten a moment in my final year as provincial in my religious community.[19] A heavy burden of tiredness had accumulated after those years of constant travel and many responsibilities. I met with my council and presented the travel that lay ahead in the next few months. Generously, the members offered to share that travel and the responsibilities it entailed. I went before the Lord deeply grateful, sensing in their generosity the sign of his understanding of my situation and his faithful love. As I sat in church, a tear of gratitude to the Lord came to my eye. It was a blessed experience of spiritual consolation.[20]

"Every Increase of Hope, Faith, and Charity"

I find it interesting that Ignatius has inverted the usual order of the three theological virtues: the classic "faith, *hope,* and charity" becomes "*hope*, faith, and charity," in which hope receives the first place and so a certain prominence. In writing the text, did Ignatius intend to give hope such prominence? One author comments simply, "He begins with confidence in God."[21] Certainly this changed order suggests the message of hope that permeates the entire set of rules.

A man is praying with Scripture one morning. Prayer has been dry for the past two weeks, and everything in him expects it to be equally dry today. Still, he is faithful and fully intends to dedicate his customary time to prayer. His text this day is Luke 5:1–11, Peter and the catch of fish. The first minutes of his prayer, as he reads through the text, are as dry as he expected. He reads the text again, and this time notices Peter's response when, through the sign of the fish, he recognizes that the Divine has come close to him in Jesus. He sees Peter fall on his knees before Jesus and say, "Depart from me, Lord, for I am a sinful man" (Lk 5:8)—"I am not holy enough, I am too sinful to be this close to you, and so, depart from me, leave me, let me be farther from you."[22] The man's attention is then caught by how Jesus responds to Peter. Jesus does not argue with him; he simply confirms Peter's belonging with him and Peter's place in his mission (Lk 5:10–11).

As this man perceives Jesus's response to Peter, something in his own heart gently lifts: "Lord, you respond to me in the same way when I sense my limitations and failures." Now he finds that he is glad to be at prayer: "Lord, you may have more yet to give me in my prayer this morning." This man is experiencing the *increase of hope* that Ignatius describes as spiritual consolation. This is a perceptible, felt experience, with an uplift of heart.[23]

A woman is at daily Mass. She loves the Mass and is present with goodwill. Her attention wanders a little at times, and when it does, she brings herself back to the flow of the prayers. The Mass reaches the consecration. The priest takes the bread, pronounces the words "This is my Body," and elevates the now consecrated Bread. As the woman gazes toward the altar, a warm and lively awareness fills her heart: "This is really you. You are truly present before me in the consecrated Bread." She is experiencing the *increase of faith* of which Ignatius speaks in rule 3. She always believed the truth of the Real Presence in the consecrated Bread and Wine, but in this moment, by God's gift, she experiences this truth more deeply with a happy uplift of heart.

The same might occur, for example, when listening to or reading Scripture. As we listen and read, the Word comes alive: with joy we sense that Jesus is speaking to us, now, through that text. We always believed that Jesus speaks to us through his Word; in this moment, however, we *experience* this truth in a lively fashion and with a warm, happy movement of the heart. Similar experiences may occur with regard to many truths of our faith: the mystery of the Holy Trinity, God as Creator of the world around us, Jesus's death and resurrection, his abiding closeness as our Savior, his providence in our lives, his presence in our neighbor (Mt 25:40), and other tenets of the faith.

The woman at daily Mass receives Communion and remains after Mass to pray for a few minutes. She feels herself deeply loved by the Lord, and her heart rests gladly in that love. She senses that this love prepares her for the day, and that she is now more ready, in Jesus, to love the others at work. She is experiencing the *increase of charity* that Ignatius describes as spiritual consolation. Again, we can all remember times when we have felt something similar, whether in prayer or in the activity of the day.

"Joy That Calls and Attracts to Heavenly Things"

Finally, Ignatius speaks of "all *interior joy* that *calls and attracts* to *heavenly things* and to *the salvation of one's soul*, quieting it and giving it peace in its Creator and Lord." "Interior" here, for Ignatius, is synonymous with "spiritual." In fact, in his *Autograph Directory*, Ignatius twice describes the joy of spiritual consolation as "spiritual joy."[24] This spiritual joy moves the heart in a specific direction: in it, the heart is *called* and *attracted* "upward" as it were, toward what Ignatius calls *heavenly things* and the *things of salvation*.

Author Evelyn Waugh describes Monsignor Ronald Knox's prayer after his entrance into the Catholic Church:

> He told a friend that in his first months as a Catholic he received the "consolations" he needed and *often ran to church* in his *impatience to begin his prayers*. He *looked forward to his meditations* as periods of pure joy. And at St. Edmund's it was his radiant devotion which most impressed his more discerning colleagues.
>
> The present Bishop of Lancaster, Dr. Flynn, writes: "My most outstanding memory of him [at St. Edmund's] is his absorption in prayer before the Blessed Sacrament. That made so profound an impression on me that one day, years after, preaching in the North on the love of God as an act of the will, which would not involve the emotions, I said: 'Don't tell me that this is all the love of God means. I have *seen* people in love with God.'"[25]

In his spiritual joy, Knox's heart is called and attracted to heavenly things and the things of salvation: he is so strongly drawn to the presence of the Blessed Sacrament that he often runs to church; he is so drawn to prayer that he is impatient to begin and looks forward to his meditation as a time of pure joy.

Such experiences exemplify the spiritual joy that Ignatius wishes to highlight in rule 3. When our hearts are filled, gently or more strongly, with joy in the Lord, then we are "called and attracted" to the things of faith and of the spiritual life in general. We delight, for example, in meditation, *lectio divina*,[26] reading Scripture, participating in Mass, praying the Liturgy of the Hours or the Rosary, serving the Lord in our respective vocations, and taking new steps to grow in the spiritual life. We need only think of past—or present—times of spiritual consolation to see this blessed dynamic at work in our lives.

In his *Autograph Directory*, Ignatius adds other nuances to the experiences of spiritual consolation given in rule 3. Consolation includes, he writes, "interior peace," "hope in the things of above," a "raising up of the mind," and "every interior movement that leaves the soul consoled in our Lord." All experiences of spiritual consolation, he writes, "are gifts of the Holy Spirit."[27] The later *Official Directory* adds still further nuances: "light, and a clearer understanding of divine things," "the raising up of the mind to God," "hope fixed in God," "perception of eternal things," "a turning toward heavenly things," "the warmth of holy love," and "any similar effects or stirrings of the heart, all of which are from the good spirit."[28]

Spiritual Consolation: Some Examples

The following are again from my journals. I give them in chronological order.

"A Sense of Peace that I Did Not Think Possible"

I had completed the manuscript of a new book and sent it to the editor. I was awaiting his appraisal of the book with some anxiety because upon it would depend whether or not the book would advance toward publication. At the time, I was a writer-in-residence at a college in Toronto. One afternoon during this time of waiting, I decided to take a short pilgrimage on foot to the Cathedral of St. Michael's:

> Yesterday I walked to St. Michael's, and it was a time of blessing. At one point, near the end of my time there, a gift was given to me, without my even asking at that moment for it, just given, of a surrender of the manuscript and the editor. I felt a sense of peace that I did not think possible until I would hear from the editor. I sense that you, Lord, can do this in me, when I cannot do it. I sense that this needs to be renewed, that it is not a one-time thing. But I *experienced* yesterday that it is possible to find peace even before an issue is resolved, that you, Lord, can do this in me. It happened while praying in the cathedral, and that seems to be my part, opening myself to this gift.

Ignatius writes in rule 3 that God, in giving consolation, "quiets the soul and gives it peace in its Creator and Lord." I still remember that gift and discovering that peace is possible in situations that cause anxiety, even before they are resolved.

"I See that This Retreat Could Open Up"

From the first time of prayer at the beginning of an eight-day Ignatian retreat:

> Just the warmth of being with you, Lord. I began by praying with Isaiah 55:1–2: "All you who are thirsty,

come to the water!"[29] But I really just wanted to be with you, Lord. As I sit here, Lord, I am happy. I see that this retreat could open up in ways that I can't foresee now. For now, there are no major burdens, only the one decision about ministry that I will need to pray about during the retreat. The retreat seems more focused on issues of growth in community, the pace of life, tiredness, writing, and prayer. The happiness is to see your goodness and to see it bear fruit.

This was a quiet time of spiritual consolation that prepared me for the retreat. I felt the "increase of hope" that Ignatius describes: the sense that God had grace in store for me in the days of retreat that lay ahead.

"I Feel a Sense of Safety"

This next reflection dates from the beginning of a retreat I gave for seminarians. I found it physically laborious to speak in the talks. I did not then realize that I was losing my voice, a process that would lead to surgeries and repeated cancellations of ministry over the next years. Yet I knew that something was not right. One day, I went to the chapel and spent some time there alone, looking at an icon of Our Lady of Tenderness. The experience stayed with me and strengthened me in the months that followed. Still today, I keep a photograph of that icon in my office, and I am looking at it now as I write this book. While giving that retreat for seminarians, I wrote:

> I stood looking at the icon, Jesus's little hand in Mary's, his small cheek against hers. I place myself there and find peace, an attraction of heart, light on various things, and a sense of safety.

As I sit looking at this icon, just four or five feet in front of it, I feel a sense of safety, of something holy, an answer to my fears about my future in my ministry and priestly life, and that the book I am writing now and the next I have in mind are in good hands. It is a place beyond my limitations. I feel *hope* where there is so often a lingering fear and anxiety. I feel peace, a joy.

If Jesus is in this place, tenderly held by Mary, kept safe by her care and love, why can I not be there, too? He is our model, the one we imitate.

That experience of being loved and kept safe, and the hope that it engendered, accompanied me through the years of struggle that followed. It still speaks to me today. It was a spiritual consolation, a gift of feeling God's love, of spiritual joy, and of an increase of hope in a time when I so needed it.

"Isaiah 40 Was Pure Mercy"

Another year, I was making my annual retreat in December. One morning, I was in the kitchen preparing breakfast. No one else was in the house, and so, since it was close to Christmas, I put on Handel's *Messiah* as a background. I enjoyed the opening orchestral movement, and then awaited the first sung piece. I had not heard *Messiah* for some time and was curious to see how the narration of Jesus's birth would begin in the oratorio.

When it did begin, the beauty of the music, of the tenor's singing, and, above all, of the words moved me deeply. The text is from the King James Bible: "Comfort ye, comfort ye my people, saith your God. Speak ye comfortably to Jerusalem, and cry unto her, that her warfare is accomplished, that her iniquity is pardoned" (Is 40:1–2). This was the beginning of the story: a message of comfort, a cry that the struggle is over, that human iniquity and failure have been forgiven.

When I shared this with the retreat director, the director suggested that I take this text and experience to prayer. I did that:

> Isaiah 40—comfort my people, tell them that their struggle is over, that their iniquity has been forgiven—was pure mercy and love for your people. They did not merit it: they were in exile for their sins and failures. It was simply mercy, as was the coming of Jesus when this text was seen in all its fullness, as it is also in regard to God's coming in my life. I write this with consolation even to tears. It is simply God's love and mercy, not my merit. My part is to be comforted and receive God's mercy.
>
> But the key is God's free intervention, consoling his people, speaking tenderly to them, lifting their guilt, ending their struggle. I think sometimes of my part as a long, hard struggle, tiring, at times exhausting, working hard, having to do the work, yet the key thing is to receive mercy, to be open to it, to say yes to it. I think that this shift is the heart of the retreat: the journey toward living in Isaiah 40.

Music, beautiful singing, and the words of Scripture were the occasion of this spiritual consolation. It brought, in Ignatius's words, "interior peace," "hope in the things of above," a "raising up of the mind," and an "interior movement" that left "the soul consoled in our Lord." I am sure that readers will recognize such times in their own spiritual experience.

In rule 4, Ignatius explores the experience contrary to spiritual consolation. We turn now to that rule.

Chapter 4

Darkness of Soul

How suddenly things had changed!
Happiness into bitterness, joy into tears!
—St. Charles of Sezze

Rule 4 is the companion to rule 3 and describes its exact opposite: spiritual *desolation*. As in rule 3, Ignatius does not give a definition but rather a list of experiences of spiritual desolation. I have italicized each:

> Fourth Rule. The fourth is of spiritual desolation. I call desolation all the contrary of the third rule, such as *darkness of soul, disturbance* in it, *movement to low and earthly things, disquiet from various agitations and temptations,* moving to *lack of confidence, without hope, without love,* finding oneself *totally slothful, tepid, sad* and, *as if separated from one's Creator and Lord.* For just as consolation is contrary to desolation, in the same way the thoughts that come from consolation are contrary to the thoughts that come from desolation.

The final sentence of rule 4 applies to rules 3 and 4 together and makes a key point about the cognitive aspect of both.

Obviously, spiritual desolation is not the happiest topic in the spiritual life! Yet after almost forty years of learning and sharing Ignatius's spiritual teaching, I believe that his teaching on spiritual desolation—what it is and how to over-come it—may be the most valuable resource he offers for the spiritual life. I say this because I also believe it true that, for most dedicated people, for most of the way on the spiritual journey, the real obstacle is spiritual desolation: the times when we become disheartened in the spiritual life and feel the pull to relinquish our prayer, our efforts to grow spiritually, and our desires to take new steps in God's service. A teaching that equips us to recognize and reject spiritual desolation is among the most valuable that can be offered us. I have wit-nessed the clarity and hope these rules give countless times over the years.

Spiritual and Nonspiritual Desolation

All that we have said about spiritual and nonspiritual con-solation applies equally to their opposites, spiritual and nonspiritual desolation. *Spiritual desolation,* like spiritual consolation, is an experience on the level of the heart. It sig-nifies a heavy movement of the heart, such as sadness, dis-couragement, anxiety, hopelessness, and the like, (and so "desolation") on the level of the spiritual life, of faith, and of our relationship with God (and so "spiritual"). A man, for example, begins a time of prayer. He does not feel the warmth of God's love this day. He struggles even to remain at prayer, and a sadness pervades his efforts. He feels far from God, with a sense that his prayer will be fruitless. This man is experiencing *heavy movements of the heart* on the level of *his relationship with God*: he is experiencing *spiritual desolation.*

Ignatius does not speak in rule 4 of a deficiency in physical energy (tiredness) or emotional energy (depression)—that is of a natural or *nonspiritual* desolation. As in rule 3, Ignatius focuses on the specifically *spiritual* level, describing specifically *spiritual* desolation.[1]

By parallel with rule 3, though Ignatius does not discuss nonspiritual desolation, this does not mean that nonspiritual desolation has no importance for the spiritual life. Just as *healthy nonspiritual consolation* is often the space into which God infuses the grace of *spiritual consolation*, so also *nonspiritual desolation*—when we are vulnerable through tiredness or depression or both—is often the space into which the enemy brings the further trap of *spiritual desolation*. The enemy readily works in our nonspiritual vulnerabilities.

Earlier (chapter 2) we explored the example of Gerald, the forty-one-year-old married man who recently returned to the Church. We described his grace-filled experience at Sunday Mass and the homily that moved him to decide to pray daily with Scripture for ten minutes. We mentioned the tense conversation with his teenage son at supper and the heaviness that filled Gerald's heart after. In terms of rule 4, Gerald experienced *nonspiritual desolation* after a discouraging interaction with his son.

Later that evening, Gerald is in his study preparing for work the next day. This is the time when he planned to speak with his wife and, with her help, begin the ten minutes the next morning. But now Gerald does not feel God's closeness, and the warm gratitude to God (spiritual consolation) that he felt at Mass that morning is gone. He feels no energy for spiritual things and no desire to pray or begin new steps in prayer. In terms of rule 4, Gerald is now experiencing *spiritual desolation*, a heaviness of heart specifically on the level of his spiritual life and relationship with God. The nonspiritual desolation created a vulnerability into which the enemy has brought the discouraging trap of spiritual desolation. Very often this will be the pattern.

It is important to note, however, that a certain amount of nonspiritual desolation is normal and even holy in a well-lived life. The mother, for example, who stays up three or four nights in a row with a sick child grows physically tired. Her tiredness derives from her love for her child and her desire to live well her vocation as a mother. Obviously, she will need, when circumstances allow, to recuperate the physical energy expended. The same may be said of the pastor who guides his parish through Holy Week or who is called to the hospital in the early morning. He, too, may feel a physical and emotional tiredness. Again, there is something holy about his nonspiritual desolation, accepted out of love for his parishioners, and again he will need, when circumstances allow, to recover the energy spent in their service.

But if there is too much and too persistent nonspiritual desolation in a person's life—if persons say, "I always feel exhausted" or "I always feel somewhat depressed"—then not only as good stewards of their health, which God calls them (and us) to be, but also *for the sake of their spiritual lives*, they need to do something about this. Many problems that we consider spiritual resolve when we pay wise attention to the needs of our humanity on the nonspiritual level.

To say this simply, I imagine that most of us have a daily routine of prayer. We esteem it, know that it helps us, and try to be faithful to it. I imagine also that I am not alone in experiencing days when I say to myself that "I just can't do it today." What very often resolves that for me is *exercise*. I get some healthy exercise, and then I am ready to pray. The problem never was that I did not want to pray; the problem was that I had not paid wise attention to a *nonspiritual* need of my humanity.

One of the best things we can do for our spiritual lives is to take wise care of our humanity on the nonspiritual (natural) level. St. Teresa of Avila writes, "Take care, then, of the body for the love of God, because at many times the body must serve the soul."[2] *For the love of God*: for the sake of our spiritual lives and for our progress in the love of God. Such prudent care closes the door to many spiritual desolations.

What we have just said indicates that, again by exact parallel with *spiritual* and *nonspiritual consolation*, the distinction between *spiritual* and *nonspiritual desolation* is both important and must not be overstressed. It is important because spiritual and nonspiritual desolation are distinct realities, calling for spiritual or nonspiritual remedies respectively. When both are used wisely—the person, for example, with appropriate psychological help is overcoming depression, and with appropriate spiritual help is simultaneously growing in prayer and love of God—then wonderful progress occurs.

For this same reason, however, the distinction must not be overstressed. As we have seen, *nonspiritual* desolation is often the space into which the enemy will bring the trap of *spiritual* desolation. When the whole person is integrated into the spiritual journey, the enemy's spiritual desolations significantly lose their power to wound.

Spiritual Desolation and the Dark Night

When I present the rules, questions regarding the relationship of these two experiences—spiritual desolation and dark night—generally arise: Are they different? Are they the same? How should we respond to the one and the other? Often the question of St. Teresa of Calcutta's spiritual darkness arises, and of how this is to be understood in the light of Ignatius's teaching on spiritual desolation. These are significant questions and merit accurate responses.

In my replies to them, I utilize the term *spiritual desolation* in Ignatius's precise sense and the term *dark night* also in John of the Cross's precise sense. Clarity regarding the two terms largely provides the answers to these questions.

By *spiritual desolation*, as just described, Ignatius understands a heavy movement of the heart (sadness, discouragement, and the like) on the level of our relationship with God. As he clearly specifies, this discouraging trap is always the work of the enemy.[3] Together with temptation to obvious sin, it is the "garden variety" tactic of the enemy, one that all dedicated persons experience on the spiritual journey. Obviously, "garden variety" does not signify "harmless." If we do not resist spiritual desolation, it will cause great spiritual damage.

The *dark night*—more specifically, the two passive dark nights, that of sense and that of spirit—in the understanding of John of the Cross, is an experience of infused contemplative prayer, felt by the person as dark and painful. Through it, God is purifying the person he is calling to higher degrees of infused contemplative (mystical) prayer, thus rendering the person capable of the increased union this prayer supposes. The dark night, therefore, in contrast with spiritual desolation, is a work of God.

Of the first dark night, that of sense, one classic author writes that it "is a prayer of simplicity" characterized by "a state of aridity" generally experienced as "bitter and painful."[4] The dark night is an experience of *prayer*, and, like all prayer, it is a gift of God. The "bitter and painful" quality it assumes specifies it as "dark" and as "night."

Another author explains, "Why are the passive nights painful? This purification process is a cure of illness and therefore involves a cutting away, a removal of the roots of spiritual maladies, and a separation from the egocentrism that wounds us." He continues, "In these beginnings of infused prayer God is communicating nothing less than Himself through a light and love that itself consumes our egocentrism. We do not, however, perceive this communication as light and love but as darkness and pain. This . . . perception is due to our incapacity and opaqueness and unlikeness to the divine. . . . Hence, in this night, one perceives the love he is receiving as dryness and emptiness."[5]

The dark night, therefore, is an experience of infused contemplative prayer felt as painful because it is purifying; it prepares the person for greater union with God through higher states of infused contemplation. The difference between this purifying experience of prayer and the discouraging lies of spiritual desolation is evident.[6] The first is a gift of God; the second is a trap of the enemy. By *accepting* the first, we grow; by *rejecting* the second, we grow.

In our own time, the experience of St. Teresa of Calcutta provides a remarkable example of a decades-long willingness to accept the dark night. Her spiritual director, Joseph Neuner, SJ, identified her long interior trial as the dark night of John of the Cross. At his request, Mother Teresa described her interior experience in writing. Years later, Neuner affirmed, "My answer to the confession of these pages was simple: there was no indication of any serious failure on her part that could explain the spiritual dryness. It was simply the dark night of which all masters of the spiritual life know."[7] According to spiritual writer Reginald Garrigou-Lagrange, OP, this night may, in some cases, serve not only to purify the individual but also "to make the already purified soul work for the salvation of its neighbor."[8] The fifty years of Mother

Teresa's night and the extraordinary fruitfulness of her life suggest this understanding of her darkness.[9]

At times, the distinction between spiritual desolation and the dark night is clouded by a broader use of "dark night." "Dark night," as an expressive metaphor, is currently applied to a wide range of struggles. In 1955, for example, Flannery O'Connor wrote that "right now the whole world seems to be going through a dark night of the soul."[10] Gerald May speaks of a "dark night of recovery" in AA members whose desperate straits have led them to begin a spiritual journey, or again of a "corporate dark night of the soul" in respect to social systems.[11] Actor and filmmaker Mel Gibson refers to a wild period in his life, a time of emptiness and void, as a "dark night of the soul."[12] More broadly, John Paul II writes that "the term dark night is now used of all of life and not just of a phase of the spiritual journey. The Saint's [John of the Cross] doctrine is now invoked in response to this unfathomable mystery of human suffering."[13]

Wider applications of the metaphor "dark night" are legitimate, in keeping with the nature of metaphor itself. For the purpose of our specific question, however, clarity requires that we retain the precise sense of the metaphor as intended by John of the Cross. When that sense is retained, the answer to the question is clear.

Having made the distinction, we must also note that a person undergoing the dark night may experience spiritual desolation as well. While enduring the "bitter and painful" purification of the dark night, the person may grow anxious and afraid, vulnerable to the discouraging lies of the enemy's spiritual desolation. In this case, the same principle holds: the dark night is to be accepted and the spiritual desolation rejected.

How will we recognize in practice the difference between spiritual desolation and the dark night? A few general observations may be offered. All dedicated persons experience spiritual desolation; not all experience or have yet experienced the dark night. Those experience the dark night whom God is now calling to infused contemplative (mystical) prayer. Generally, those whom God calls to the dark night are generous with the Lord and evidence a certain spiritual maturity.

The responsibility to distinguish accurately between the two, however, lies not with the person but with a competent spiritual director. Such questions in individual experience should be brought to wise and competent spiritual direction.

Desolation and Dryness

Another question arises periodically when I present the rules: What about dryness? Is dryness in the spiritual life a form of spiritual desolation? If, for example, persons experience dryness when they try to pray or go about their day, are they in spiritual desolation? Is dryness the same as spiritual desolation, or is it something different? As with the earlier questions, clear answers matter because they dictate the appropriate response to this experience.

The Directories

Ignatius knew that practical advice, beyond that given in the book of the *Spiritual Exercises*, was necessary for directors of the Exercises. He therefore drafted or verbally dictated several brief commentaries of this kind, a work completed in subsequent years by the early Jesuits. These commentaries are known as the *Directories* for the Spiritual Exercises.[14] We will refer to them here and at various points in this book.

When Ignatius lists various experiences of spiritual desolation in rule 4, he does not mention dryness. In his *Autograph Directory*, however, when Ignatius again names experiences of spiritual desolation, he does include dryness (*sequedad*) among them.[15] Highlighting the contrariety between consolation and desolation, Ignatius writes that desolation may be experienced as "dryness against tears," that is, against—the contrary of— the tears that express the love of God felt in consolation.[16]

Many of the directories follow Ignatius in this. Juan Alfonso de Polanco, for example, includes "aridity" among the forms of desolation.[17] Diego Miró describes desolation as "sadness, want of trust, lack of love, and dryness, as is said in the fourth rule."[18] Here Miró expresses his conviction that dryness, though not explicitly mentioned, is to be understood as included in Ignatius's fourth rule. The *Official Directory* likewise includes dryness among the experiences of desolation.[19] The *Short Directory* amplifies the description: desolation may be felt as "a dryness of affect, and darkness of mind, as is said in the fourth rule."[20] In desolation, therefore, the person may experience a darkness, a confusion, on the cognitive level and a dryness, an aridity, on the affective level.

Forms of Dryness

In dryness, then, persons experience the opposite of the affective warmth of spiritual consolation and the physical tears that may express it: as they pray, as they live the spiritual life and their relationship with God, they are dry, arid, devoid of uplifting affective stirrings. When is this experience spiritual desolation as Ignatius describes it in rule 4? The answer depends upon the specific form of dryness these persons experience. As with other terms in the spiritual life, the same word can signify many different things.

A first form of dryness may result simply from lack of formation in prayer. Persons of good will desire to pray and make sincere attempts to do so. Because these persons, however, have never received formation in prayer, they flounder, unsure of how to proceed: their prayer is dry. The need here is exposure to classic and effective forms of prayer: *lectio divina*, Ignatian meditation or imaginative contemplation, the Liturgy of the Hours, and so forth. Once these persons learn how to pray, the floundering will cease, and this form of dryness will be overcome.[21]

Dryness may also arise from negligence in the life of prayer or from an inconsistency between a person's prayer and life. If such persons weaken in fidelity to prayer, no longer dedicate consistent time to it, or no longer prepare in the way they find helpful, dryness may result. Likewise, behavior contrary to the Gospel may also cause prayer to feel dry: the disharmony between prayer and life will render prayer more difficult—more dry.[22]

Yet another experience of "dryness" may result from solid growth in prayer. A point may arrive when God now calls such persons to a more simplified form of prayer. The earlier, more active and discursive methods no longer assist as before, while the new and simpler way of praying is not yet firmly established. This is a healthy "dryness" and a sign of growth. Competent spiritual direction will greatly assist such persons to negotiate this blessed passage in prayer.

Dryness may again result when persons need to share with God a burden, fear, shame, or anxiety that fills their hearts—and have as yet been unable to do so. They experience dryness: nothing seems to help in prayer, the time passes slowly and with distractions, and the prayer they attempt appears to lack life.

A husband and wife sit across the table from each other at dinner. He knows that she holds a burden in her heart that she has not been able to express and share with him. Until the burden is expressed and shared, they will struggle to speak together with their habitual ease and communion. Their conversation will remain on a superficial level—it will feel dry—while both know that something deeper needs to be communicated. A man once told me that for eleven years his prayer had been dry. A few questions revealed that his young son had died eleven years earlier. When, after some hesitancy and with some courage, he shared with the Lord the stored-up pain and anger in his heart, the dryness ceased and prayer flowed again.

Other forms of dryness may result from nonspiritual factors. When persons are physically exhausted, they may find their prayer dry: they simply do not have the physical energy to pray in their usual way. Adequate rest will resolve this "dryness." Something similar may result from depletion of emotional energy. Persons who have expended great emotional energy in difficult situations and who try to pray may also find that their prayer is dry: they are affectively spent and struggle to be emotionally present to their prayer. Healthy ways of replenishing emotional energy will resolve this "dryness" as well.

None of these forms of dryness are experiences of spiritual desolation.[23] Each has its individual cause and so its individual remedy. Good spiritual direction will be sensitive to the cause of such persons' individual experiences of dryness and so assist them to respond appropriately, helping them to eliminate its cause or—should such "dryness" indicate growth toward simplified prayer—assisting them to negotiate it well.

If, however, the dryness bears the mark of spiritual desolation—affective aridity coupled with discouragement, a sense of distance from God, a weakening of hope, various temptations, and the like—then such persons will recognize the enemy at work and hear the call to active and energetic resistance.

Qualities of Spiritual Desolation

Through the years, as I have studied and taught these rules, received the sharing of many, and experienced the rules personally, I have noted various qualities of spiritual desolation. I will share and discuss them here.

A Sense of Irreparable Disaster

One morning, on a day of physical struggles and tiredness—and so of nonspiritual vulnerability to spiritual desolation—I was able to name this quality of spiritual desolation. If it is strong enough, spiritual desolation may bring a sense of irreparable disaster. Its message is this: "Things are going badly for you. You are in a bad way spiritually, and things will continue to go badly. It's all over. The harm can't be undone. Even if it could, you won't take the necessary steps. You won't change. Don't think it's ever going to be different."

This is simply one more lie of the enemy. We are only in a time of spiritual desolation, not in a time of irreparable disaster. Growth is always the work of God's love and grace, and that is always available. When in spiritual desolation, I find it helpful to name this lie explicitly: "No, nothing is over. It is never too late. All the doors to God and growth are open."

Spiritual Desolation Presents Itself
as Our Spiritual Identity

This quality of spiritual desolation touches the heart of its burden. If we believe the lie that equates our *experience of spiritual desolation* with our *spiritual identity*, the desolation will grow very heavy.

A woman rises one morning and prepares to pray. This day, she does not feel God's closeness and has little desire for prayer. The spiritual desolation (voice of the enemy) says to her, "Do you see who you are (identity)? You are *a person who does not love prayer.*" No, she is a person who loves God and prays faithfully, a person whom God is permitting to experience spiritual desolation on this particular morning for reasons of a love that Ignatius will describe later in the rules.

A man may one day feel far from God, as though God were a million miles away. He feels very alone as he tries to serve the Lord at work and at home. The spiritual desolation (voice of the enemy) says to him, "Do you see who you are (identity)? You are *a person far from God.*" Again, no, he is a person who loves and serves the Lord faithfully, a person whom God is permitting to experience spiritual desolation this day.

A priest is taking a new initiative in his parish from which he hopes much spiritual benefit will come. This day he is tired and discouraged. He struggles to pray and finds himself doubting that much fruit will ever result from so much labor. The spiritual desolation (voice of the enemy) says to him, "Do you see who you are (identity)? You are *a person who does not have much confidence in God.*" Once again, no, he is person who, with trust in God, is taking new initiatives but whom God is permitting this day to experience spiritual desolation.

Obviously, if these persons or any of us believe the lie that equates the experience of spiritual desolation with our spiritual identity, much discouragement and pain will ensue. If we are aware of and reject this lie, much of the burden of the desolation will lift. I have often seen how the unmasking of this lie sets captives free.[24]

There Is No Shame in Experiencing Spiritual Desolation

This point—that there is no shame in experiencing spiritual desolation—cannot be repeated too often. When I present the rules, I repeat it many times. No one has yet told me that I say it too often!

People who love the Lord frequently feel shame when they experience spiritual desolation. Their unspoken thought, were it expressed, would be something like this: "If I really loved the Lord the way I should; if I were as faithful to prayer, to God's service, to my vocation, as I should be; if I were as dedicated to living my faith as I should be, I would not feel this heaviness and this lack of energy for spiritual things." Often linked to this is an also unarticulated sense that somehow "I am the only one" who experiences such sadness, lack of fervor, and discouragement in the spiritual life: "If other people could see me now, so unwilling to pray, just wanting to pick up the smartphone again or flop in front of the television . . . "

I describe this space of the heart with reverence since I know how heavy and painful such thoughts and feelings can be. We all experience times of spiritual desolation. Generally, without Ignatius's help, we do not even have a language for them or a way of understanding them, let alone of articulating them to others. And so we carry them in silence, and alone.

It is liberating to know that spiritual desolation is an ordinary experience in the spiritual life, that every disciple of the Lord for two thousand years—including the canonized saints—has undergone this experience, that there is no shame in experiencing spiritual desolation, that times of spiritual desolation are normal in a well-lived spiritual life (*SpirEx* 6), and that, therefore, *we are not the only ones.* Experiencing spiritual desolation is simply part of what it means to live the spiritual life in a fallen, redeemed, and loved world. What *does matter* is to live the discerning life: to be aware of spiritual desolation when it is present, to name it for the lie of the enemy that it is, and to reject it. The principle focus of these fourteen rules is to help us do precisely that.

Spiritual Consolation and Spiritual Desolation Together?

Is it possible to experience both spiritual consolation and spiritual desolation simultaneously? The commentators offer various answers. Some who answer positively do so by introducing distinctions such as essential spiritual consolation and contingent spiritual consolation, or substantial consolation and sensible consolation.[25] Such distinctions are possible and clarify certain questions, but it is well to note that Ignatius does not make them and does not consider them necessary for the practical application of the rules—his single interest. I believe it wise in this, as throughout, to follow Ignatius's own pedagogical choices. Unless we do so, the rules quickly become too complicated to use.

Can one experience spiritual consolation and spiritual desolation simultaneously? Ignatius feels no need to address this question explicitly. His consistent manner of speaking in the rules, however, supplies a clear answer. Already in rules 1

and 2, Ignatius highlights the contrariety between the action
of the good spirit and the enemy: if one spirit does one thing,
the other will do exactly the opposite. This contrariety holds
through the entire set of rules: "I call desolation all the contrary of the third rule," "just as consolation is contrary to
desolation," "the thoughts that come from consolation are
contrary to the thoughts that come from desolation" (rule 4);
"As in consolation the good spirit guides and counsels us
more, so in desolation the bad spirit" (rule 5); "Let one
who is in desolation consider how the Lord has left him in
trial. . . . For the Lord has taken away from him his great
fervor, abundant love, and intense grace [that is, his spiritual consolation]" (rule 7); "Let one who is consoled seek
to humble himself. . . . On the contrary, let one who is in
desolation think that he can do much" (rule 11), and so forth
throughout the rules.

Ignatius speaks of a "time of desolation" (rule 5), of being
"in desolation" (rule 6), of "one who is in desolation" (rules
7, 8, 11), of "finding ourselves desolate" (rule 9), and of
"the desolation that will come after" a time of consolation
(rule 10). He likewise speaks of "one who is in consolation"
(rule 10). Ignatius never speaks of the two as simultaneous,
or of a person as experiencing both spiritual consolation and
spiritual desolation at the same time. His language in rule 10
renders explicit his perception that the one experience *follows* the other rather than mingles with it: "Let the one who
is *in consolation* think how he will conduct himself *in the
desolation* that *will come after*."

Minimally, then, we may say that for his purpose—that is,
to help us apply the rules well—Ignatius feels no need to discuss a situation in which one might experience both consolation and desolation together. From the practical perspective,

in applying the rules, I believe it is best to follow his lead. I think it is clear, however, that Ignatius himself understands spiritual consolation and spiritual desolation to be mutually exclusive experiences: they do not blend but rather succeed each other in time.[26]

Experiences of Spiritual Desolation

Ignatius names a number of experiences of spiritual desolation in rule 4. Persons in spiritual desolation may experience *darkness of soul.* They feel a burden in their spiritual lives, do not understand what is happening, and go forward with a heavy sense that things are bad and likely to get worse. They may also experience a *disturbance* in their hearts, a lack of serenity, a sense of turmoil and restlessness in their lives of faith.

In spiritual consolation, persons feel an "upward" call and attraction toward heavenly things and the things of salvation (rule 3); in spiritual desolation, exactly the opposite pull is felt. Now these persons experience a *movement to low and earthly things*: "material comforts, gratification of the body in various ways, memories of such things from the past, immersion in the empty trivia of the surrounding society, diversion through the media, the Internet, busyness, superficial conversation and similar occupations."[27]

Philip is a man who loves the Lord. He usually ends his day at 10:00 p.m. with some minutes of reading Scripture and the examen prayer.[28] This has been a day of spiritual desolation, however, and this evening Philip feels no inclination to pray. As he sits at his desk, a few inches in front of one hand is the Bible, and a few inches in front of the other is his smartphone. Nothing in Philip now wants to reach out for the Bible, and everything in him wants to reach out for the smartphone—and one touch of the screen will become fifty, then a hundred . . . or more. Philip is experiencing the *movement to low and earthly things* that characterizes spiritual desolation. We may repeat once again that there is no shame in experiencing this pull: this is simply what happens in living the spiritual life in a fallen, redeemed, and loved world. What matters critically is that Philip be aware, understand what is happening, and reject the pull toward low and earthly things—that is, that he live the discerning life.

In spiritual desolation, persons further experience *disquiet from various agitations and temptations*. Their hearts are troubled, disquieted, and various temptations float in and out of the desolation: "Why don't you let your prayer go till later? You can let yourself see that. It doesn't have to get too far out of hand . . . " and similar deceptive suggestions of the enemy. Let us note Ignatius's pairing of *spiritual desolation* (heaviness of heart in our spiritual lives) and *temptation* (deceptive suggestions of the enemy). We will see this pairing again in rule 7, and Ignatius will focus specifically on temptation in the final three rules (rules 12–14). We may expect, then, that temptations will generally accompany the affective heaviness of spiritual desolation.

In spiritual consolation, persons experience an increase of hope, faith, and charity; in spiritual desolation, they feel exactly the contrary: a movement toward *lack of confidence*, and a sense of being *without hope* and *without love*. As Philip sits at his desk at 10:00 p.m. in desolation, he finds himself thinking, "Look at you! You'll never be a man of prayer. You'll never really love the Lord. All your efforts to grow spiritually will never lead to much (*lack of confidence*). Why pray tonight? Nothing is going to come from it. And what is the point of getting up early to go to the men's breakfast in

the parish? Nothing will change (*without hope*)." As Philip
sits at his desk, he feels no warmth of God's love and of love
for others in God (*without love*). There is no shame in any of
this; what matters is that Philip be aware, understand what is
happening, and take action.

Persons in desolation experience themselves as *totally*—
a powerful adverb—*slothful* (without energy for spiritual
things), *tepid* (without fervor), and *sad* (without joy). They
may be faithful to prayer, to involvement in the parish, and to
the effort to love, but all is heavy and joyless.

Finally, Ignatius writes, persons in spiritual desolation feel
as if separated from their Creator and Lord. The words "as
if" give the lie of desolation: God is Emmanuel (Mt 1:23),
ever with us to the close of the age (Mt 28:20), providing
even in the smallest details of our lives (Lk 12:6–7). The feeling, however, in spiritual desolation is that "I am here, and
you, God, are very far away. I am alone." As Philip sits at his
desk at 10:00 p.m., he may well feel "as if separated from his
Creator and Lord," alone in the heaviness of his heart and
exposed to temptation.

The beauty of all this—to use a somewhat unexpected
word when speaking of spiritual desolation—is that *everything about it is a lie*: either an outright lie or a truth that
desolation skews and mixes with a lie. When we perceive this,
captives are set free to reject the lie and walk firmly toward
the Lord they love.

In his *Autograph Directory*, Ignatius makes explicit the
exact contrariety of spiritual consolation and spiritual desolation. After describing spiritual consolation, he continues,
"Desolation is the contrary . . . such as war against peace,
sadness against spiritual joy, hope in low things against hope
in things of above, low love against high love, dryness against

tears, and turning the mind to low things against the raising up of the mind."[29]

The same contrariety holds between the *thoughts that arise from spiritual consolation* and the *thoughts that arise from spiritual desolation.* Just as the *affective* experiences of spiritual consolation and spiritual desolation are contrary, so too the *thoughts* that arise from the one and the other are contrary.

When Gerald (see chapter 2) attends Sunday Mass and hears the homily on Luke 11:1–13, with the invitation to pray with Scripture for ten minutes each day, his heart is warmed with gratitude to God for the change that has occurred in his life. He feels God's closeness and love, and a quiet joy fills his heart. Gerald is experiencing spiritual consolation.

As his heart experiences this, *thoughts arise from the spiritual consolation*: "If praying once a week at Sunday Mass already makes this difference, what would happen if I did what Father is suggesting and prayed daily?" And again: "I could arrange my morning to get ten minutes each day. Actually, all I have to do is ask my wife for help since she has been doing this for some years. She will be happy to help me, to show me how to find the readings and get started." As you will remember, Gerald decides that he will speak with his wife that evening and will begin this practice the next morning.

At supper that evening, the conversation with his teenage son does not resolve well, and Gerald is discouraged. He is now in his study, preparing for work the next morning. Gerald remembers that he had planned to speak at this time with his wife about the ten minutes with Scripture. But now he does not feel God's closeness; there is no warmth, no peace, and no attraction to new steps in prayer. Gerald is experiencing spiritual desolation.

As his heart experiences this, *thoughts arise from the spiritual desolation*: "Who are you kidding? You've been away from the Church for twenty years. You've never even read Scripture. What makes you think you'll understand anything written there? Why approach your wife about a practice that is bound to fail? You'll just embarrass yourself and her. You had a nice experience at Mass this morning, but that doesn't change anything, and it is not going to last."

As is evident, the thoughts that arise from spiritual consolation are *exactly the contrary* of those that arise from spiritual desolation. Again, discernment is key. If Gerald is aware of and can name these two experiences, he will also know how to respond to the thoughts that arise from the one and the other.

Spiritual Desolation: Some Examples

Several experiences of spiritual desolation follow. I give them as I recorded them in my journals.

"A Heaviness in My Heart This Morning"

The following is from the time when I was in the parish near home, writing and helping my mother who was alone:

> As I sit here in church this morning, there is a heaviness in my heart. Part of it is poor sleep last night, and part also is the uncertainty of how to deal with the situation at home. I felt too alone yesterday and without much energy.
>
> I think, though, that the enemy's lie is getting mixed into the natural tiredness after three weeks of this intense routine. The voice says quietly, "You are alone. You are getting tired, and it's your own fault. You are pushing too hard, and you can't do this anymore. You'll

do the work, but it will be with fatigue, and so you'll miss things in the writing, and your creativity will be dulled. You'll get to the end of this writing time utterly worn out and then have to pick up with your travel for ministry. This is all going to be grinding, hard work. It will be fruitful, yes, but terribly hard. And you won't really have the time you need to finish. The warmth of the closeness of the Father, Jesus, and the Holy Spirit that you experienced in the retreat will fade . . . "

That's a lot! Father, Jesus, Holy Spirit, help me, protect me, and show me the way. Mary, be with me throughout this day.

Objectively, the work has gone well thus far. It has been very fruitful. I am tired to some degree, and part of it is the delicate balance in knowing how to help at home.

When I prayed the Liturgy of the Hours in church yesterday afternoon, my spirits rose. I think more prayer can help at these times.

Further accusing voices: "The part you are writing now is not very good, and this book is not going to turn out well. Your writing and ministry are all coming to an end, winding down . . . "

As I write this, it seems quite an attack. I will need to talk this out with Ed.

This will all change and lift, and probably I'll see some of this change today. I think this book will be helpful. I'm just in that uncertain period of waiting for the first reactions.

I found it very helpful at the time to review in writing what I was experiencing. In terms of the rules, though I was not thinking of such categories then, this was an application of rules 6 (prayer and examination in time of desolation), 8 (trust in God that the desolation will pass), and 13 (talk with a wise and competent spiritual person). As I remember that day, I can see the difference this review made and how it helped me live the day with more trust in God. As one author comments, the difference between "myself-in-desolation," just submerged in it, and "myself-reflecting-on-myself-in-desolation," that is, examining it objectively before the Lord, is great.[30]

"The Enemy Claims Power over the Future"

I wrote this next entry after a further surgery, when I could not yet see what lay ahead. The following are notes on a conversation of spiritual direction:

> Ed spoke of the fear about the "what-ifs." This is the taunting of the enemy, meant to discourage you, claiming power over the future. You'll never return to active ministry, never be able to share community life as before. The enemy wants you to focus on what is dark, and to pull you into the future seen in this way.
>
> The Holy Spirit is helping you to pray in this, and Mary is present to you. Turn quickly to the Lord, ask Mary's intercession, in such times.
>
> The enemy is all about the negatives, the nos. The truth, even on a medical level, is that there is progress, and you are getting stronger. The medical situations are moving ahead. There is real hope, and the Lord with his love is with you.
>
> So, be quick to turn away from the negative thoughts. Don't even open the door! Renounce the lies. Even imagining what might happen is a temptation. Be in the

present, be open to his grace today, surrender to his will today. As Ed said this, I realized that this I could do.

Surrender to his Heart as best you can today. The surrender is not a surrender to "the worst" but to his faithful love for you. This is the one you surrender to.

I found it very helpful to talk about this spiritual desolation and receive guidance regarding the enemy's discouraging tactics (rule 13). This was a nonspiritual vulnerability after a surgery that gave the enemy an opening for spiritual desolation. A common trait of spiritual desolation—the enemy's claim of power over the future, always seen in a dark light—was also evident that day. Ed's advice to reject this tactic of the enemy immediately reflected Ignatius's counsel in rule 12: resist in the very beginning, before the burden can grow. Ed was right, too, that objectively things were improving on the medical level. In the nonspiritual and spiritual desolation, I found it hard to see that on my own, and it was encouraging to hear Ed and recognize the truth of what he said.

The Thoughts that Arise in Consolation and Desolation

I had just returned from giving an eight-day Ignatian retreat. Those days had been blessed, and I was grateful. But I was also tired. The following occurred shortly after the drive home, when I was back in community. I wrote this later that evening:

I was just back after the retreat and the drive home. It was that vulnerable space I have long recognized, right after giving a retreat, when suddenly the people are no longer there. All the busyness and goodness of involvement with them is gone, and I am alone, feeling the tiredness after expending energy for those days.

I was in my room, feeling alone and burdened, not wanting to pray the Liturgy of the Hours or do anything other than just get a novel and eat food that I knew I really didn't need. I felt that the rest of the day was going to be like this, alone, exhausted, heavy, and without energy for prayer.

Then, as I unpacked, I put on a CD of the Divine Mercy Chaplet set to music. I had heard it a few weeks before and liked it. My heart lifted right away. The beauty of the melody and of the prayer spoke to me: "For the sake of the sorrowful passion, have mercy on us and on the whole world" just repeated over and over with a lovely melody. It was a prayer for mercy, and it seemed just right for that moment.

My energy came back. I did the practical tasks that needed doing, planned ahead for the things I would need to do the next day, and felt renewed desire for them. I found myself thinking of the goodness of the retreat that had just finished with much gratitude to the Lord. I got some needed exercise, and the rest of the day went well.

As I review this experience, again I see spiritual desolation arising in a space of nonspiritual vulnerability: a time of being alone and tired. Prayer made all the difference, in this case with the help of a prayer set to music that I liked. This was an experience of Ignatius's counsel to pray in time of spiritual desolation (rule 6). I was not thinking of rule 6 at the time! In some inarticulate way, however, I knew that I needed help, and this seemed a way to look for it.

In this experience, I also note the contrary nature of the thoughts that arose in the desolation and then in the consolation that followed. In the nonspiritual and spiritual desolation all seemed dark. I felt alone and helpless, unable to pray, bound inevitably to sink into isolation and some form of escape, with a sense that the rest of the day would be spent this way.

In the spiritual consolation that followed, my heart lifted and my energy returned. I was ready to pray, and took the nonspiritually healthy step of exercising, further increasing my energy. I no longer felt a need to escape, but was able to address the tasks at hand and prepare for the coming day. My heart felt gratitude to the Lord for the goodness of the retreat just concluded. I was struck to see the truth of Ignatius's words in rule 4, that the thoughts arising in spiritual consolation will be exactly the contrary of those that arise in spiritual desolation.

Such is spiritual desolation as Ignatius describes it in rule 4. As we turn now to rule 5, we will note a shift in the rules. In his title statement (be aware, understand, take action), Ignatius gave the basic paradigm for discernment. In rules 1 and 2, he clarified how the good spirit and enemy work in those heading away from or toward God. In rules 3 and 4, he described the two basic spiritual movements he invites us to discern: spiritual consolation and spiritual desolation. At this point, we possess the basic elements of discernment. Ignatius will now assist us to apply them in daily life.

Chapter 5

In Time of Desolation
Never Make a Change

A decision that you have taken in the light, do not give up in time of darkness.

—Words of a Spiritual Director

When I teach these rules, my heart always lifts when we reach rule 5. It is simple, clear, and enormously helpful. It is the rule that people never forget, even fifteen, twenty, or more years after learning it. When people speak about the difference the rules have made in their lives, generally rule 5 is mentioned.

As I begin my presentation of rule 5, I beg those present never to forget this rule. I tell them that rule 5 will bring us safely through almost any darkness we may encounter in the spiritual life. I say this not only because rule 5 is rich in itself, but also because I have so often witnessed its benefit in experience, both my own and that of others. I have always felt that there is a special grace attached to rule 5.

The text reads:

Fifth Rule. The fifth: In time of desolation never make a change, but be firm and constant in the proposals and determination in which one was the day preceding such desolation, or in the determination in which one was in the preceding consolation. Because, as in consolation the good spirit guides and counsels us more, so in desolation the bad spirit, with whose counsels we cannot find the way to a right decision.

The first sentence gives the guideline. It contains eight words never to be forgotten: "In time of desolation never make a change." *In time of desolation never make a change.* Generally, when I teach rule 5, I repeat these words three times, inviting the people to say them with me. It is an exercise worth doing—even right now.

The second sentence gives the reason for the guideline: "Because, as in *consolation* the *good spirit* guides and counsels us more, so in *desolation* the *bad spirit*, with whose counsels we cannot find the way to a right decision." We will look more closely at Ignatius's text and then offer examples of this rule in application.

"In Time of Desolation"

Rule 5 applies whenever persons are *right now* in a *time of spiritual desolation*. Vincent's project at work does not go well this morning, and he is discouraged. On his lunch hour, he normally attends Mass in a nearby church. Today Vincent does not go. As the afternoon and evening unfold, still feeling disheartened, he omits all his habitual prayer. This evening, Vincent is in his room, feeling far from God and with no desire for spiritual things. Vincent is now in *a time of spiritual desolation*: rule 5 applies.

Laura's college-age daughter called this morning, and the conversation was tense. She, too, feels discouraged, and the discouragement remains as the hours pass. At three in the afternoon, Laura sits alone in the kitchen with a cup of coffee. At this time, she normally prays part of the Liturgy of the Hours. Today Laura has no desire for this prayer or for any other. She feels alone, far from God, and disheartened. Laura, too, is in *a time of spiritual desolation*: rule 5 applies.

When Ignatius, who never uses a superfluous word, speaks of desolation, he does not always repeat the adjective "spiritual." Always, however, this adjective is understood: the desolation he intends throughout the rules and so in rule 5 is *spiritual* desolation (see rule 4). We may note, however, that rule 5 will generally apply on the *nonspiritual* level as well. A woman, for example, who is struggling with depression meets with her counselor and says, "I think I'm going to quit my job and move." Her counselor is likely to reply in words similar to these: "You know, this may not be the best time for you to make such changes. Let's work through the depression first, and then we can revisit this question."

But in rule 5, Ignatius addresses the specifically spiritual level. If I may supply the adjectives Ignatius presumes in his text, the guideline of rule 5 reads as follows: In time of *spiritual desolation*, never make a change to any *spiritual proposal* that you had in place before the desolation began.

"Never"

Ignatius's adverbs are expressive in general and seldom more so than here. Rule 5 is, to borrow an expression from a philosopher, a *categorical imperative*: it admits of no exceptions.[1] It is enough to know that I am in spiritual desolation and thinking of changing some spiritual practice that, before this desolation began, I had planned I would do—Vincent normally prays with Scripture in the evening, Laura with the

Liturgy of the Hours in midafternoon, and both, in a time of spiritual desolation, are thinking of omitting that practice— and I know that I *should not make that change.*

Precisely because it admits of no exceptions, rule 5 is clear and may be applied unhesitatingly in practice. This rule admits of no exceptions because "in desolation the *bad spirit*" guides and counsels us, "with whose counsels we *cannot* find the way to a right decision."

"Firm and Constant"

In time of spiritual desolation we *should not* make a change; what we *should* do is remain "firm and constant" in what we had planned to do before the desolation began. *Firm and constant*: this is a classic Ignatian doublet, an exercise in synonymous parallelism, in which both members of the doublet contribute to the total sense the author wishes to express. Ignatius's practice is similar to the synonymous parallelism employed in Hebrew poetry; in it, the same sentiment is repeated in different but equivalent words: "*Make me to know your ways*, O Lord; *teach me your paths*" (Ps 25:4), "The Lord is my *rock*, and my *fortress*" (Ps 18:2).[2] The two elements are similar, and each, with its own nuances, strengthens the full sense the writer wishes to convey.

Ignatius employs this device throughout the *Spiritual Exercises*, and repeatedly in the rules. Thus, for example, in rule 1: "leading them to imagine sensual *delights* and *pleasures*," "to make them grow in their *vices* and *sins*," "*stinging* and *biting* their consciences." In rule 2, the good spirit gives "*courage* and *strength*," "*easing* and *taking away* all obstacles." The use of these doublets is even clearer in the original Spanish: *delectaciones y placeres, vicios y pecados, punzándoles y remordiéndoles, ánimo y fuerzas, facilitando y quitando*, and the like.

Here, in rule 5, Ignatius tells us that when tempted to change our spiritual proposals in time of spiritual desolation, we should, on the contrary, remain *firm* and *constant* in what we had planned before the desolation began. *Firm*: that is, not giving way, not moving; and *constant*: that is, maintaining over time this firm refusal to give way. The person is to hold fast *unwaveringly* to what was planned and do so *throughout the duration of the spiritual desolation*. *Firm and constant*: this is a rich spiritual stance and a reminder deeply needed in a culture of sound bites, tweets, and hesitation to commit.

"In the Proposals and Determination"

Ignatius immediately presents us with a further doublet: *proposals and determination*. It is these that we should not change in time of spiritual desolation, but should maintain with firmness and constancy.

When persons conclude their examination of conscience, they "*propose* amendment with his grace" (*SpirEx* 43). When they seek to overcome a particular sin or defect, upon rising in the morning they "*propose* to guard themselves with diligence" from it (*SpirEx* 24). When they feel sorrow for their sins, this sorrow is accompanied by "a firm *proposal* not to commit those or any other sins" (*SpirEx* 82). As is evident, for Ignatius the word *proposal* denotes a firm choice, diligently pursued, in the spiritual life.

Determination, for Ignatius, expresses a "firm resolution," "an explicitly stated decision," and "decisions that call for a commitment."[3] Thus, when persons at prayer hear Jesus's invitation to join him in the work of redemption, if their hearts are moved by love, they will answer that "I wish and desire, and it is my deliberate *determination*" to follow Jesus even in the most challenging aspects of his life (*SpirEx* 98). Likewise, when they are discerning God's will, Ignatius invites them to consider the present choice in the light of life's end. And, he continues, "entirely in conformity" with that light "I will make my *determination*" (*SpirEx* 186).[4]

Proposals and determination is followed by a second and more extended doublet: "in which one was *the day preceding such desolation*, or in the determination in which one was *in the preceding consolation*." Ignatius thus specifies that these proposals and determinations were in place in *the time before* the desolation began ("the day preceding") or in *the spiritual experience* that preceded the desolation ("in the preceding consolation"). In both cases, the persons look to their spiritual situation *before* the desolation began.

A key point in Ignatian discernment is touched here. If persons have spiritual *proposals and determinations* in place—for example, to go on that retreat, to attend Mass this weekday, to discuss this matter in spiritual direction, or to rise early tomorrow for prayer—and in time of spiritual desolation a thought of a *change* arises—this other retreat might be better, I should not go to Mass this weekday because of other commitments, this is not the right time to raise that matter in spiritual direction, tomorrow I should take things at a slower pace and will pray later in the day—Ignatius never counsels these persons to weigh the respective merits of the earlier proposal and the new ("Wouldn't this other retreat be better for me? Perhaps I'm not quite ready for the one I signed up for. Maybe the different theme of the other retreat would help me more right now. But still, I do feel attracted to the one I signed up for. Maybe I shouldn't attend any retreat right now when I can't see clearly . . . "). To attempt this would be to enter a quagmire from which these persons would likely emerge only with difficulty.

Rather than weigh *the respective merits* of the former and new proposals, Ignatius simply invites these persons to consider *the time in which they arose*: Did the former spiritual proposal arise *before* the spiritual desolation began? And has the new proposal arisen *in the time* of this spiritual desolation? Then these persons have all the clarity they need for action: they should not change their former proposals but remain firm and constant in them.[5] Ignatius has found a clear and usable guideline to assist us in otherwise confusing situations. And the stakes are high! Firmness in such proposals or the absence of firmness will have much to say about our spiritual progress.

"Guides and Counsels Us More"

When Ignatius employs the phrase "guides and counsels us more" in rule 5, how are we to understand the word "more" (*más*)?[6] As one commentator notes, "This 'more' has caused the translators much labor."[7] The word "more" is found in Ignatius's own *Autograph* manuscript.[8] It is removed and interpreted in the official Latin translation called the *Vulgate*.[9] It was first omitted and later added in another early Latin translation titled the *Versio Prima*.[10]

This same divergence is found in contemporary translations. In his classic translation, for example, Louis Puhl, SJ, omits "more."[11] Jules Toner, SJ, translates "*más*" as "generally" in the translation that begins his *Commentary*, and later omits "generally" when reproducing the rule for discussion.[12] In my translation, I included the word "more" in keeping with my aim to render Ignatius's own words as faithfully as possible.[13]

What, then, does Ignatius intend when he writes that "in consolation the good spirit guides and counsels us *more*"? More than what? Gil aptly summarizes three possible replies.[14]

In a first interpretation, "more" signifies that the good spirit guides and counsels us always but more in the time of spiritual consolation than at other times. This interpretation highlights the intensification of the good spirit's work in time of spiritual consolation.

In a second, "more" signifies that in time of spiritual consolation the good spirit guides and counsels us more than the bad spirit. In this interpretation, both the good and the bad spirits may guide and counsel in time of spiritual consolation, but the good spirit counsels more and the bad spirit less in such times.

A third mode of understanding "more" is found in the interpretative rendering of the Vulgate translation: "In fact, while anyone enjoys that consolation that we described earlier, he is not guided by his own spirit but by the promptings of the good spirit."[15] In this case, the comparison lies between the person's own spirit and the good spirit: in time of spiritual consolation, the good spirit guides and counsels us more than our own thoughts and perceptions.

All three interpretations are possible, the first and the third without difficulty, and the second if properly understood. To understand the second interpretation correctly, we may return to the final sentence of rule 4 as discussed in the preceding chapter.

We have seen Ignatius's understanding that the thoughts that arise from spiritual consolation are contrary to the thoughts that arise from spiritual desolation. The thoughts

that arise from *spiritual consolation* are of the *good spirit*;
those that arise from *spiritual desolation* are of the *bad spirit*.
Any thoughts, therefore, that arise from—are born directly
out of—spiritual consolation are of the good spirit.[16] Any
thoughts that arise from—are born directly out of—spiritual
desolation are of the bad spirit. The simplicity and clarity of
this teaching allows us to apply rule 5 without hesitation:
all we need to know is that we are in spiritual desolation,
and then we know with certitude that any changes to our
spiritual proposals that arise out of that desolation are of the
bad spirit and so to be rejected. This is why Ignatius can so
confidently employ the adverb "never."

It is possible, however, that in a time of spiritual consolation other thoughts that *do not arise from*—are not
born directly out of—the spiritual consolation may present themselves. These thoughts might be of the bad spirit.
Thus, for example, a man is praying and experiences
warm spiritual consolation. In the joy of this consolation,
he finds himself grateful to God, desiring to respond to
God's love, and asking God to show him how to grow in
his service. As this occurs, suddenly a troubling thought
comes to him: "How do you know that you are not just
imagining all of this?"[17] This thought comes *during* the
time of spiritual consolation, but it clearly *does not come
from*—is not born directly out of—the spiritual consolation. This thought comes *from outside* the spiritual consolation and in all likelihood is of the bad spirit. Understood
in this sense, the second interpretation given above is also
possible.[18]

Obviously, Ignatius does not ask that one who employs
rule 5 sift such interpretations! Rule 5 is simple, clear, and
readily applicable: Are you in a time of spiritual desolation?

And are you, in a time of spiritual desolation, considering changing a spiritual proposal that you had in place before the desolation began? Then you have all the clarity you need: you know that you should not make this change, but remain firm and constant in what you had planned to do before the desolation began.

Two Questions

Some examples will illustrate rule 5 in practice. A woman usually arrives home from work at 5:00 p.m. A year ago, she began praying evening prayer from the Liturgy of the Hours before preparing her supper. She enjoys this prayer that renews her awareness of the Lord as the evening begins, and she is happy to find herself growing in love of the psalms.

Three days ago, a tense conversation with a fellow worker left her angry and discouraged. In the following days, it was harder to pray, though she maintained her daily times of prayer. Today she went to Mass on her lunch hour but was distracted and felt spiritually dry as she left church. She did not feel God's closeness this day and had no energy for spiritual things.

Now she has arrived home from work. She remembers that this is the time when she prays evening prayer. But she feels no desire for it this day. She finds herself thinking, "Maybe I'll just let it go now and pray it later in the evening."

Two questions: Is this woman in a time of spiritual desolation? The answer is obviously yes: she feels spiritually "tepid" and "as if separated from her Creator and Lord." Is this woman, in a time of spiritual desolation, thinking of changing a spiritual proposal that was in place before this desolation began? Again the answer is clearly yes: her spiritual "proposal" of praying evening prayer after work has been in place for a year, and she knows its fruitfulness. Whenever the answer to these two questions is yes, what does Ignatius counsel us? What should this woman do when she has returned home and before she begins to prepare supper? She should not make a change, but should pray evening prayer at 5:00 p.m., exactly as planned before the desolation began.

A man goes to confession regularly and finds the sacrament helpful. This coming Saturday, following his customary pattern, would be the next time to go. He plans, therefore, to go to confession on Saturday at 4:00 p.m. when confessions are heard in the church. Prayer, however, has been dry for the past few weeks, and it has been hard to be faithful. On more than one occasion, in fact, the man has omitted his normal times of prayer. He is not sure what is wrong and is troubled. Recently he finds himself anxious when he tries to pray, and he is even beginning to lose hope of ever having a true life of prayer.

Now it is Saturday morning. The man remembers that he planned to go to confession that afternoon. But now the feelings are different: "Maybe I'm not in the best spiritual shape to go to confession. It will just be difficult and embarrassing when I'm feeling like this. It might be better to wait till next Saturday. Honestly, I just don't feel like it right now."

Two questions. Is this man in a time of spiritual desolation? The answer is obviously yes: he is experiencing "darkness of soul," confused by what is happening spiritually; he is "disquieted from various agitations" and is "moving to lack of confidence" that he will ever have a true life of prayer. Is this man, in a time of spiritual desolation, thinking of changing a spiritual proposal that he had in place before the desolation began? Again the answer is clearly yes: for a long time now, he has gone regularly to confession on Saturday every so many weeks, and this Saturday would be the next time according to his habitual practice. Whenever the answer to these two questions is yes, what does Ignatius counsel us? What should this man do this Saturday afternoon at 4:00 p.m.? He should not make a change, but go to confession exactly as planned before the desolation began.

Both the woman and the man may find that if they follow rule 5, do not make the changes suggested in the spiritual desolation, and faithfully maintain—perhaps with some courage—their earlier proposals, that this time of prayer and this confession will bear special fruit. In the woman's case, it may be the beginning of the end of her desolation. In the man's case, God's loving forgiveness and the priest's spiritual counsel may lift his heart and give him new hope. There is a reason why the enemy attacks our proposals in time of spiritual desolation!

Such examples could be multiplied: a woman who plans to speak with her spiritual director in their next meeting about a problem that has long burdened her; a businessman who plans to join the parish financial council; a young professional who decides to rise a little earlier and pray before going to work, and many similar situations. In time of spiritual desolation, the enemy will attack and attempt to lead us to change these "proposals." The same two questions will provide us all the clarity we need: Am I in a time of spiritual desolation? And am I, in this time of spiritual desolation, thinking of changing a spiritual proposal that I had in place before this desolation began? If, with God's grace, the clear light of rule 5, and a grace-inspired courage, we are willing to remain firm and constant in these proposals, much harm will be avoided and much fruit will result.

In Tolkien's *The Lord of the Rings*, when Frodo is on the verge of the darkest part of his journey, he encounters Lady Galadriel. She is a figure of great wisdom, goodness, and nobility. Lady Galadriel gives Frodo a small crystal phial, filled with white light, and tells him that it will be a light for him in the dark when every other light goes out.[19] *A light in the dark when every other light goes out*: that is what rule 5 can be for us. In time of spiritual desolation, when everything in us cries out that we were wrong before; that the spiritual plans and proposals—how we will pray, how we will serve the Lord, even our vocational choices—we thought were clear and right, we now see were mistaken and must be changed; when everything in us says that this change is urgent and must be made *now*, then rule 5 will be for us a light in the dark when every other light goes out. The two questions are all we need. If we call them to mind and apply them, we will never go astray.

Said with reverence, how many times have we seen people make changes to their spiritual proposals in time of spiritual desolation, relinquishing their prayer, ceasing to speak with their spiritual directors, withdrawing from service in the parish or attendance in a parish group, even making vocational changes? Said also with much reverence, we may recall times that we have made such changes when in spiritual desolation. These changes were always harmful. It is important to add, however, that the story is not over, and God's grace and love can open all doors and show us the way forward.

But once we have learned rule 5 and assimilated its wisdom, we will grow less and less exposed to such harm. This is Ignatius's intention in offering us rule 5.

When Helpful Changes May Be Considered

When, therefore, may helpful changes be considered? Never in time of spiritual desolation! This is the emphatic counsel of rule 5. But rule 5 does not say that helpful changes in our spiritual proposals, changes that will truly lead to spiritual progress, may never be considered.

Such changes may be considered in time of spiritual consolation, when "the good spirit guides and counsels us more," or simply in a time of spiritual calm.[20] Ignatius speaks of this last as the "tranquil time" (*SpirEx* 177), when we are neither in the joy of spiritual consolation nor the heaviness of spiritual desolation, but calm and able to use our "natural powers freely and tranquilly" (*SpirEx* 177). This, too, is a rich spiritual space in which we may love and serve the Lord.

We will often find, however, that those changes that seemed so necessary and urgent in time of spiritual desolation no longer seem so at all when the desolation has passed. Toner comments, "Ten times out of ten we will be glad that we waited and do not have to live with consequences of a decision made in circumstances which call that decision into question."[21] *Ten times out of ten*: this is another way to express Ignatius's "never."

Rule 5: Some Examples

I cannot express adequately how grateful I am for rule 5 in my own life. Many, many times, it has made all the difference, helping me avoid decisions that, often only a short time later, I could see would have been harmful.

One experience repeated several times in my early years of priesthood. The work of my religious community involves giving retreats, and shortly after my ordination I began to do this. Many of these were weekend retreats for groups in a retreat house. I would arrive on Friday afternoon, get settled, share supper with the people, and then, at perhaps 7:00 p.m., we would gather in the chapel to begin the retreat.

I would hand out the schedule I had prepared for the weekend, with the various times of talks, personal prayer, Mass, meals, and prayer together in chapel. Then I would give the first talk, about thirty minutes. When I finished, we would enter into silence. Some would remain in chapel to pray. Others would go quietly to their rooms.

Afterward, there I would be, alone in my room, with all the vulnerabilities of a new priest beginning a new ministry. Obviously there was no feedback yet. I would sit in my room wondering: "How did the beginning go? Is the schedule right? Am I packing too much into the weekend and demanding too much of them? Did they like the first talk? Did I say anything helpful? Did they not like it? Will some decide this retreat is not worth their time? Will I find cars missing from the parking lot in the morning? Maybe I need to lighten the schedule . . . "

What I am describing is nonspiritual desolation arising from the vulnerabilities of a new priest who has not yet received feedback on his efforts. I suspect that I am not alone in this; each of us experiences this in our respective callings! The non-spiritual desolation could easily become spiritual, however, as it would get harder to pray and trust in the Lord's love.

Then, in all this anxiety and confusion, I would remember rule 5. I would say to myself, "No, this is no time for you to make any changes to what you planned for this retreat. You stay exactly with what you planned." And it would always work out well.

This Is the Last Time

A similar experience, again related to retreat work, stays clearly in my mind. For many years I had led weekend retreats for a wonderful group of laypeople in a large city. I enjoyed working with them and admired the faithful lives and dedication of the leaders.

This particular year I arrived for another of these retreats. In earlier retreats, I had spoken on the topics of my books, themes regarding prayer and discernment. This time the leaders asked that I speak on a different, though related, topic. I had not given many retreats on this new topic, and as the retreat began, I wondered how it would be received by this group.

We began on Friday evening with a first talk, and then entered into silence. As Saturday unfolded, I found my heart growing heavier and heavier. Each talk was harder to give than the last. In my individual meetings with retreatants, they—appropriately!—spoke of their needs and did not address mine—that is, my need to know how they were finding the retreat.

I will never forget our final meeting for prayer that Saturday evening. We gathered in the chapel at 9:00 p.m. The organizers had prepared a lovely version of night prayer from the Liturgy of the Hours, with some other prayers. The whole exercise lasted about a half hour. As those thirty minutes progressed, I found myself deeply discouraged and unhappy, so much so that I simply wanted to get up and leave the chapel. If I could have done this without being noticed, I would certainly have left. Just to remain there as the prayer continued became almost unbearable. Finally, when at last we finished, I disappeared to my room.

I woke early the next morning, a few hours before our first gathering in common. The heaviness and darkness still filled my heart and mind. As I began the day, I found myself thinking that perhaps it was time to end these retreats, that maybe I had already given all that I could to this group, and that it might be time for them to find another retreat director. I saw myself speaking to the leaders that afternoon, after the group had left, and gently telling them that this would be the last retreat.

But as these early hours progressed, alone in my room, I sensed that something was wrong. I knew that I needed to examine what was happening. In the quiet of that Sunday morning, I took my journal and began to write. I described what I was experiencing and the thoughts that were arising. As I did so, something clicked, and I realized that this was exactly the situation Ignatius discussed in rule 5. I was in spiritual desolation, and in a time of spiritual desolation was considering a change to a long-standing spiritual proposal: the giving of annual retreats for this group. I remember writing that this was no time to make any decision about future work with this group, that I needed to stay the course on this final day of retreat, and wait for a clearer mind to review decisions about the future.

That Sunday morning I wrote the following:

Rising. I have found this retreat awful, all except for the one-on-one meetings. I don't know what it is. Maybe this topic is not really sufficient for a whole weekend? Maybe I'm tired of this setting and this group, and it's just time to stop or interrupt for a time. Maybe this is just desolation. I'll find out more today when we begin talking again, and I get the evaluations.

But this has been very hard. I was too alone yesterday, without feedback. By last evening, I couldn't stand it. Maybe it's just that I'm tired and on the edge of a cold.

What happened next was a small thing, but it helped me greatly. The time for breakfast arrived, and I left my room and headed down the corridor toward the dining room. As I walked, I met one of the organizers. Because we were in silence, she did not say anything. But she smiled at me as we passed. Affectively speaking, that stopped me in my tracks. If she was smiling, this retreat could not be such a disaster! She never knew how much she did for me with a simple smile.

We finished the retreat at lunch and, after the group left, the leaders and I stayed to review the evaluations. They were very positive. The next day, I wrote in my journal:

About the retreat this weekend. Now I experience consolation. There is a happiness in my heart, and I feel nourished by the retreat. Now my thoughts are that we should continue these retreats. There is energy in the Lord in them, and the people desire them. There may be ways of adapting them now, building on what we've already done, so that now we can go deeper.

The following year I returned, and we continued with these retreats.

This is why I am so grateful to St. Ignatius for rule 5. What if I had not recognized that I was considering *a change* in a time of *spiritual desolation*? The "thoughts that come from desolation" (rule 4) can seem very compelling in that time of darkness. Without rule 5, the door to a fruitful ministry would have been shut that morning. In this instance and so many others, the wisdom of rule 5 has blessed me.

I Don't Want to Be Here Anymore

On this occasion, I returned to our community after a week of travel for a retreat. It had been a fruitful time, but it had also been demanding. Jetlag was involved as well. This was again that tired space after the richness of ministry. Four days after I returned, I rose and went to chapel for prayer. During that time, I wrote:

> Don't make changes in desolation, in the worn-out days after a trip. I am feeling that I don't want to be here any longer, that I've been stationed here too long, that I'll be tired as long as I remain here, that it is time to ask for a transfer. I don't want to go through these tired days after a trip anymore.
>
> I am also thinking of giving up the travel for retreats and seminars of this kind, that it is time to stop this and reserve my energies for other work.

Rule 5 was in play once more. This time I saw it clearly and recognized that the two changes I was thinking of making, both significant—asking for a transfer to another house of the community and ending much of the ministry I had been doing—were suggested in a time of spiritual desolation. Later I discussed this in spiritual direction, and Ed confirmed the application of rule 5 to my experience that morning:

> Recognize the strong desolation you were feeling and that sense that "I have to get out of here and go to a different community." You don't want to be working out

of this desolation. If the Lord wants a change, it will not come in this way.

Rule 5 is a great friend on the spiritual journey. It tells us what we *should not do* in time of spiritual desolation. Its companion, rule 6, will tell us what we *should do* in time of such desolation.

Chapter 6

Spiritual Means for a
Spiritual Struggle

*We ought never be discouraged because
of any trial . . . nor ever abandon
any exercise or duty or anything else.
If you can do nothing else, at least
stand before the Cross and say, "Jesus!
Jesus! I entrust myself to our Lord Jesus
Christ."*

—St. Catherine of Siena

Ignatius now proposes an active response to the enemy's tactic of spiritual desolation, a message charged with hope and energy. He writes:

Sixth Rule. The sixth: although in desolation we should not change our first proposals, it is very advantageous to change ourselves intensely against the desolation itself, as by insisting more upon prayer, meditation, upon much examination, and upon extending ourselves in some suitable way of doing penance.

The first line, "although in desolation we should not change our first proposals," summarizes the preceding rule: in time of spiritual desolation never change a spiritual proposal that was in place before the desolation began. Having urged us to stand our ground in time of desolation, Ignatius now counsels us *to resist the desolation itself*: "it is very advantageous to change ourselves intensely *against the desolation* itself."

Ignatius supplies four spiritual means for this resistance: *prayer* of petition, by which we seek God's help to remain firm in the trial; *meditation* on truths of faith that can sustain us in the struggle; careful *examination* of how the desolation began and subsequently unfolded so that we will see how to combat it effectively; and suitable *penance* as a refusal to flee helplessly from the desolation into some form of empty diversion. Employed together, these four tools supply a formidable assault on the discouragement and lies of the enemy's desolations.

Two Rules in Combination

As rules 1 (persons moving away from God) and 2 (persons moving toward God) form a pair, and as rules 3 (spiritual consolation) and 4 (spiritual desolation) do likewise, so also do rules 5 and 6.[1] Each rule, while expressing a specific guideline in itself, can be understood fully only in combination with the other. Ignatius renders this pairing explicit by beginning rule 6 with a summary of rule 5, and then showing its completion in rule 6: "although in desolation we should not change our first proposals [rule 5], it is very advantageous to change ourselves intensely against the desolation itself [rule 6]." The pairing is also clear in the deliberate repetition of the verb "change": we do not *change* (the transitive verb *mudar*) our *proposals* (rule 5), but we do *change ourselves* (the reflexive verb *mudarse*) (rule 6).

In rule 6, Ignatius thus immediately sounds a note of great hope, completing and surpassing rule 5: in time of spiritual desolation, not only should we resist the enemy's attempts to undo our former spiritual proposals (rule 5), but we can and should strive actively to reject the desolation itself (rule 6). Ignatius does not say that the best we can do in desolation is to remain firm in our former proposals (rule 5) but that much more is possible: in time of desolation, with hope, with energy, with the spiritual means at our disposal, and with confidence in God's grace, we can strive actively *to reject the desolation itself.* This changing of ourselves against the desolation is, he tells us, *very advantageous*—that is, much sorrow will be avoided and much good will result from this active effort.

Philip, for example (chapter 4), sits at his desk at 10:00 p.m., alone in his room. Work has not gone well in the preceding days, and he is discouraged (nonspiritual desolation). In his heaviness of heart, it has been harder to feel God's love and more difficult to pray (spiritual desolation). Normally at 10:00 p.m., Philip reads from Scripture for ten minutes and prays the examen prayer, reviewing the day with the Lord. Tonight he feels no desire to do so, and everything in him just wants to turn on the television or begin surfing websites on his smartphone (rule 4: movement to low and earthly things). Rule 5 tells Philip that, though it will cost some courage, he should make no change to his spiritual proposal for 10:00 p.m., but pick up the Bible and begin to read as usual. Rule 6 tells Philip that he can do even more: he can *change himself* against the desolation itself through prayer, meditation, examination, and suitable penance.

At times, when I teach rule 6, I see a light dawn in the eyes of some listeners: to know that God never asks us passively to endure spiritual desolation until somehow it passes, but that we are always called actively to resist it, *sets captives free.* A man once told me this: "I thought that in time of desolation there was nothing I could do, that I just had to retire at the end of the day with these awful burdens. To find out that there *is* something that I can do, that I don't have simply to wallow in this, changes everything." Another, a former football player, told me that he thinks of rules 5 and 6 in terms of defense and offense: "I like rule 5 because it says that we defend our territory and don't let the enemy into it. But I especially like rule 6 because that tells us to go right at the enemy and defeat him." Another shared a similar analogy: "When I was in Little League, I played shortstop. When the ball was hit and was coming toward me, the coach told me to charge the ball and not just wait for it to reach me so that I'd have to take whatever bounce I would get. I see rule 6 like that: we don't simply remain passive in desolation, but we use the spiritual tools to reject it."

Desolation and the Cross

Often, when I present Ignatius's call to change ourselves intensely against spiritual desolation, questions like these arise: Doesn't God allow trials in our lives? And do we not grow by faithfully enduring them? How, then, can Ignatius say that our call in time of spiritual desolation is to resist and reject it? These questions merit clear replies. Such clarity permits us to understand rule 6 more precisely, and so sets us free to follow Ignatius's counsel without hesitation.

Jesus tells us that "if anyone wishes to come after me, he must deny himself and take up his cross daily and follow me" (Lk 9:23).[2] Paul likewise preaches that "through many tribulations we must enter the kingdom of God" (Acts 14:22).[3] Our Christian tradition describes such tribulations with the word Jesus himself employs, that is, the *cross*: difficult situations of health, for example, that persist though we do all we can to care for our health, or the weight of responsibilities inherent in our vocations as spouses, parents, priests, religious, workers in the business world and the like.[4] When our crosses are carried with Christ, our Good Fridays, like his, lead to an Easter Sunday—to blessings of grace and new life in us and through us for others.

The Servant of God Élisabeth Leseur writes, "Suffering is the great law of the spiritual world. . . . We will only know later the work accomplished by our suffering and our sacrifices. It all goes to the heart of God, and there, joined to the redemptive treasure, it expands in souls in the form of grace."[5] Christians share in the same redemptive pattern of Christ: "Our sufferings and our sacrifices," Elisabeth affirms, "expand in souls in the form of grace." These trials—these crosses—lie within God's providence in our lives and are to be borne faithfully, though not alone, but in communion with Christ: "If anyone wishes *to come after me*, he must deny himself and take up his cross daily and *follow me*."

Such *crosses* of health and responsibilities, however, are very different from the enemy's tactic of *spiritual desolation*, that is, his lies and discouraging insinuations. Spiritual desolation, as rule 6 so emphatically indicates, is *never* to be borne passively, but is *always* actively to be rejected.

Martha is a sixty-five-year-old married woman. Her marriage and family are sources of joy for her, and her relationship with the Lord has deepened over the years.

Diabetes runs in her family, and in her forties, Martha found that she was diabetic. She is faithful to the appropriate diet, and regularly takes the medication indicated. Ten years ago, a neuropathy developed in her feet with its accompanying pain. Some days are harder than others.

Martha's eldest daughter had many struggles in her marriage and is now separated from her husband. Martha has been a pillar of strength for her daughter, helping her and her children over the years in their difficult situation. The company for which Martha's husband works has laid off many workers, and she and her husband wonder what they will do should he be laid off as well.

Martha does her best to face these issues with prayer and trust in the Lord. This is not always easy, and at times she grows discouraged. As the years pass, however, she worries less and turns more easily to the Lord in times of pain and struggle. Her family finds her an increasing source of strength as these various issues unfold.

Martha is a woman who loves the Lord and for whom the *cross* has taken the form of physical struggles, familial issues, and financial concerns. As she does her human and spiritual best to deal with these matters, she is faithfully carrying the cross (Lk 9:23) and is growing correspondingly in the Lord.

Jessica is a thirty-six-year-old single, professional woman. She returns from work one Wednesday, burdened by the struggles experienced that day. She is discouraged and feels no desire to pray as she usually does when back from work: Why should she bother? Nothing will change even if she prays. Jessica does not feel God's closeness and love. The energy she generally finds for spiritual things is gone. On Wednesday evenings, Jessica normally goes to the parish for Bible study. This evening she has no wish to go. All she wants is to head to the refrigerator and sit in front of the television.

Jessica realizes that she needs to examine what is happening. She recognizes that she is experiencing desolation and turns to the Lord for help. She asks for the courage to resist the desolation and chooses to pray as usual. She also decides that she will go to the Bible study as she usually does on Wednesday evening.

Jessica is experiencing *spiritual desolation*. By being aware of this and using the appropriate means to reject it, Jessica will grow in faithful love of God.

Martha and all who share in their own lives the experience of the cross, grow by *faithfully carrying* this cross, using the spiritual and human means that can help. Jessica and all who share in their own lives the experience of spiritual desolation, grow by *faithfully resisting* the desolation and its discouraging lies.

Rule 6 is a beacon of light, calling captives to freedom in time of spiritual desolation. *Simply to know* that this is the call—to change ourselves, actively and intensely, with courage and trust in the Lord, against the desolation by using the spiritual aids at our disposal—awakens enormous hope and releases spiritual energy.

Four Spiritual Means: Prayer, Meditation, Examination, Penance

Ignatius supplies four spiritual means for this resistance to desolation: prayer, meditation, much examination, and suitable penance. While these means may be employed in many spiritual contexts, in rule 6 Ignatius directs them specifically to the person now experiencing spiritual desolation. Practiced in this situation and in the manner Ignatius describes, each will be, as he indicates, "very advantageous" to the one in desolation.

Ignatius asks persons in desolation to "insist more" upon these four means. In the immediate context of the rule—the Ignatian retreat—persons are already utilizing these four means. Ignatius now counsels them, in their time of spiritual desolation, consciously to increase their use of each as a means of combatting the desolation. Applied to daily life, rule 6 presumes an ongoing life of prayer, meditation, examination, and some form of suitable penance. In time of desolation, persons are consciously to increase their exercise of these spiritual means in order to combat the desolation.

A young man once told me that he had always thought that resistance to desolation simply involved an increased effort of will: "You have to try harder, and that is all there is to it." To learn from Ignatius's rules that much more—the many spiritual tools that Ignatius supplies—is available to assist our efforts was for him a great source of encouragement. In rule 6, Ignatius presents four of these. We will examine each in the light of concrete experience.

Prayer

The first "tool" is prayer of petition: simply to turn to the Holy Trinity, to the individual Persons of the Trinity—Father, Son, and Holy Spirit—or to the intercession of Mary and the other saints, and *ask for help*.[6] I think that Ignatius may deliberately have listed this as the *first* means for resisting desolation—that is, that prayer of petition is the primary means: just to ask, in time of desolation, for the help of the omnipotent and infinitely loving God and the intercession of the saints whose love constantly embraces us (*SpirEx* 232). This means is available to us always and in all circumstances.

Philip is alone in his room at 10:00 p.m. after the discouraging day. Already he has omitted his habitual prayer that day. Now Philip sits at his desk, poised between the Bible that he usually reads at this time and the smartphone. Nothing in him wants to pick up the Bible, and everything in him wants to flee into mindless and potentially harmful surfing on the Web. Philip feels helpless, bound to fall—*and he turns to Jesus and asks for help.* "Lord, I could fall. I feel so weak. Please be with me, and give me the strength I need." Philip has exercised the first means that Ignatius supplies: he has turned to the God who promises, "Ask, and it will be given you" (Mt 7:7) and has prayed for help.[7]

All of us can easily recognize such moments in our own experience and different circumstances in life. Our first call is to do what Philip does here: simply to turn to God and *ask for help.*

In the residence of my community, my office stands at the end of a corridor of offices. Behind it is the back stairwell, little frequented during the day. My own room is directly above my office. When I am at home, I often walk the flight of stairs—eight steps up, a landing, then eight steps more—between my office and my room. Over the years, the short time of that walk, in the quiet of that stairwell, has become a place of prayer for help in desolation.

The following has repeated often: As the day unfolds, I will be vaguely aware that something is weighing on me. In the brief moments as I walk those stairs, I will recognize that I am in desolation, and I will make a short, simple prayer for help. A few hours later, with an uplift of heart, I will realize that I am no longer in desolation. Something has intervened—an encouraging email, a phone call, a conversation, a time of prayer—and the desolation has passed. Then I remember the prayer in the stairwell. Each time this happens, I am further confirmed in the power of simply *asking God's help* in time of desolation.

For the same reason, I have become grateful for the Liturgy of the Hours, this periodic return throughout the day to prayer with the psalms.[8] Several times a day—five for those who pray it fully, two or three for those who pray it in part—the Liturgy of the Hours calls one to prayer. I find that often, in times of desolation, this prayer marks the difference between immersion in desolation and the beginning of resistance. I begin praying the psalms with some reluctance, and the first minutes generally are difficult. Gradually, however, my heart opens to the prayer, and I feel less alone: the desolation begins to lift.

The same may be said of any prayer (Mass, *lectio divina*, meditation, imaginative contemplation, reading of Scripture, the Rosary, vocal prayers) we habitually make at various points of the day—upon rising, commuting to work, during the lunch hour, in the quiet of the evening, or before retiring. Such regular times help us exercise Ignatius's first counsel in desolation: to turn to God in prayer and ask for help.

The Servant of God Élisabeth Leseur writes, "In arid times, when duty seems difficult and daily responsibilities have no attraction, when all spiritual consolation is denied us and the beautiful light that illumines life is veiled, in these times humble prayer alone can steady us and give us hour by hour and day by day the determination to act 'against our will.'"[9]

A woman once told me of a friend of hers who, when in desolation, says to her, "I'm going down to church to do some rule 6!" I loved it: a perfect application of Ignatius's invitation to turn more insistently to prayer in time of desolation.

"The Burden Has Largely Lifted"

The following are personal experiences. The first is from my journal on a day in April, some years ago:

This afternoon I returned to the house feeling tired. The research needed for this book I am writing is demanding, and I feel the pace. I answered some emails and then, feeling exhausted and discouraged, ate some food I did not need and picked up a novel. Father Matthew walked by my office and did not stop. This awakened fears that he may be unhappy with our recent conversation about organizing the house.

I can see now that I was trying to solve my need alone, as Ed says we so often do. But I had to get working on the talk I will be giving to the students in a few days. This drove me to the chapel, my first prayer this afternoon since this heaviness started. I've been in the chapel now for fifteen minutes, and I note that the emotional burden has largely lifted: I am not alone. Now I look forward more to the talk as well.

Such experiences, especially when I see them repeat, teach me the power of prayer in overcoming desolation.

"Jesus, Look upon Me with Healing and Love"

Writing has been a significant part of my life now for years. It is a setting in which I can experience the battle with spiritual desolation that we all share in our individual callings. These next paragraphs are from an entry in the same journal, some months after that just quoted. This was an early morning, while writing the same book:

I am tired this morning and not sure why. Is it stress? Rising too early? I don't know how to change this. I feel game for the task of writing, committed to it, but I feel as though this will take weeks of tiredness, of heaviness, of burden. . .

Mary, please love me with a mother's love, and show me the way, beyond my lack of wisdom. Please guide me as I write, and make this book fruitful. Holy Spirit, please grant me wisdom. Jesus, look upon me with healing and love. Father, let me know today that I am beloved in your heart.

There is some struggle here again, this great tiredness, this "soft" discouragement. The enemy is in this some-where, and I don't see this clearly. It is time to talk once more with Ed.

This experience incorporates several of Ignatius's counsels, primarily that of turning to prayer in time of desolation. I find that such prayer always helps, first because I feel less alone, and then because experience has taught me that, in ways I cannot foresee, God does answer such prayers. I also experienced here the examination Ignatius counsels later in this rule: by looking at the desolation, I was able to sense that the enemy was at work and that I needed help to understand this more clearly (rule 13). I am grateful to Ignatius for sup-plying me with a wisdom that assists me daily in this way.

"I Learned Again that I Am Not Alone"

Some years later, again during a time of writing:

I got back from giving the retreat two days ago and am feeling the post-trip time of desolation. I feel worn. This morning I did some writing and then some spiritual direction in midafternoon. After that, I had no more energy. I was tempted not to go to evening prayer and supper with the others. I prayed to the Father for help. I did go to evening prayer and it went well. Supper was wonderful; the others asked about the retreat, and it was good to share about it. I learned again that I am not alone. The Father does respond.

I sense how the enemy, in times like this of desolation, tells me that the chapters I'm writing will be of poor quality. The contrary is true. I made very good progress today, and was ready to write after one day of rest.

This time, too, turning to God in prayer made all the difference.

"I Sensed When It Changed"

Ten months later, in the ordinary ebb and flow of life:

After lunch today, a time of desolation. I forgot the meeting with Father Charles, and it was embarrassing to get the phone call about that. Above all, there is the burden about the future of my ministry and how the conversations will go. I picked up a novel and ate food that I didn't need. Then I said Mass and asked the help of the Father, Mary's intercession also (I said the Mass of Mary, the Mother of Divine Hope), and things changed. I worked all afternoon and faced all the issues. I sensed during the Mass when it changed.

I keep learning that fleeing desolation into some form of diversion does not help, and that turning to prayer does. The first is solitary; the second is relational, and that makes all the difference.

Meditation

Sixteenth-century Jesuit Jerónimo Ripalda writes that one in desolation "should increase his prayer and meditation *against what the desolation is telling him.*"[10] Ripalda's words capture perfectly the sense of the meditation Ignatius recommends in rule 6: this is a meditating on God's Word, on truths of faith, and on the memory of God's past fidelities, that directly counters the discouraging lies of *what the desolation is telling the person.*

I have seen people do this in many beautiful ways. Some have favorite scriptural passages they call to mind in desolation. One man told me that in desolation he reflects on Psalm 46:10, "Be still, and know that I am God."[11] A priest encourages those he guides to return in time of desolation to biblical passages in which they have encountered God in a special way. A woman tells me that she has her "antidesolation" hymn and sings it in time of desolation. I love this! Its refrain especially, as she sings it, assures her of God's faithful love. Another woman has a favorite poem with a similar message and recites it in time of desolation. All of these have found personal ways to meditate "against what the desolation is telling them": they are doing precisely what Ignatius recommends in rule 6.

I think of this as filling our spiritual quiver with spiritual arrows, and having these ready for times of desolation. Because we have prepared in advance, we can employ these meditative "arrows" all the more quickly against desolation when we experience it.

One such spiritual arrow has helped me for many years. I had been stationed outside the country for several years and then was called back to work with our seminarians. The move involved not only a cultural readjustment but also a work for which I did not feel prepared. Other factors, too, rendered the situation difficult. As the months passed, the burden grew.

One winter's evening, I stepped off the subway and began walking toward our house, about a quarter of a mile away. I still remember the dark of that evening, the cold, the headlights and noise of rush-hour traffic on the street alongside, and the snow piled by the sidewalk. Each step was taking me closer to a task that had become very heavy. I found myself saying to the Lord, "Lord, why is this happening? I'm just trying to do the best I can." Then I found these words in my heart: "I have been here before." *I have been here before*— that is, "Lord, there have been other times in my life when I have felt what I am feeling now, and I can now look back on them and see more clearly how you blessed me through them. I can trust that someday I will look back on this time also and see what you, Lord, are giving me through it." The burden did not lift completely, but something did change. My heart grew just a little lighter, because I could believe that this experience, too, was within God's providence in my life, and that someday, at least in some measure, I would understand why.

Those words, "I have been here before," are one of my points of meditation in time of desolation. They remind me that God has seen me faithfully through former times of desolation and even made them channels of growth. When I recall these words, I feel a beginning of hope, and the desolation gets a little easier to bear. This is one personal way in which I find Ignatius's counsel of meditation "against what the desolation is telling me" of great help. Have we identified our own ways?

Some years ago, I met a wonderful woman religious then in her seventies and now with the Lord. She told me that when she got into a "low"—in Ignatian terms, a time of desolation—she would turn to the Lord and say, "You've carried me for fifty-five years of religious life. You won't drop me in this little thing either." It was a perfect application of rule 6: a reflection, in time of desolation, on God's past fidelity that strengthens the person to resist present desolation.

I think of Jesus faced with the tempter in the desert (Mt 4:1–11). He immediately responds to the tactics of the enemy with the Word of God, and the enemy is defeated. To call to mind pertinent passages from Scripture—to meditate on them—in time of desolation greatly encourages the one in desolation.

Evagrius of Pontus, a fourth-century monk, proposed this way of responding to the enemy in his book *Talking Back* (*Antirrhêtikos*).[12] In this little volume, Evagrius gathers 498 biblical passages to be employed against various tactics of the enemy. A number apply directly to Ignatius's counsel of meditation in time of desolation.

The soul, Evagrius writes, that "due to the sadness that comes upon it, thinks that the Lord has not heard its groaning," will benefit from Exodus 2:23–24: "The children of Israel groaned because of their tasks, and cried, and their cry because of their tasks went up to God. And God heard their groanings."[13] Further, "Against the soul's thought that supposes it is tested beyond its strength," Evagrius proposes 1 Corinthians 10:13: "God is faithful, and he will not let you be tested beyond your strength, but with the testing he will also provide the way out so that you may be able to endure it."[14] Again, "Against the soul that succumbs to listlessness and becomes filled with thoughts of sadness," Evagrius proposes Psalm 46:1, "Why are you sad, my soul? And why do you trouble me? Hope in God, for I will give thanks to him, the salvation of my countenance and my God."[15] The many examples establish the principle: in time of desolation, *meditate*. Which passages from Scripture will help us in time of desolation? Can we name some of these passages?

"Consolation Has Returned"

At the conclusion of a time of prayer some years ago:

> I began this time of prayer feeling far from you, Lord. The seminar yesterday went well, but it left me tired, and it was hard to pray yesterday. I asked Mary to lead me to you. Again I invited you into my "thin film of grayness." And my heart has lifted. I thought of the words of Isaiah, "The Lord delights in you" (Is 62:4).[16] I could not feel this as I started. Now, it is warmer. Lord, it is always the same: the key is to invite you into the grayness, the self-doubt, the question as to how you see me. I feel happier, ready for the day. Consolation has returned.

I do find that this is the key: to invite the Lord into my experience of desolation and to remember his words of love. This lifts my heart and helps me reject the desolation.

"Everything Changed for the Better"

Some years later, looking back on the day:

> Just back from overseas travel and tired from the travel. My first meeting was at 10:00 a.m., and I had to be ready for that. But I just couldn't get started on the day. My feeling was that it would be like this all day, that I wouldn't even say Mass or pray the Liturgy of the Hours because I was so tired, that the whole day would be lonely and heavy. Now I can see the signs of desolation in such feelings and thoughts.

Then I had the thought of listening to a CD on discernment that had been given to me. When I did, instantly everything changed for the better. The heaviness lifted, and I got started on the day. I offered to say the noon Mass and did. I joined the others for our weekly meeting and spent time sharing with one of them especially about my trip. As I write this, I am spending my time in prayer before the Blessed Sacrament. I can see that listening to the CD was a form of the meditation of which Ignatius speaks in rule 6.

I am amazed at the energy I have. I am still tired, but the heaviness is gone. Now I have just the normal tiredness from a trip, and it is not heavy.

As is evident, many of these experiences of spiritual desolation begin, for me, in times of tiredness from travel or writing. Such tiredness is a normal nonspiritual consequence of expending physical and emotional energy. I know that I need to respond to it with healthy nonspiritual remedies: sleep, proper meals, relaxation, sharing in community, and exercise. But I know, too, that the enemy readily works in that nonspiritual vulnerability, and that with it I can also experience spiritual desolation, feeling distant from God, without energy for prayer, and with the discouragement that typifies desolation. This was an experience in which the spiritual desolation entered through a nonspiritual vulnerability (physical tiredness from travel), and an experience in which meditation—through the content of the CD—lifted the spiritual desolation. At that point, only the nonspiritual vulnerability remained and that, consequently, was much easier to address. These same principles apply to all of us in our different circumstances of life.

Much Examination

Over the years, I have come to appreciate the wisdom of this counsel: in time of spiritual desolation, do not flee the burden by seeking some form of diversion—food, a novel, a movie, the Internet, simple busyness—but stop and *examine* what is happening. I find that when I am in spiritual desolation, the undiscerning, unreflective, unaware tendency is to avoid it by some such diversion. I suspect that I am not alone in this!

Experience teaches me over and over that flight into diversion does not resolve desolation. When we close the refrigerator for the final time, when we turn off the tablet or smartphone, when the movie finishes—the "aspirin" has worn off but the symptoms are still there, perhaps even a little heavier because we know that we have succumbed to the desolation.

Ignatius counsels us to do just the opposite: instead of fleeing, *examine* what is happening. I find that this initially can take some courage. I also find that when I do stop fleeing and examine the desolation, things begin to get better.

Questions to Examine

When I examine what is happening, I ask myself two questions: What am I feeling? And, how did this get started? Both questions are of great help to me. First, *what am I feeling?* Simply to recognize that "I'm in desolation" is very freeing. This recognition changes the experience from a sense of overwhelming, all-encompassing burden to a spiritual experience that I can name and to which I can respond. The difference is enormous: we cannot deal with an overwhelming burden, but we can deal with a specific spiritual experience. Just to examine what I'm feeling and reach the point in which I can recognize it as spiritual desolation is already a beginning of liberation.[17]

Second, *how did this get started*? When I can pinpoint the beginning of the desolation, the sense of liberation grows stronger. Again, we cannot deal with a confusing, dark cloud of heaviness. But we *can* deal with a situation that, for example, began when we received that email or phone message at ten this morning, when we got the results of the test from the doctor, or when we felt discouraged to see ourselves react again in a way we had hoped to have overcome. Often enough, we also realize that before that moment, we were at peace, perhaps even in consolation. Once we see when and how the desolation began, we can make decisions regarding how to reject it: I'll call that person, I'll make a follow-up appointment with the doctor to discuss remedies, I'll prepare for that situation so that I am not caught off guard next time, I'll take this to further prayer, I'll talk with this person who can help me. In this way, we are set free to *respond* in the Lord rather than simply *react*.[18]

This Examination in Practice

In his *Spiritual Exercises*, Ignatius supplies various times of examination. After a period of prayer, for example, he invites the person to review the prayer (*SpirEx* 77). This excellent practice can be done briefly in daily life after a time of *lectio divina*, imaginative contemplation, reflective meditation, or any form of quiet prayer we find helpful. Were there experiences of spiritual consolation? More to the point of rule 6, were there experiences of spiritual desolation? What were the feelings and thoughts? How did we respond? I find that often just making time for quiet prayer already leads to clarity. The diversions are removed, I face what is happening in my heart and thoughts, and I begin to see more clearly. If I also review the prayer, this clarity is likely to increase.

Ignatius also offers us the daily examen prayer—a rendering of the classic examination of conscience that incorporates
discernment into the prayer. Elsewhere I have discussed the
examen prayer in detail.[19] If we desire to grow in our capacity to examine spiritual desolation, praying this daily examen
may be the best practice we can adopt. If we do pray it, then
at least once a day we will stop explicitly to examine the spiritual movements of our hearts. Among many other benefits, the
examen ensures that, should we be in spiritual desolation, no
day will pass without the "much examination" to which Ignatius call us in rule 6. I find the examen prayer a great blessing
both in time of desolation and also in general.

Finally, we can stop at any time to examine an experience
of spiritual desolation. When we feel a burden on our hearts,
a few minutes taken from the day's busyness can make a great
difference. I do this at times between phone calls, if I can get
a few minutes, or walking from one meeting to another. Jesuit
author Keith Townsend describes this as a "quick flash of discerning awareness" in the midst of the day.[20] Sometimes we
will see quickly what we are feeling and how it began; then we
can already plan how to respond. At other times, clarity may
not come immediately. Nonetheless, even a quick examination, if that is all time permits at the moment, already begins
to lift our burden and prepares us for the less hurried time
when we can examine our spiritual desolation more fully.

A woman who is a nurse told me that, at times, she senses
that something is not right in her heart. Because the busyness
of the hospital day does not permit her to stop and examine
it then, she "parks" it, as it were, near her heart. When she
rides the commuter train home from work, with the Lord
she examines the heaviness. This is a beautiful application of
Ignatius's "much examination" in time of desolation.

Some may find that writing this examination helps to see things more clearly. In a classic line, Francis Bacon affirms that "reading makes a full man; conference a ready man; and writing an exact man."[21] Writing what we experience may, in fact, help us to grasp it more exactly. I find that when spiritual desolation seems so knotted and confused that I cannot see clearly, describing the experience in writing helps me separate the threads and understand better what is happening. Generally, I rise from this exercise with a lighter heart and a clearer sense of how to proceed. Would we find such journaling helpful in time of spiritual desolation? Experience and reflection on that experience will help answer this question.[22]

What if we do our best to examine the spiritual desolation and still cannot find clarity? For Ignatius, the discerning life is never lived alone. The best recourse in this case is to talk with a person of spiritual wisdom and competence. We will return to this when we discuss rule 13.

Suitable Penance

In time of spiritual desolation, when the heaviness urges us to flee into diversion and gratification, Ignatius invites us to stand our ground with suitable penance. Said with a slight change of vocabulary, he urges us to stand firm with *suitable gestures of penitential courage.*

The penance is to be *suitable*—not unsuitable, that is, without due measure or in some way inappropriate for the person. And, as a little reflection readily reveals, when we are burdened by desolation such acts may require *courage.* The difference between indulging in diversion, simply surrendering to it, and engaging in some suitable form of restraint is great. The first discourages us further; the second begins to set us free.

These penitential gestures may be objectively small: a person waits ten minutes to head to the refrigerator again, waits fifteen minutes before going online, smiles at another when indisposed to do so, performs a simple service for another, undertakes that little task that has been waiting for several days, chooses to exercise rather than watch television, and many similar "suitable" gestures of penitential courage. These "small" gestures have great power to lift the discouraging sense of helplessness that desolation insinuates. When we take even one small step with the Spirit, the Spirit prepares the next and the next—and the downward trajectory of desolation collapses.

"Doing the Small Things Helped"

As I've mentioned, sometimes just getting exercise makes the difference: after that, I am ready to pray and take positive steps to reject spiritual desolation. Sometimes resisting the flight into diversion by dedicating myself to the small tasks at hand helps in a similar way.

One day I had been busy at my tasks through midmorning. Then I received a disappointing email. I had hoped for another's help on one aspect of a writing project, and this email expressed a gracious refusal. Since my hopes had been high, my disappointment was correspondingly great. The following is from the day's examen:

> When I received the email, I felt myself slip into desolation. I knew that I needed to resist or it could grow. What helped was the choice to do the small, concrete things that I could do. I had an errand waiting to be done at some point, and went out and did it right away. I reordered some notes, replaced the candles in the

chapel, prepared for a talk I had to give later, prayed the Liturgy of the Hours, and got exercise. It all helped, and the desolation did not take charge of the day.

While this may not be precisely what Ignatius intends by "suitable penance," I believe it is very much the dynamic he intends: in time of spiritual desolation, rather than flee into diversion and gratification, we stand our ground with suitable gestures of penitential courage. I have come to believe, too, that no such gesture is too small. Experience will teach us which gestures are suitable for us, and it will teach us their power as well.

Rule 6 in Synthesis

What will happen to Philip in desolation at 10:00 p.m. or Laura at 3:00 p.m., if both, with trust in God's grace, turn to God with a heartfelt *prayer of petition*, asking for the help they so much need; *call to mind and meditate on* the truths of faith, scriptural verses, and memories of God's fidelity in the past that assure them of his help in this darkness as well; *examine* what they are feeling and how this got started, gaining new insight into the present heaviness; and rather than reach for the smartphone or remote control, make *suitable gestures of penitential courage*, breaking the discouraging descent into diversion? And what will happen in our times of desolation if we do these things?

What will *not* happen is a helpless and prolonged surrender to the desolation. What *will* happen, as God's grace blesses our efforts, is that the desolation will weigh less and will be less likely to endure: captives are beginning to be set free. Rule 6 is a great gift for the journey.

Chapter 7

When You Think that You
Can't, Know that You Can

> *In some way, suffering ceases to be suf-
> fering at the moment it finds a meaning.*
> —Viktor Frankl

In his desire to help us resist desolation, Ignatius now turns
to our *thoughts*. He has already advised us to avoid harmful
changes (rule 5) and to adopt helpful changes (rule 6). Now
he urges us *think* in a certain way during times of desolation.
These thoughts, he tells us, will strengthen us to resist the
desolation. The text of rule 7 follows. In it, the governing
word is the initial verb *consider*:

> Seventh Rule. The seventh: let one who is in desolation
> consider how the Lord has left him in trial in his natu-
> ral powers, so that he may resist the various agitations
> and temptations of the enemy; since he can resist with the
> divine help, which always remains with him, though he
> does not clearly feel it; for the Lord has taken away from
> him his great fervor, abundant love and intense grace, leav-
> ing him, however, sufficient grace for eternal salvation.

The way we think significantly affects our spiritual lives.
This is an important principle to which Ignatius has already

referred (rule 4, final sentence) and to which he will return repeatedly (rules 8, 10, and 11).[1]

At times, psychiatrists, psychologists, or counselors are present when I teach the rules. A number have noted the parallel between Ignatius's procedure in the rules—inviting us to adopt certain ways of thinking as a help to overcoming spiritual desolation—and their own use of cognitive behavioral therapy in helping persons surmount emotional struggles. In each case, the choice to adopt thoughts that better reflect the truth of the situation significantly relieves the burden. Five hundred years ago, Ignatius applied this principle to the spiritual life.

Ignatius invites persons in spiritual desolation—the disheartened Philip alone in his room at 10:00 p.m., the discouraged Laura at the kitchen table in midafternoon, and us all when in desolation—to *consider* three interrelated thoughts: that this spiritual desolation is a trial; that God's purpose in permitting the trial is to provide them an opportunity to resist desolation and so grow in the ability to resist; and that they can indeed resist because, though they do not feel it, God is giving them all the grace they need to resist the desolation. We will explore these below.

Two Experiences of Grace

In rule 7, as in the preceding rules, Ignatius continues to speak of *spiritual consolation* and *spiritual desolation*. This rule is for "one who is in desolation," and from whom the Lord "has taken away . . . his great fervor, abundant love, and intense grace"—that is, his spiritual consolation.

At this point, however, Ignatius introduces a new category. Though God has taken away the *intense grace* of spiritual consolation—that is, the warm, perceptibly felt, uplifting grace of spiritual consolation—he has not taken away all grace. Even when the grace of spiritual consolation is absent and the burden of spiritual desolation is present, God is still giving grace. This is, Ignatius affirms, "the divine help, which always remains with him, though he does not clearly feel it." Ignatius titles this divine help *sufficient grace*—all the grace the person needs to persevere safely through the desolation and stay on course toward eternal salvation: "leaving him, however, sufficient grace for eternal salvation."

Intense grace and *sufficient* grace: these are experiential terms.[2] *Intense grace* is the perceptible, uplifting grace of spiritual consolation; *sufficient grace* is largely unfelt—"though he does not clearly feel it"—but very real, and supplies all the strength the person needs to resist the desolation.

At times, the term "hard consolation" has been used to describe this sufficient grace.[3] I have always found this phrase difficult to accept, both because Ignatius never uses it and it creates confusion in those who apply the rules to their experience: Is this difficult experience, this heaviness of heart, spiritual desolation (of the enemy) or is it "hard consolation" (of the good spirit)? Obviously, depending on the answer, our responses to it will be very different.

I understand why this phrase "hard consolation" arose. When warm spiritual consolation is absent and heavy spiritual desolation is present, God's grace is still at work. We witness people who, in the darkness of spiritual desolation, with great courage remain faithful to their spiritual and vocational commitments. Grace is clearly at work, even in the absence of warm spiritual consolation as we have described it thus far. This deep, fortifying grace, experienced without warmth, at work in the darkness of desolation is then titled "hard consolation":

it is a work of God, of grace (and so, in this understanding, "consolation") experienced without warmth (and so, "hard").

After years of working with Ignatius's rules, I realized that Ignatius himself addresses this largely unfelt but effective grace. In rule 7, he simply calls it "sufficient grace": all the grace the person needs to resist the desolation. Ignatius repeats this vocabulary in rule 11: the one in desolation should think that "he can do much with God's sufficient grace to resist all his enemies." I find it best to avoid the confusing phrase "hard consolation" and to adhere to Ignatius's own vocabulary: though God does at times take away the *intense* (felt) grace of spiritual consolation, he never takes away the (largely unfelt but real) *sufficient* grace that permits us to resist desolation.

When Philip at 10:00 p.m., burdened by spiritual desolation, *feels* helpless to resist, and feels that he will inevitably succumb to "low and earthly things," he can *know* with certitude that he *can* resist, because God is giving him sufficient grace to resist. When he does reach out for the Bible rather than the smartphone, we witness God's sufficient grace at work in time of spiritual desolation.

Not every work of grace is spiritual consolation, which always involves a perceptible, happy, uplifting movement of the heart. God's grace is not limited to spiritual consolation alone, and Ignatius, in keeping with our age-old tradition (1 Cor 10:13), is confident that even in time of spiritual desolation, that grace will always be *sufficient*.

The Thoughts that Strengthen

As mentioned, Ignatius supplies three thoughts that strengthen, one following on the other. We will review them in sequence.

"The Lord Has Left Him in Trial"

If Philip at 10:00 p.m. and Laura in midafternoon can *consider* this thought—that this experience is not just meaningless pain, not just an empty fate, but rather a *trial* permitted *by the Lord*—they will be greatly heartened to resist the enemy's discouraging lies. Suffering that has no meaning quickly becomes unendurable: if they perceive the desolation as meaningless pain, Philip will likely reach for the smartphone, and Laura for the remote control—as will we in similar circumstances.

But when suffering acquires meaning, it can be borne. This is the first thought to consider *right in the time of desolation*: This difficult experience is not meaningless. It lies within God's providence in my life. It is a *trial* that the Lord is permitting (Acts 14:22).

From his experiences in the concentration camps of Nazi Germany, psychiatrist Viktor Frankl wrote his classic book, *Man's Search for Meaning*. Observing with a professional eye, Frankl learned the difference between those who survived and those who did not. Those who found meaning in their suffering—wives and children whom they were determined to see again, a life's work to be completed, and the like—survived; those who found no meaning in their pain, succumbed.

In time of spiritual desolation, Ignatius writes, consider that this is a *trial* within the providence of a loving God (see rule 9). Pointless affliction cannot be withstood; a trial permitted by the Lord can.

People have told me the difference that this thought makes. When we see spiritual desolation simply as "my failure, my inadequacy," each experience of it discourages. But when we understand desolation as a trial permitted by God, to be borne with trust in God and the fruitfulness of which we learn by experience, everything changes. Here, too, captives are set free, and energy is released to resist and reject the desolation. As we will see, Ignatius will return to this reflection in rule 9.

"So that He May Resist"

We grow in patience by exercising the act of patience in situations in which we could easily become impatient. We grow in prayer by exercising the act of prayer, day after day. We grow in love of neighbor by exercising that love in concrete situations as the years go by. Said more abstractly, we grow in good habits (virtues) by repeatedly exercising the act of those good habits.

The same is true of the ability to reject spiritual desolation. We grow in this ability by experiencing spiritual desolation, and while in it, exercising the act of resisting the desolation. As we do this repeatedly over the years, we grow in the ability to reject desolation. If it is true, as I have suggested, that for most of us, for most of the way on the spiritual journey, spiritual desolation is the main obstacle, then few abilities are of greater value in the spiritual life than this.

God permits the trial of spiritual desolation, Ignatius says, for this very reason: *so that we may resist the desolation* and, by resisting, grow in the ability to resist it. Such is the second thought that Ignatius asks us to consider in time of spiritual desolation.

Early in my priesthood, for two consecutive years, I made my annual eight-day retreat without a director. This was certainly unwise. In both years, the same thing happened: by the fourth day, I found myself struggling with spiritual desolation.

At the time, a retired Jesuit whom I knew, Father William Reed, was living in this retreat house. He had been a professor all his life, a good religious and a fine priest. Both years, on that fourth day, I called his room and asked if we could meet. Each time, the same thing happened. Father Reed set a time, and at that time, I knocked on his door. When I did, I heard his voice from within, saying, "Come in." When I opened the door and saw him, instantly I began to feel peace.

He was very much the professor! His room and desk overflowed with books and papers. Amid them all, he sat in his rocking chair with his pipe. What immediately calmed me was Father Reed's deep sense of serenity. You had the feeling, looking at him, that this was a man who knew life's struggles, had experienced them, and had reached a state in which he would no longer be easily shaken by them. For me, as a young priest burdened by desolation, simply to see him brought peace. Both times, after our conversation, I left strengthened in that peace and ready to resume the retreat.

I imagine that most of us know persons like this. Generally, though not always, they are people in the latter decades of life. Such persons are pillars of strength for the rest of us, and we willingly converse with them. How did they reach this point? How do persons attain this seemingly unshakable state of peace and wisdom? Most often, I believe, this occurs through undergoing trials over the years, and faithfully enduring them. Having witnessed God's faithful love in their struggles, such persons' peace deepens as they face life and all it may bring (Ps 23).

This is the thought Ignatius counsels us to consider in the trial of desolation: that God has left us in this trial *so that we may resist* the desolation and, by resisting, grow in the ability to resist it. Each time we do resist an experience of desolation, two things happen: we are set free from the discouraging lies of that desolation, and we grow in the ability to resist future desolation. This thought, considered in time of desolation, will strengthen us to resist that desolation.

Achille Gagliardi, SJ (1537–1607), in the first extensive commentary on these rules, offers a comparison to illustrate rule 7 and why God allows the trial of desolation.[4] When teaching a child to write, the teacher first guides the hand of the pupil with his own. Then he removes his hand and allows the child to form the letters on his own.

Obviously, Gagliardi comments, in the first case the letters are better formed than in the second. In the first case, the teacher largely forms the letters; in the second, the child's lack of skill dictates the shaping of the letters. The teacher, however, is better pleased with the letters in the second case, for if the teacher constantly held the child's hand, the child would never learn to form letters by himself.

Gagliardi applies the metaphor: "In a similar way, works that are done in the fervor of consolation are almost of God since they are performed with the delight of that consolation, by which we are drawn to accomplishing good acts with ease. In desolation, however, we are left to ourselves (though not without God's grace), so that by engaging our own energy in our works and actions, we may grow in strength, as we see in the seventh rule."[5] God leaves us in the trial of desolation so that by resisting, "we may grow in strength, as we see in the seventh rule."

"Since He Can Resist"

This is one of the most hopeful statements in the entire set of rules! There is what I call "the litany of spiritual desolation."

This litany is the following: "I can't, I can't, I can't, I can't, I can't . . . I can't go to prayer today, I can't finish this time of prayer, I can't take part in the Bible study this evening, I can't spend a day longer with these people, I can't go on in this vocation . . . I can't, I can't, I can't . . . " And when in desolation everything in us cries out that we can't, Ignatius urges us to consider *that we can*, because though we do not clearly feel it—the intense grace has been taken away—God is giving us sufficient grace to resist the desolation.[6] If we *consider* this truth in time of desolation, the desolation's power to harm us will greatly diminish.

Two young boys are learning to ride a bicycle. The first is convinced that he can learn to ride. The second is convinced that he cannot. The outcome is already largely determined: the first will likely learn to ride; the second is unlikely to do so. In the first case, difficulties will not dishearten the young boy but will be accepted as part of the learning. In the second, the same difficulties will further convince the boy that he cannot learn to ride.

If Philip at 10:00 p.m. in his room and Laura in midafternoon in her kitchen are convinced that they cannot resist the desolation, in all likelihood they will succumb. If both *consider* right *in the desolation*, as they sit in their respective rooms, that *they can resist*, and further consider the reason why they can resist—because though they do not clearly feel it, God is giving them all the grace (sufficient grace) they need to resist—they are much more likely, in fact, to resist. Such is the power of this third interrelated thought that Ignatius proposes in rule 7.

In a time of deep desolation, Jesuit poet Gerard Manley Hopkins penned a lovely verse that describes exactly the choice to consider that we can resist:

Not, I'll not, carrion comfort, Despair, not feast on thee;
Not untwist—slack they may be—these last strands of man
In me, ór, most weary, cry *I can no more*. I can;
Can something, hope, wish day come, not choose not
    to be.[7]

In the depth of his desolation, Hopkins turns to God, rejects the thought that *"I can no more"*—the emphasis is his—and chooses to affirm that "I can." In this, he perfectly exemplifies rule 7.

What if, then, in time of desolation, we sit for a few minutes in silence before the Lord—in church, alone in our rooms, out walking, while driving, or as we exercise—and choose to call to mind these thoughts: that this desolation is a trial within God's providence, that the purpose of the trial is to provide an opportunity to resist desolation and so grow in the capacity to resist, and that we can resist because God is giving sufficient grace to resist? What will happen to the course of our desolation? In all likelihood, we will in fact resist it; it will not harm us.

Rule 7: Some Examples

Over the years, rule 7 has been a help for me in time of desolation. I provide here a few simple illustrations.

"I Could Clearly Feel the Dynamic of Rule 7"

The following is from a day that began in spiritual desolation. There were several causes: troubling situations in the world and in this country, concerns for ministry and the spiritual life, and the death of a man who had been a friend and helper for many years. At midday I wrote:

My spirits have gradually risen today. The conversation with John helped. It revealed to me that some of my fears had no basis.

This morning at Mass I could clearly feel the dynamic of rule 7, that I could consider what I could not clearly feel. I see the need to consider, to think, when I cannot feel. And slowly it helped. Now, after the conversation with John, I see consolation returning more. In the desolation and discouragement of this morning, I did not see this.

The day continues to be filled with blessings: a good meeting with the doctor and an email from the editor who is open to the future books I proposed.

That evening:

The day started so tired and heavy, and got better. The phone conversation this evening helped in dealing with the death and funeral. I continue to feel joy about the prospect of future writing.

Experiences of this kind have taught me the efficacy of rule 7, of the choice to consider God's faithful love and grace even when I do not feel it. As on this day, rule 7 helps me in the struggle against desolation.

"I Can't Do This"

At the conclusion of a time of prayer that morning:

I started this time of prayer with that sense that "I can't do this," that I just can't because I'm too tired. That there is some tiredness is true. But before, I would have believed this feeling of helplessness and filled the time for prayer with reading related in some way to the spiritual life, so as to "get through" the time.

Now, after talking about this with Ed, I realize that that sense that "I can't" is a lie of the enemy. Ed helped me to see this, and I experienced it today.

The prayer then warmed with a sense of the Father's presence, and a sense of Jesus with me in the Blessed Sacrament. I end with more warmth.

I find it liberating to challenge the "I can't" of spiritual desolation. Experience teaches me the difference this can make. A certain measure of objective physical tiredness is very different than an overwhelming, disheartened sense that "I just can't pray today." When, turning to the Lord and following Ignatius's guidance, I see the enemy's lie, I am set free to pray. At times, as this day, the experience then reverses: desolation disappears and consolation emerges.

"And Peace Quietly Comes"

This next experience occurred halfway through an eight-day Ignatian retreat. It was an overcast October day. I was the only one in the building who was on retreat; all the others were part of a program of spiritual formation. For that reason, too, I felt alone. I had come to the retreat tired, and some tiredness was still present.

That afternoon, at the end of an hour of prayer, I described the experience. As I reread it now, I see more clearly than I could then the nature of "the thoughts that come from desolation":

The struggle continues. I am tired. This is like in my final months as provincial when I was so tired. All the

spiritual advice was good, but I was still tired. It is like
telling beautiful truths to a person who needs sleep. He
still needs sleep.

I am afraid of the soul-searing work of writing the
book that lies ahead.

I am aware that there is desolation in this. I turn to
the Father, and I ask Mary's help, but I still feel the burden. Before there were two of us on retreat, but now the
other has finished, and I am the only one. I sense that the
enemy uses this, too.

I consciously choose to turn to the Father, to ask
Mary's help. And peace quietly comes. Speaking my
prayer out loud helps, considering what I cannot clearly
feel: your presence, your faithfulness, and your love.
Then I felt, at least a bit, the assurance that I am not
alone. I thought of Jesus's words, "I am not alone,
because the Father is with me" (Jn 16:32).[8] I never saw
the second part of this verse before, "because the Father
is with me."

I write this sitting by the lake's edge, looking across
to the docks and church, under the cloudy skies.

I think that the enemy is at work in this, who does
not want me to find energy and hope in writing this new
book. Just to say the Father's name leaves me feeling
less alone. The heaviness lifts, and some sense of hope
dawns. To turn to you, Father, and to know that I am
not alone, that your love and grace, your salvation are
with me, and that you, Jesus, are with me too, strengthens me in this battle.

This has been an hour of spiritual struggle. I end with
more peace.

As I review this entry, I am struck by the heaviness of the thoughts that arise in desolation (rule 4, final sentence). A work in which I delight, that is, writing, appeared to me then as "soul-searingly" heavy. I felt tired and alone.

In this desolation, rule 7 was again a faithful friend. The choice to consider what I could not clearly feel in the desolation—that is, the Father's love, fidelity, and grace; Jesus's saving power; and Mary's loving intercession—began to tip the balance away from desolation and toward a beginning, at least, of peace and hope. For this reason, as for so many others, I am grateful to Ignatius for his rules.

Chapter 8

"Let Him Think that He Will Soon Be Consoled"

> *Therefore, be steadfast in your resolutions. Stay in the boat in which he has placed you, and let the storm come. Long live Jesus! You will not perish. He may sleep, but at the opportune time he will awaken to restore your calm.*
> —St. Pio of Pietrelcina

In rule 8, Ignatius writes:

> Eighth Rule. The eighth: let one who is in desolation work to be in patience, which is contrary to the vexations that come to him, and let him think that he will soon be consoled, diligently using the means against such desolation, as is said in the sixth rule.

Rule 8, like the three preceding rules, supplies means to help resist spiritual desolation. The rule contains three related parts: the call to *patience* in time of spiritual desolation; an invitation to *think* in a way that will sustain this patience, that is, to consider that consolation will return soon; and a renewed encouragement to employ the *active means* (prayer, meditation, examination, and penance) described in rule 6. We will examine each of these three.

"Work to Be in Patience"

"Let one who is in desolation work to be in patience, which is contrary to the vexations that come to him." *Work to be in patience.* My wording here, somewhat clumsy in English, is a literal translation of Ignatius's Spanish, *trabaje de estar en paciencia.* I translated literally to capture the effect of Ignatius's words: that to remain *patient* in time of desolation will require *work.* A certain effort will be necessary to exercise the patience so key in time of desolation.

This patience, Ignatius tells us, "is contrary to the vexations that come" in the time of spiritual desolation. Desolation presents itself with urgency: things are going badly, everything is confusing, you can't go on this way, you are regressing, you'll never make real progress, you've gotten things all wrong, you must make this change immediately—anxiety, pressure, burden, urgency—and the answer is the *patience* that "is *contrary* to the *vexations*" that come in time of desolation.[1]

The word "patience" derives from the Latin verb *patior,* which means to bear, to suffer, to endure.[2] This is the virtue of the person *who will not give up,* who will not surrender to the vexations of the desolation, but who will stand firm, working to be in patience, resisting, while God permits the desolation to endure. "Patience," writes Gagliardi, "is directly opposed to desolation and is the only antidote to it."[3]

A man, for example, planned to pray for an hour and now finds the hour desolate. He *will not give up,* will not surrender to the urgency of the desolation, but will stay the full sixty minutes as planned. He will work to be in patience, which is contrary to the vexations the desolation brings him. A woman is leading the Bible study in her parish and loves it, finding it a rich source of personal spiritual growth as well. The recent weeks, however, have been desolate. In her desolation she feels "slothful, tepid, and sad" (rule 4), with no desire to lead the Bible study group. Yet she *will not give up*, but working to be in patience, will lead the group as usual.

A woman told me that she heard a talk in which the speaker mentioned times that seem overwhelming. In such situations, the speaker counseled just living one hour at a time. The woman told me that sometimes twenty minutes at a time is all she can do. In a different setting, a man endured repeated surgeries on his leg and a long, slow recovery. He said that he learned, month after month, how you can endure. Both this woman and this man, in their respective settings, have worked to be in patience in difficult times. Such patience, Ignatius tells us, is the key virtue in time of spiritual desolation; it is the "antidote to it."

In her journal, spiritual writer Caryll Houselander describes a difficult time, and writes, "My heart is cold, my thoughts are cold, my soul is cold, but my will is on fire; in that fire I will forge a sword of service."[4] Dominican mystic and preacher Johannes Tauler calls for patience in desolation when he writes, "No one can fully understand all the good that lies hidden in this stern trial of desolation of spirit, this dark and frozen spiritual winter—supposing always that one holds his mind steady and firm in patient endurance."[5] In a magnificent passage in *The Lord of the Rings*, J. R. R. Tolkien describes this "patience" in the hobbit Sam at the darkest point of the quest: just when hope appears to die in his heart, hopelessness is transformed into new strength. Sam's will grows firm, and nothing, neither despair nor weariness nor endless miles to traverse, will stop him from faithfully pursuing his task.[6]

What if we sought a similar grace from God in time of desolation, the grace of a will on fire, of firmness in patient endurance, and of a will that neither despair nor weariness could subdue? This grace enables us to "work to be in patience" when spiritual desolation is present.

"Let Him Think that He Will Soon Be Consoled"

Ignatius, however, does not simply counsel us to work to be in patience: he supplies further means that greatly facilitate this "work." The first is a *thought* to be considered in time of desolation: that we will *soon be consoled*. This thought comprises three elements: that the present desolation will pass, that consolation will return, and that it will return much sooner than the desolation is telling us.

The adverb "soon" is powerful here. Desolation, as we have said, (falsely) claims power to predict our spiritual future. And the prediction is always dark. It shows Philip at 10:00 p.m. endless weeks and months of similar desolation; it shows Laura alone in midafternoon unending days of discouraging emptiness. If we believe this lie, desolation will be very hard to resist. In the face of this lie, Ignatius asks persons who are right now in spiritual desolation to think that they will *soon* be consoled—much sooner than the desolation is telling them. The hope this truth engenders is evident.[7]

Two Patients in a Hospital Room

Here is a hospital room with two beds. In each is a patient with different symptoms but roughly the same physical discomfort. The doctor enters the room. He stops at the bed of the first patient, reviews the patient's charts, and asks some questions. The doctor says to the patient, "I know that you are feeling some discomfort, and I wish I could tell you otherwise, but I need to let you know that you will feel this discomfort for several weeks yet."

The doctor then approaches the second patient. Again he reviews the charts and asks some questions. He says to the patient, "I know that you are feeling some discomfort, but I can tell you that by tomorrow you'll be feeling as good as new." The doctor then leaves the room.

How do these two patients, both experiencing roughly the same discomfort, react? The first falls back on his bed, stares out the window, and then picks up the remote control, flipping mindlessly through the channels. The long weeks of discomfort that lie ahead dishearten him, and he feels little energy for anything constructive.

The second, however, calls his wife immediately, and they plan for his return home. He also calls his boss, and they begin discussing the next project he will undertake at work. Already his thoughts turn creatively to this task. He moves about the room, packing his belongings. He finds himself desiring exercise and walks the corridor, speaking cheerfully to those he meets.

The doctor's words do not change the physical discomfort that both patients feel. The knowledge, however, that this discomfort will endure at length or pass soon changes everything. Our spiritual situation when in desolation, Ignatius tells us, is that of the second patient. If in time of desolation we can *think*, consider, call to mind this truth, that consolation will return *soon*, the spiritual discomfort of the present desolation will be much easier to endure.

"Was It Like This Yesterday?"

These are not just words! If we do as Ignatius counsels, and in time of desolation call to mind this truth—that we will

soon be consoled—we will experience the energizing difference it makes.

Some years ago, I met a faithful religious woman whom I
will call Sister Mary. She was seventy-five at the time, and is
now with the Lord. She told me that when she experienced
desolation, she would say to herself, "Was it like this yesterday?" This was a perfect application of Ignatius's rule 8
and his counsel to consider that consolation will return soon.
Sister Mary's practice was this: in time of desolation, she consciously adverted to the fact that the desolation lasts only
for a time: "Was it like this yesterday? No, there was a time
before this desolation began when I did not feel this burden."
That thought helped break the desolation's hold on her and
raised her awareness that consolation would return.

At times, I have done the following: When I sense that I
am in desolation, I take my journal and describe what I am
feeling. Then, with rule 8 in mind, I add, "This desolation
will pass. There will come a time when I will read what I am
writing now and will no longer be in desolation." And such
is always the case. When I write those words, it is an *act
of hope*, of trust in God's love and in the truth of Ignatius's
rule 8. When I reread them after the desolation has passed
and consolation has returned, it is *an experience* of the truth
of this rule. Each time I do this, I am strengthened in readiness to do it again in future desolation. For me personally,
this practice more than any other helps me grow in applying
rule 8.

A related exercise also helps me live rule 8. At times, when
in desolation, I take my journal and reread experiences of
past—sometimes very recent—spiritual consolation. These
may have arisen in prayer, in ministry, through relationships,
or in many settings. I find my heart lift as I recall these. When

I do this, I learn that I can resist desolation not only by combating it directly but also by remembering past consolation. As with Sister Mary, that remembrance assures me that the present desolation will pass and that consolation will return.

If Philip at 10:00 p.m. and Laura in midafternoon believe the lie that present desolation will continue at length, they will struggle to resist it. But if they consider the truth—that this desolation will pass and that consolation will return much sooner than the desolation is telling them—they will be greatly heartened to resist it. Can we call this thought to mind in desolation? What will happen if we do?

"Just Knowing that the Desolation Will End"

A young man told me of a weekend retreat he had made. During it, he experienced times of both consolation and desolation. He said, "Just knowing that the desolation will end really helps."

A priest arrived in his new parish. The parishioners were angry because of recent events in the parish, and they projected their anger onto the new pastor. He found himself desolate, and so reread the rules. When he reached rule 8, he saw Ignatius's counsel to consider that the desolation will not last forever, and that consolation will return. His heart lifted as he read. He told me that rule 8 has become his favorite rule.

A woman went out one day and looked at the sky, which was partly cloudy. She noted how the sun was darkened when a cloud passed in front of it. Then the cloud would pass, and the sun would shine again. She thought, "The sun is always there, shining, even when I don't see it." That simple experience, she said, helped her remember that God's love is always at work in her life, even when things seem dark. This is a lovely way to remember that the clouds of desolation will pass, and that the sun of consolation will return much sooner than the desolation seeks to tell us.

"Diligently Using the Means"

Ignatius supplies a second help to aid us work to be in patience: not only a *thought* but also *action*, and specifically the four means named in rule 6: "diligently using the means against such desolation, as is said in the sixth rule." Most literally, Ignatius invites us to use *las diligencias* listed in the sixth rule: prayer of petition, meditation on truths that can sustain us in desolation, much examination of how the desolation began and developed, and suitable gestures of penitential courage. The vocabulary (*diligencias*) indicates a use of these four means with energy and dedication—with *diligence*.

The complete sense of rule 8 is thus that we strive to remain *patient*, faithful, and enduring in time of desolation, and that two things will help us do this: the *thought* that consolation will return soon, and a *diligent application* of prayer, meditation, examination, and penance. As the years pass, I have come to see more and more the efficacy of this rule.

The Law of Undulation

This phrase, "the law of undulation," is from writer C. S. Lewis, and it expresses perfectly the presupposition that underlies rule 8.[8] Lewis writes of human persons that "their nearest approach to constancy . . . is undulation—the repeated return to a level from which they repeatedly fall back, a series of troughs and peaks."[9]

Underlying rule 8 (and later rule 10) is Ignatius's understanding that the law of undulation applies also to spiritual movements: spiritual consolation will last for a time, and eventually spiritual desolation will return. That desolation, too, will last only for a time—less than the desolation would have us believe—and then spiritual consolation will return. These alternations are *normal* in the spiritual life.[10]

Ignatius learned this early in his conversion. After his life-changing confession at the monastery of Montserrat, he settled in nearby Manresa where he would spend the next months. He tells us that "he began to experience great variations in his soul, finding himself at times so empty that he found no taste in prayer, nor in hearing Mass, nor in any other prayer that he made. At other times, the contrary of this came to him, so much so and so suddenly that it seemed the sadness and desolation left him like one who removes a cape from another's shoulders."[11] Ignatius's later *Spiritual Diary* testifies amply to both consolation and desolation in his later and more mature spiritual experience as well.

Often, when I present rule 8 and speak of these alternations as normal, I sense the relief in the hearers: "I'm normal!" I can feel the lifting of a burden in the group. We all experience these "ups and downs" in the spiritual life, but often have no vocabulary for them and do not know how or with whom to share them. We think that we should not experience such alternations, that if we were more advanced spiritually we would not, and that others do not struggle with these "undulations" as we do. The truth is very different: such alternations are normal spiritual experience. No saint, and no one who has ever loved the Lord, has walked any other road.

Writer Madeleine L'Engle affirms that "the growth of love is not a straight line, but a series of hills and valleys."[12] Jesuit Thomas Green writes matter-of-factly, "Desolations will come; they are, in fact, as normal a part of human life as are rainy days."[13] I like the calm tone of this sentence. Rainy days, to pursue the metaphor further, are an inconvenience, but if we never had them other serious problems would arise. Once again, there is no shame in experiencing spiritual desolation: it is as normal a part of human life as are rainy days. What does matter is discernment: to be aware of, name, and reject the desolation.

A man said that for many years he had believed that, when he was good, God would give him the "lollipop" of consolation. When he "messed up," God would permit the enemy to "beat him up" for a while with desolation.[14] He lived this way for years before learning of Ignatius's teaching on discernment. To know that the alternation of consolation and desolation is a normal ebb and flow in the spiritual life set him free. Now he knew that he did not just have to "white-knuckle" the times of desolation, but that he could discern them (be aware, understand, take action), and that the call was always to resist and reject the desolation.

People sometimes ask, "What is to be expected regarding these alternations? Will we experience the same amount of spiritual consolation and spiritual desolation? More of one than the other? If so, of which? Are we always either in spiritual consolation or in spiritual desolation? Do all have essentially the same experience of both, or do different persons experience different patterns?" These are good questions!

We have already spoken of what Ignatius calls "the tranquil time" (chapter 5). He explains, "I said a tranquil time, when the soul is not agitated by various spirits and uses its natural powers freely and tranquilly" (*SpirEx* 177). In this spiritual condition, persons experience neither the joy of spiritual consolation nor the heaviness of spiritual desolation: they are "not agitated by various spirits." On the contrary, they are tranquil, in a state of calm, in which they can use their "natural powers freely and tranquilly," that is, they can think, recall, choose, imagine, and the like, with freedom and peace.

This "tranquil time" is, obviously, a rich space in which persons may love and serve the Lord. If we review our own spiritual experience, we will all recognize such "tranquil times"—that is, times when, if we examine our hearts, we would say, "I do not think that I am experiencing the joy of spiritual consolation, but neither am I feeling the heaviness of spiritual desolation. Things seem to be calm and tranquil." We may experience such times briefly or more at length.

In Ignatius's understanding, therefore, we are not always either in spiritual consolation or in spiritual desolation. At times, we may experience neither, and continue to love and serve the Lord "using our natural powers freely and tranquilly."

With regard to the proportion of spiritual consolation relative to spiritual desolation, no universal rule can be given. Each person's experience is individual and lies within God's loving providence in that person's life. Our part is to dispose ourselves—through prayer and living the Word of Christ—to receive spiritual consolation and to accept it when God gives it, and likewise to resist and reject spiritual desolation when God permits the enemy to bring us this trial. When we do this with our imperfect but sincere best, we may leave the proportion of spiritual consolation and desolation to God's providence, sure that his loving wisdom best knows what will help us progress on the spiritual journey.

Rule 8: Some Examples

As mentioned, sometimes when I feel knotted with a desolation that I cannot understand, I take my journal and describe in writing what I am feeling. I find this helps a great deal. Generally, when I have expressed it all on paper, I gain a better sense of what is happening. The knot unties to some degree, and I see the several strands of which it is composed. This gives me greater clarity about what I need to do.

That exercise also becomes an experience of rule 8. On one occasion when I did this, I concluded, "I feel better fifty minutes into this hour than the desolation let me suspect could happen." On another occasion, "Even as I write, things do not seem so dark. Desolation claims power over the future. See rule 8." I keep learning that desolation will pass much sooner than the enemy would have me believe. The lie that present desolation will simply continue is effective if we believe it, but it is only a lie.

"The Moment When It Hit Me"

International travel for meetings and various conferences was part of my role as provincial. At times, after these travels, I would spend a few days in a retreat house to rest and prepare for the next tasks. On one such day, I wrote:

> Yesterday was a much more peaceful and consoled day than the desolate days before. Prayer yesterday in the morning was consoling. But there was that moment even before prayer when it hit me that the desolation of the preceding days could change so easily, that I didn't need three or four days for this to happen. This was a grace, and it was linked to prayer with Jesus.

As I reread this entry now, I remember that experience. My feeling was that the desolation could not change until after the days needed to recover from tiredness. Then I found, with delight, that the desolation had simply vanished, even before

I began my prayer that day. I learn from this and similar experiences that desolation presents itself as hard to dislodge, as only ceasing reluctantly after long and hard effort. This day it disappeared much more quickly than I had thought possible. I believe that these are experiences of the *soon* that Ignatius calls us to consider in time of desolation.

"I Trust that This Desolation Will Pass"

On this day, I strove to apply rule 8:

> Up this morning with desolation. A momentary struggle to get started in my time of prayer, falling asleep at times. Father, Jesus, help me. I trust that you have good things in store for me today.
>
> The feeling is that the day will go badly, will be unproductive with no progress on the book, and that this will continue all week. Mary, I need you. Rule 8: I trust that this desolation will pass, and that as I review the day this evening, I will see the fruitfulness of it.
>
> So, respond to emails, work on the book, and exercise today.

This was a conscious choice to call rule 8 to mind in a time of desolation: to *consider* that this desolation would pass, trusting that by evening, in my examen, I would see something of this. That act of trust in Ignatius's words also gave me the courage to plan positively for the day and to fill it with constructive activity. In such times, I find rule 8 a true blessing.

Chapter 9

"It Is Better for You that I Go"

> God wishes to test you like gold in the
> furnace. The dross is consumed by the
> fire, but the pure gold remains, and its
> value increases.
>
> —St. Jerome Emiliani

"It is better for you that I go" (Jn 16:7): I cited these words of
Jesus in my earlier book when introducing rule 9.[1] Since then
I have repeated them many times when presenting rule 9, and
my appreciation of their richness has grown. It is Holy Thurs-
day night, and Jesus has told his disciples, "Now I am going
to the one who sent me." He knows that the intimation of his
impending departure saddens his disciples and so continues,
"Because I told you this, grief has filled your hearts." Then
Jesus adds, "But I tell you the truth, it is better for you that I
go. For if I do not go, the Advocate will not come to you. But
if I go, I will send him to you" (Jn 16:5–7)[2]—that is, if I do
not ask you to go through the temporary, painful separation
of my passion and death, the work of redemption will not be
completed, the Church will not be born, and the Spirit will
not be poured out upon you to equip you for the task that lies
ahead. But if I go, all of this will occur.

I tell you, it is better for you that I go. These are powerful
words for the whole of the spiritual life and for discernment

of spirits in particular. Why does God allow us to experience the darkness of spiritual desolation in which we feel "as if separated from our Creator and Lord" (rule 4)? Could not God spare those who love him this trial? Why does a God who loves us permit us to undergo the heaviness of spiritual desolation? The answer is precisely because God loves us, and that, at times, in his loving providence he knows that *it is better that I go*, that is, if I do not ask you to go through the temporary darkness of spiritual desolation, certain kinds of growth that I wish to give you will not be attained. But if I do ask you to undergo spiritual desolation, and you strive to resist and reject it, this growth will be imparted.

In rule 9, Ignatius writes, "There are three principal causes for which we find ourselves desolate." "Cause" here signifies God's reason in allowing the desolation.[3] Ignatius highlights three of these—these are the "principal" causes for which God permits desolation. In each case, implicitly or explicitly, Ignatius indicates the fruit that God wishes to give through this experience. If we perceive God's cause— his reason for allowing the spiritual desolation in our own experience—the desolation will be easier to resist, and we will more likely gain the fruit God wishes to give by permitting it.

Ignatius, therefore, does not ask "Why does a God who loves us permit us to undergo spiritual desolation?" for speculative reasons. As always—this is a book of spiritual *exercises*—his aim is practical. If we can grasp why God is allowing *this experience* of spiritual desolation, we will be strengthened to reject it and so grow spiritually as God intends. We will examine and exemplify God's three reasons for permitting spiritual desolation.

"Through Our Faults"

Ignatius states the first of these: "The first is because we are tepid, slothful, or negligent in our spiritual exercises, and so through our faults spiritual consolation withdraws from us." In rule 4, Ignatius described spiritual desolation as "finding oneself totally slothful, tepid, sad." The vocabulary here in rule 9 is similar, but the two experiences are very different. In rule 4, Ignatius described a *feeling* of tepidity and slothfulness as qualities of a spiritual desolation *already present*. In rule 9, he intends an *actual* tepidity, sloth, or negligence *that precedes* spiritual desolation, and that God seeks to heal by permitting desolation to follow.[4]

We may note the precision of Ignatius's language at this point in rule 9. He does not affirm that *God* gives the spiritual desolation. There are, he tells us, three principal reasons "for which we find ourselves desolate." Again, when we are tepid, slothful, or negligent, "spiritual consolation withdraws from us." As said earlier, God does not give spiritual desolation but permits the enemy to bring it for reasons of a love that Ignatius describes in this rule.

Six months ago, Diane began dedicating twenty minutes to prayer each morning. Before the activity of the day, she would spend these minutes meditating on the Gospel of the day's Mass. Diane grew to love this practice and experienced its fruits. She found that, since she began this prayer, her faith was more alive. Sunday Mass now meant more to her, and Diane felt God's presence more readily throughout the day. She grew more patient with her children and more loving in general. Diane knew that the change in her had become a blessing for the whole family.

Three weeks ago, all of her children caught a severe flu. There were visits to the doctor and largely sleepless nights. At the same time, Diane's husband was working overtime on a pressing business project, and she had less help at home than usual. Christmas was close, and the season also added to the pace of life. In the midst of chaotic days, of constant demands on Diane's time and energy, and a growing tiredness, the twenty minutes of prayer in the morning were swept away.

The children's illness passed, Diane's husband completed his project, and the holiday season ended. Life returned to its normal pace. Today, several weeks later, Diane is driving to school to meet the children. As she drives, she realizes that she no longer feels the closeness with the Lord that she has loved in this past year. Her faith seems less alive, her confidence in God diminished, and her sense of God's love less present. Diane finds herself missing and desiring her former daily relationship with God. She then realizes that she has not resumed the twenty minutes of prayer dropped some weeks earlier in the time of pressure. Now that she perceives this, Diane immediately resolves to begin again the next day.

Such is the first reason why God may allow spiritual desolation. When persons who love God and are generally progressing toward him regress in a specific aspect of the spiritual life, God may allow desolation as a "wake-up call." The discomfort of the desolation alerts the person to the area of regression and so to reintegrate it into a life generally progressing toward God.

In a lovely phrase, Ignatius comments that God our Lord, "who loves me more than I love myself," disposes this for our healing in the time of "our faults."[5] Elsewhere Ignatius expresses similar sentiments: "Blessed be our most wise Father, who is . . . so tender when he chastises."[6]

At times, when I am discouraged, I will attempt to flee into diversion through reading a novel, checking the news again on the Internet, eating food that I do not need, and the like. When I do this, sometimes a sense of emptiness grows so strong that I am almost "driven" to pray. When I do turn to prayer, the emptiness lifts, and often consolation returns with a sense of peace and warmth. I no longer feel alone: God "who loves me more than I love myself" has called me, through desolation, to the prayer I so needed.

In chapter 1, commenting on the "stinging and biting" action of the good spirit in those heading "from mortal sin to mortal sin," I noted the parallel between rule 1 and the first reason of rule 9. In both, God's action is uncomfortable, dramatically so in the "stinging and biting" of the conscience described in rule 1, and more quietly so, through permitting spiritual desolation in rule 9, the first reason. In both cases, God's love is at work, calling the person who is regressing back to the one Love that can fulfill the human heart. In rule 1, the regression involves the total direction of the person's spiritual life (moving away from God), and in rule 9, it involves smaller areas (within a life generally progressing toward God). In both, however, the dynamic is the same.

"To Try Us"

In rule 7, Ignatius already spoke of spiritual desolation as a *trial*. He does so again in rule 9, but from a different perspective. In rule 7, Ignatius asked us to consider that desolation is a trial in which the call is to resist, because we can resist. In rule 9, he focuses on the learning and growth that derive from the trial of desolation when we faithfully resist it.

Ignatius writes, "The second, to try us and see how much we are and how much we extend ourselves in his service without so much payment of consolations and increased graces."

To try us: as in rule 7, Ignatius presents spiritual desolation as a trial. From this trial, something is learned, something is gained: to try us *and see*.

Translated literally, the text reads: "The second, to try us for how much we are, and how much we extend ourselves in his service and praise without so much payment of consolations and increased graces."[7] Who learns from this trial? Who sees? Certainly, God already knows "how much we are, and how much we extend ourselves in his service and praise" when we do not receive spiritual consolation in "payment" for our efforts.

In prayer, we tell God of our hopes, sorrows, joys, and requests, not because God does not know these, but because sharing them with God in prayer disposes our hearts to receive what God desires to give us. In like manner, the trial of desolation reveals not to God but to us "how much we are, and how much we extend ourselves in his service and praise" when consolation is absent. Such learning greatly assists us on the spiritual journey.

Augustine writes, "Is God then so ignorant of things, so unacquainted with the human heart that he has to find out about a man by testing him? Of course not. It is in order that a person may find out about himself. . . . There are things in a person that are hidden from the person in whom they are. They will not come out, or be opened, or discovered, except through tests and trials and temptations. If God stops testing, it means the master has stopped teaching."[8] Teresa of Avila writes, "Try us, O Lord, you who know the truth, in order that we may know ourselves."[9]

An important point follows. When I teach rule 9 and we explore God's second reason for allowing us to experience spiritual desolation, I raise a question—adding that I do not wish a verbal answer. The question is simply a way to high-light a possible view of spiritual desolation. "How many of us," I ask, "if we were to say why God allows us to experi-ence spiritual desolation, would consider the question fully answered in Ignatius's rule 9, first reason, 'because we are tepid, slothful, or negligent in our spiritual exercises'?" In this view, if God permits us to experience spiritual desola-tion this is *always* because we are in some way at fault: tepid, slothful, or negligent.

Ignatius's view is evidently different. Our faults are *one* reason for which God may permit spiritual desolation, but only one. Two additional reasons follow, neither of them linked to any negligence on our part. When we perceive this, we are further strengthened to resist desolation.

In 1538, Doctor Pedro Ortiz made the Spiritual Exercises under the direction of Ignatius. Ortiz kept notes of these Exercises, and in them he writes, "Divine consolation may be lost in two manners: one is because of our own culpability through sin . . . and in the second manner, we may lose divine consolation of the soul without fault, since divine provi-dence at times freely withdraws it from the soul, because of the many advantages and benefits of this, as will be said."[10] A similar point emerges: not all loss of consolation arises because of our faults.

In the second reason we are considering at present, God permits the spiritual desolation as a *trial* from which we learn and grow. Writing to a woman burdened by physical and spiritual trials, Ignatius affirms, "So great is his loving kind-ness that, if it were good for us, he would on his part be more inclined to keep us always consoled rather than afflicted, even in this life. But as the condition of our misery in this present state requires that at times he visit us with trials instead of delights, we can see in this his fatherly and supreme mercy that he confines our trials to the brief course of this life and not without an occasional mingling of many consolations."[11] Augustine notes that "our pilgrimage on earth cannot be exempt from trial. We progress by means of trial. No one knows himself except through trial, or receives a crown except after victory, or strives except against an enemy or temptations."[12] More succinctly, Teresa of Avila writes, "God never sends a trial without immediately compensating for it by some favor."[13]

"And That Remedy Included Countless Graces"

When Ignatius arrived at the University of Paris to begin his studies, he lodged with Pierre Favre and Francis Xavier. All three would later be canonized saints.

Pierre was a man of great goodness and sensitivity, yet prone to inner turmoil. Of the four years he spent in Paris with Ignatius, Pierre writes, "Our Lord, then, instructed me in so many ways, giving me remedies against so many bouts of depression that came that way to me that I would never be able to remember them. However, I can say that no distress or worry, scruple, hesitation, fear, or any other kind of evil spirit that I was able to feel to a notable degree ever came to me without my finding, at the same time or a few days after, its true remedy in God our Lord. He would grant me grace to ask, to seek, and to knock for that grace. And that remedy included countless graces to recognize and to experience the different spirits, with which I was getting more acquainted from day to day, for the Lord had left in me those goads, which never let me remain lukewarm."[14]

Why does God allow Pierre to undergo so many struggles with "bouts of depression . . . distress . . . worry, scruple, hesitation, fear, or any other kind of evil spirit"? Could not God, whom Pierre loved so deeply, have spared him these trials?

God permits us to experience spiritual desolation, Ignatius writes, to *try us* and *see*: so that through the trial of desolation, we see in new ways, grow in spiritual learning, and progress in spiritual wisdom. In the paragraph cited, Pierre lists various ways in which, through these trials, he comes *to see*.

None of these spiritual trials, writes Pierre, "ever came to me without my finding, at the same time or a few days after, its true remedy in God our Lord." Each time God permits "distress . . . worry, scruple, hesitation, fear, or any other kind of evil spirit," God assists Pierre to find "its true remedy in God our Lord." God gives this remedy quickly, sometimes immediately, and always without long delay, "at the same time or a few days after." Pierre knows that his search for such remedies is itself God's gift of grace: "He would grant me grace to ask, to seek, and to knock for that grace."

Pierre learns that in his trials of spiritual desolation God's grace is at work, strengthening him to seek the remedy and always, without fail, guiding him to find that remedy. Pierre's desolations are a time of *trial* in which he comes to *see*.

This remedy supplies an abundance of grace: it "included countless graces." This abundant grace is specifically directed toward growth in discernment, "countless graces to recognize and to experience the different spirits." As Pierre undergoes these trials and receives these remedies, he grows "more acquainted from day to day" with such spirits and how to discern them. Pierre further recognizes that God permits these trials as "goads, which never let me remain lukewarm." God, in permitting such trials, provides Pierre with an ongoing "goad" toward fervent spiritual life.

Pierre's desolations are indeed trials from which much is seen—through which he grows greatly in spiritual wisdom and energy. Such, Ignatius says, is a second reason for which God may permit the trial of spiritual desolation.

Obviously, none of us relishes such trials! But God, "who loves us more than we love ourselves," may permit them in order to give us such growth. When we review our own spiritual experience, we see the truth of this. Certain kinds of growth arise through the joy and light of spiritual consolation. Other kinds, however, normally are given only through the trial of spiritual desolation. Often the heaviness of desolation has almost compelled us to take steps that led to rich spiritual growth: to pray in new ways, approach the sacraments more frequently, consult with a spiritual guide, begin spiritual reading, join a group in the parish, make a retreat, and similar measures.

In times of desolation we learn, in a blessed way, to be humble. We learn also, "in the flesh," that God is trustworthy and that he brings us safely through these trials. Because God loves us, Ignatius affirms, at times he will permit the trial of desolation as an opportunity for growth.[15]

"All Is the Gift and Grace of God"

The third reason for which God may permit spiritual desolation is "to give us true recognition and understanding so that we may interiorly feel that it is not ours to attain or maintain increased devotion, intense love, tears or any other spiritual consolation, but that all is the gift and grace of God our Lord; and so that we may not build a nest in something belonging to another, raising our mind in some pride or vainglory, attributing to ourselves the devotion or the other parts of the spiritual consolation."[16]

Ignatius develops this third reason at greater length than the two preceding combined, and at greater length than the full text of several other rules.[17] It would seem, then, that Ignatius, who avoids all superfluous words in these rules, attaches a special importance to this third reason and so describes it at length.[18]

A semicolon divides the text into two parts: "that all is the gift and grace of God our Lord; and so that we may not build a nest."[19] This may be a further example of Ignatius's use of doublets—in this case with more developed parts than usual—to convey his complete meaning.

God's third reason for permitting spiritual desolation, Ignatius writes, is to give us *"true recognition and understanding so that we may interiorly feel."* In permitting the desolation, God desires to give us a gift on both the cognitive ("true recognition and understanding") and affective ("interiorly feel") levels—on the levels of both head and heart.

Through the experience of spiritual desolation, we learn with both head and heart "that it is *not ours* to *attain* or *maintain* increased devotion, intense love, tears or any other *spiritual consolation.*" A man is blessed with spiritual consolation for several days and rejoices in the gift. Then a time of spiritual desolation follows. In the time of desolation, he learns that it is *not his*—not his doing—when consolation first comes ("to attain") or when it remains for some time ("to maintain"). He experiences, in the time of desolation, that all spiritual consolation "is the *gift* and *grace* of God our Lord."

In the second term of the doublet, Ignatius completes this understanding with a further nuance. Having learned, through the experience of spiritual desolation, that all spiritual consolation is the gift and grace of God, we will not then "build a nest in something belonging to another." Ignatius immediately explains the metaphor: "raising our mind in some pride or vainglory, attributing to ourselves the devotion or the other parts of the spiritual consolation."

When the man who experienced the days of consolation now finds himself in desolation, he will not easily "raise his mind in some pride or vainglory" over the consolation experienced. The present struggle with desolation deters him from "attributing to himself the devotion or the other parts of the spiritual consolation." Thus, through the experience of spiritual desolation, he is protected from the harm that might arise from "some pride or vainglory" when consolation is present. This roots him in the rich biblical space of humility (Mt 5:3; 11:29; Lk 1:47–49), which for Ignatius is the gateway to all other virtue (*SpirEx* 146).

Many of us will recognize in our own experience the dynamic Ignatius describes in rule 9, the third reason. If we recall times of spiritual consolation, perhaps days, weeks, or longer, we know that in such times we can tend, largely without conscious choice, to feel that we have "attained or maintained" at least a measure of what we experience, and so to "build a nest in something belonging to another." When desolation returns and we find it hard to pray or dedicate ourselves to spiritual things "without such grace or consolation" (rule 11), we are rooted again in humble awareness that all spiritual consolation is the "gift and grace of God." This humility prepares us to receive the further work of God's grace (1 Pt 5:5).

Three Expressions of Love

At this point, Ignatius has supplied a rich reply to the question that underlies rule 9: Why does a God who loves us, and whom we are seeking to love, permit us to experience the heaviness of spiritual desolation? God does so, Ignatius tells us, *to heal us* from areas of regression in our spiritual lives (first reason), to provide *opportunities for growth* (second reason), and to *save us from a possible pitfall* (third reason).[20] Understood in the light of God's loving providence, spiritual desolation grows easier to resist.

Here rule 9 links with rule 6. In that earlier rule, Ignatius called us to "much examination" when burdened by spiritual desolation. When we make that examination, we might ask if one of God's three reasons is at work. If we can identify either the first, second, or third reason, then we have gained light on how to respond to the desolation.

Is there an area of regression ("we are tepid, slothful, or negligent")? If we detect such an area, then we can make the needed adjustments. What if we examine and cannot readily find such an area? We should never "scratch until we bleed"! If, after a sincere and serene examination, we cannot identify an area of regression, then we may assume that God is permitting the desolation for the second or third reason.

Rule 9: Some Examples

Once more, I offer examples from personal experience. These teach me concrete ways in which rule 9 sheds light on desolation.

"Things that Need to Surface and Be Healed"

I quote the following from my journal of an eight-day Ignatian retreat. At this point, I was several days into the retreat:

> It is still just good to be here, even though not much seems to be happening in the way I would desire.

I feel tired and somewhat worn this evening, understandably, after a full day of retreat and having exercised this morning and biked to the store to get some things I needed. Then I could hear this discouraging voice: "See, it's all falling apart. It's over (the retreat). You've ruined it."

I see the partial truth in this: yes, I am tired after a spiritually and physically full day. But then the accusations start. I see how this pattern often repeats in my life. Some physical issue arises, tiredness, vocal struggles, or something else. In this vulnerability, discouraging thoughts and accusations arise: "See, you're not working the way you should. Things are going badly and will continue to go badly. It's your fault." Then I experience a time of desolation.

Here, in the silence of the retreat, I see this pattern more clearly. Yes, there can be a physical issue, but that is what it is. The accusing, discouraging voice is a different reality. I see that the desolation of this evening of retreat is happening not because the retreat is going badly, but because it is going well. Things that need to surface and be healed are now being touched as the retreat deepens.

I understood this experience, and still understand it, as an example of rule 9, the second reason. This was a trial from which something became clearer to me: a pattern that often occurred in daily life but that I found harder to identify when pressed by activity. In the quiet, reflective space of the retreat, this experience of desolation helped me see a pattern, and that allowed me to work on it. The desolation was not pleasant—it never is! But I could see why God, in his providence, allowed it to surface at this point of the retreat. Through this experience, my personal review of it, and conversation about it with the retreat director the next day, valuable learning emerged in a way that would help in the months to come.

On another occasion much like this, Ed said:

> It is important for you to hear that your experience of desolation does not mean that you are doing something wrong. The Lord is touching a place where he desires to give you new strength and hope. This is about a pattern that you've experienced a long time, and where the enemy can come in. As you did this time, stay faithful, follow the wisdom of the rules that you teach to others, journal about this, ask Mary's intercession. See the place of vulnerability and the pattern. You knew this, but there is a new clarity now.

I found his words helpful: this experience of desolation did not mean that I was doing something wrong (rule 9, first reason) but rather that through it God wanted to help me learn (second reason). Such learning would strengthen me against similar tactics of the enemy in the future.

"I Think This Was the Meaning"

The following occurred while waiting to learn if I would be transferred to another of our religious communities with a new ministry. The waiting continued throughout the summer. As it did, I found myself burdened and frustrated, engaging in interior complaints. In meetings of spiritual direction, my director helped me to pray with this issue. That summer, I spent a time of vacation with one of our communities. At the end of those days, I wrote the following:

> This has been a blessed vacation and a warm ending with all. Lord, I thank you.

I trust in your leading, Lord, in what lies ahead, how the superiors making the decision will interact, whether or not I will be transferred, and all that may come. I think now that this was the meaning of the delay before and during this summer, when I had the opportunity to sit down and discuss this with Ed in spiritual direction: to surrender in a new way to the Lord's leading, to trust that leading.

I find peace in this. Lord, help me to grow through this. I trust you as I return and resume the writing of the new book.

Here, too, I see something of the dynamic of rule 9, the second reason, at work. As the months passed and no decision arrived, frustration and anxiety surfaced. I cannot say I handled this well! Spiritual direction helped, and I did make sincere efforts to bring this to prayer. Certainly, I experienced desolation along the way.

The rest and relaxation of a vacation helped, I believe, to reflect and pray about this delay more fruitfully. I found that this "trial" called me to surrender the frustration and anxiety, and to trust concretely in God's providence for the future: from this trial, something was seen. This "seeing," this learning, while still waiting for the decision, encouraged me in the moment and strengthened me for what would lie ahead.

Rule 9 is the final rule of a subset (rules 5–9) within the rules directed to the person now experiencing spiritual desolation. Each rule (rules 5–6: the changes we should not and should make; rule 7: a trial that we can resist; rule 8: patience, and awareness that consolation will return soon; rule 9: the fruits that God wants to give in permitting desolation) equips us to resist desolation when we are in a time of desolation. In rule 10, Ignatius will turn to spiritual consolation as a gift that, if lived in the manner he will propose, can strengthen us to resist future desolation even before that desolation begins.

Chapter 10

"One Who Is in Consolation"

> *Such spiritual consolations are great*
> *gifts that God gives souls, much greater*
> *than all the riches and honors of the*
> *world.*
>
> —St. Alphonsus de Liguori

The tenth rule is the shortest of the fourteen: "The tenth: let the one who is in consolation think how he will conduct himself in the desolation that will come after, taking new strength for that time." This rule centers on the person now in *spiritual consolation*, and it invites this person to *think*, during the consolation, in a way that will lead to *new strength* for resisting spiritual desolation when it eventually returns.

Should We Accept Spiritual Consolation?

What about spiritual consolation? Should we accept it? This question is not superfluous! Over the years, I have learned that it is helpful to address it, and I find rule 10, focused on spiritual consolation, the appropriate place to do so.

People are, at times, unsure of whether or not they should accept and rejoice in spiritual consolation. Is it not better to seek "the God of consolations" rather than "the consolations of God"? What of John of the Cross's strictures on spiritual gluttony?[1] Spiritual consolations come and go: Is it not best to serve God with a firm will rather than depend on such fluctuating experiences? Might God be more pleased that we serve him so? Such questions are raised with sincere good will, and they are important.

From the outset, Ignatius advised us that his rules serve to become aware of, understand, and take action in response to "the different movements that are caused in the soul" (title statement). Some of these movements are good, of God—as Ignatius explains in rule 3, they are spiritually consoling. When they are, Ignatius says, the appropriate action is to receive them: *las buenas para recibir*—"the good [movements] to *receive* them." Ignatius never speaks of grasping at spiritual consolations or demanding them as a condition for serving God, but rather of disposing ourselves through a faithful spiritual life and then receiving with gratitude the spiritual consolations that God chooses to give. What other response should we make to any gift of God's grace? God gives spiritual consolation for a reason. By means of it, he wishes to impart a light and strength we greatly need on the spiritual journey.

In a letter to Francis Borgia, a future canonized saint, Ignatius invites him to seek God's "most holy gifts," and then explains why. By these gifts, Ignatius writes, "I understand those that are beyond the reach of our own powers, which we cannot attain at will, since they are rather a pure gift of him who bestows them and who alone can give every good. These gifts with his Divine Majesty as their end are an increase in the intensity of faith, hope, and charity, joy and spiritual repose, tears, intense consolation, elevation of mind, divine impressions and illuminations, together with all other spiritual relish and understanding that have these gifts as their objects."[2] A comparison of this text with rule 3 makes evident that when Ignatius speaks of God's "most holy gifts," he intends spiritual consolation.

Ignatius then explains to Francis why we should seek such gifts. His words reply to the questions raised above: "I do not mean to say that we should seek them merely for the satisfaction or pleasure they give us. We know, however, that without them all our thoughts, words, and actions are of themselves tainted, cold, disordered; while with them they become clear and warm and upright for God's greater service. It is for this reason that we should desire these gifts, or some of them, and spiritual graces; that is, insofar as they are a help to us, to God's greater glory."[3] Because we love the Lord and desire to serve the Lord as fully as we can, and because spiritual consolation assists us to do so, our response to spiritual consolation is to *receive* this gift when God gives it. Spiritual consolation is, as Ignatius writes, "a help to us, to God's greater glory."[4]

We all know by experience the difference that spiritual consolation makes. Without it, as Ignatius tells Francis, we are cold; with it, "all our thoughts, words, and actions . . . become clear and warm and upright for God's greater service." At such times, we love God and others in God, we pray, and we serve with energy and efficacy. We rightly bless God for such times.

With regard to John of the Cross and spiritual consolation, Jesuit author Augustin Poulain writes, "St. John of the Cross is not speaking to all Christians indiscriminately when he counsels the rejection of sensible consolations. He is only concerned with those who are beginning to enjoy the mystic state, and he simply asks them to give it the preference when it encounters any obstacle in devotions of the sensible order and the pleasure felt in them. When no such conflict occurs, we must resort to all the means that can lead us towards God."[5]

John of the Cross writes for those whom God has now called to infused, mystical contemplation; Ignatius—himself a mystic—generally writes for those at an earlier stage of the spiritual life. What would hinder growth in the more advanced mystical stage greatly blesses it in the earlier, more common stage. And, as is apparent from Ignatius's letter to Francis Borgia, he fully coincides with John of the Cross in rejecting spiritual gluttony: we do not seek spiritual consolations "merely for the satisfaction or pleasure they give us," but we receive and rejoice in them when God gives them because "they are a help to us, to God's greater glory."

"The Heavenly Peace that Came over My Soul"

The holy men and women of our spiritual tradition have always known this. They welcomed the growth that God gives through spiritual consolation. In my earlier book, I quoted a letter of St. Elizabeth Seton in which she recounts an experience of rich spiritual consolation at age fifteen.[6] On a warm, sunny day in May, she sets out into the woods, finds a chestnut tree with moss under it, and stops there, "with a heart as innocent as human heart could be, filled even with enthusiastic love to God and admiration of his works."

She continues, "God was my Father, my all. I prayed, sang hymns, cried, laughed, talking to myself of how far he could place me above all sorrow. Then I laid still to enjoy the heavenly peace that came over my soul; and I am sure, in the two hours so enjoyed, grew ten years in the spiritual life." With the sure intuition of the saints, Elizabeth knows that her call in time of spiritual consolation is to receive the gift. Having received it, she grows greatly: "in the two hours so enjoyed, grew ten years in the spiritual life."

In his biography of St. Francis of Assisi, St. Bonaventure writes, "Francis would never let any call of the Spirit go unanswered; when he experienced it, he would make the most of it and enjoy the consolation afforded him in this way for as long as God permitted it. If he was on a journey, and felt the near approach of God's Spirit, he would stop and let his companions go on, while he drank in the joy of this new inspiration; he refused to offer God's grace an ineffectual welcome (cf. 2 Cor 6:1)."[7]

Here, too, a saint perceives the call in time of spiritual consolation: "He would make the most of it and enjoy the consolation afforded him in this way for as long as God permitted it. . . . He refused to offer God's grace an ineffectual welcome." Again, the motive is the desire to receive the grace that God gives through spiritual consolation so that it can bear fruit. Francis fully exemplifies Ignatius's perspective on spiritual consolations: "It is for this reason that we should desire these gifts . . . that is, insofar as they are a help to us, to God's greater glory."

"Prayer This Morning Changed the Day"

One December morning, during a period of writing, the following occurred. It was a simple experience and one that all will recognize in their own prayer and circumstances. I offer it as one example of why Ignatius invites us to receive spiritual consolation. When prayer ended that morning, I wrote the following:

> This was a blessed time of prayer. I came oppressed, burdened, and desolate, not knowing how I would write with this heaviness in my heart. I just put all this in words to Jesus, seeing his gaze of love, the love with which he looked upon his disciples.

I realized that there is nothing weighing on my freedom to be with Jesus, and the heaviness broke. Peace and warmth returned, with a sense of being loved. I found myself ready to begin the writing again this day.

At this point, I felt no desire to say much more. This was a clear experience of relating to the Lord what was in my heart and receiving his response of consolation.

That evening, in the examen prayer:

Prayer this morning changed the day. Writing was fruitful. I finished the chapter I was writing and began the next. All went well, with new energy for writing this book.

Such experiences teach me the wisdom of Ignatius's counsel to *receive* spiritual consolation when God chooses to give it. I experience the light and strength it gives, the fresh hope that I can accomplish what the Lord asks and do so with a certain joy. Spiritual consolation is indeed "a help to us, to God's greater glory."

"Something Was Touched in Me"

At this point, I was engaged in teaching about the spiritual life. One of the other teachers had given a talk, and I found that my views differed on several points. I did not know how to address this. The next morning, I wrote these words:

Since the talk yesterday morning, my heart has been somewhat heavy. When we met briefly at lunch, I wasn't as warm as I would have wished, though I don't think this was even noticed. I do not know how to resolve this since it is an intellectual issue. I would like to talk to Ed, but that will not be possible for some days.

Then, before the Blessed Sacrament, with Jesus, I thought of his words to Mary, "Woman, behold your son" (Jn 19:26). Something was touched in me, something melted. I didn't get any answers, but a sense that it will work out, and the sense that now I can smile warmly and genuinely if we meet.

I see in this an experience of spiritual consolation, a gift of God's love: the lifting of a burden, a sense of warmth in Mary's love, an increased ability to love in a situation of slight tension, and a confidence that I would be given a way to handle the intellectual issues. Again, accepting consolation brought strength and hope.

"Taking New Strength for That Time"

To receive spiritual consolation when God gives it is, therefore, the primary call in time of spiritual consolation. We should never let anything—even rule 10—weigh on our freedom simply to accept spiritual consolation and be strengthened by it.

Rule 10 highlights, however, an additional good that can be gained from spiritual consolation: in the warmth and joy of spiritual consolation, we can also "take new strength" for resisting future desolation. If we do this, when the desolation does return, we will find it much easier to resist and reject.

Elizabeth Seton, for example, during those two hours simply receives God's abundant consolation, and in so doing grows "ten years in the spiritual life." The blessed warmth of that consolation, however, remains beyond those two hours—in fact, many years later Elizabeth can recall and describe that experience. We might easily imagine Elizabeth at prayer that evening, still joyful in the consolation received. This could well be a time in which she might "think how she will conduct herself in the desolation that will come after" and "take new strength for that time."

The same will be true for all of us. On a day, several days, a week, or longer of consolation, there will be a time when, with the Lord, we can look ahead to future desolation and take new strength for that time. If we do this, a further good will be added to the primary good of spiritual consolation.

When I ask myself how often I think to do this in time of spiritual consolation, my answer is that I am not sure. Certainly, I could do it more. I know that when I do apply rule 10, I find it very beneficial. When I do, spiritual desolation does not catch me unprepared, does not take me totally by surprise, and so I can resist more quickly.

The dynamic of rule 10 is similar to that of Joseph and the seven years of plenty followed by the seven years of famine (Gn 41). During the years of plenty, Joseph stores up grain *that he does not need*, but that will be crucial for survival in the years of famine that follow. Gagliardi applies a different comparison: "When a man is on a journey, he eats heartily so that he will be strengthened for the labors of the journey soon to follow."[8]

We may note that once again, in rule 10, Ignatius invites us to *think*, to live the reflective spiritual life. "Let one who is in consolation," he writes, "*think* how he will conduct himself in the desolation that will come after."

How do we take in strength for future desolation? In my earlier book, I discussed various ways we might do this.[9] I will list them here and then add further considerations:

- In the warmth of spiritual consolation, we can offer *prayers* of petition for strength in future desolation.

- We can *meditate*, in the joy of consolation, on truths of faith—favorite verses from the Bible, for example—that will sustain us in desolation.

- We can *reflect*, when in consolation, on the value of desolation for growth, as in rule 9.

- We can *review* with the Lord past personal growth through desolation, deepening our trust that God will give growth through future desolation as well.

- We can *resolve*, in the clarity of consolation, to make no changes in time of desolation, as in rule 5.

- In the peace of consolation, we can *refresh* these fourteen rules so that we will have them at our spiritual fingertips when, in desolation, we will need them.

- Finally, we can look ahead to specific, recurring occasions of desolation and *prepare* for them.

Over the years, I have seen people apply rule 10 in many creative ways. One woman told me that she taped a list of the rules to the door of her room and keeps another in the car she drives to work daily. She says that seeing the rules in writing often saves her from falling into desolation. Another showed me a brief summary of the rules that she carries in her wallet. A man shared his practice of praying periodically with the rules, at times just one, at times several.

Another woman underlines passages of Scripture that speak to her in consolation, and returns to them in desolation. Yet another shared a lovely practice: when in consolation, she writes herself a letter and places it in a box. When desolation has returned, she goes to the box and reads the letter. Another finds journaling a help: when in consolation, she looks back in her journal to times of desolation and reviews them now in the light of consolation.

In my life, as mentioned, I find that the time after a retreat or seminar, when I am tired and the people are no longer present, can be an occasion for spiritual desolation. I find myself in an airport or on a plane, alone and tired. In that space, the trap of spiritual desolation can enter the normal nonspiritual desolation that follows a similar expenditure of energy. The desolation may persist after I return home, in the time when I attempt to rest and recover my energy. When I am spiritually aware, therefore, in the airport and on the plane I already pray for help to resist spiritual desolation. If we know that certain situations render us vulnerable to spiritual desolation, rule 10 invites us to "take in strength" before that desolation can even begin.

When I present the rules, I invite all to dedicate five or ten minutes to planning how they will "take new strength" in time of consolation. I promise them—and I do not doubt the validity of this promise—that those few minutes will pay rich dividends in the spiritual life. May I invite the reader to do the same?

Over the years, I have seen that it is not enough simply to learn these rules. We also need a way to keep them fresh in our consciousness if we wish them to make a practical difference in our lives. Each person will find his or her way of doing this. One of the great gifts in my life is that I teach these rules repeatedly every year. When I do, my awareness of them is renewed, and I find them easier to apply.

Rule 10: Some Examples

As with the preceding rules, I again offer examples from my journals. In such experiences, this rule, too, comes alive for me.

"Reviewing This Experience Helps Me 'Take New Strength'"

The following occurred six weeks after my father's death, a fact that explains much of what took place. I had traveled across the country to give a weekend seminar on prayer. I had not presented this seminar often and was still learning how to organize the material, the right mix of talks, time for prayer, and discussion. This uncertainty also entered into the experience. We had completed the first day of the seminar, and on Saturday evening held a social time. With so much in my heart, I found that difficult.

I awoke early on Sunday morning, went to the church and sat there, journal in hand, writing out the experience:

> Rising, and before the Blessed Sacrament. Lord, I don't feel well, tired, and troubled that I didn't hold up well during the social, which went quite late, later for me with jet lag. The day is just beginning, and I already feel worn, frustrated that I seem so often to be in this situation, unable to get the rest I need and so face weariness during these trips and after.
>
> My loss of Dad continues to weigh on me, and also concern for Mother's situation, now alone. We need to find the right way to help her.
>
> Perhaps the principal thing right now is that a day of seminar lies ahead, and I do not yet see how to structure it. This is one of those learning experiences when I offer a new seminar, and I am learning, but these are hard ones for me.

Lord, please help me to find a way for this day. You have so often in the past.

As so often, writing out all of this helps to untie the "knot." As this time ends: Thank you, Lord. I now see the way to structure this day, and I think it will go well.

At the end of the day:

It went really well, and I am very happy about it.

The following morning:

Looking back on yesterday morning when all seemed so black. Now I'm very happy about it all. That Saturday afternoon desolation on a weekend of teaching: watch for it in the future! Reviewing this experience helps me to "take new strength" for future desolation in this same situation.

Each time I review an experience like this I find that I note similar experiences more quickly when they again arise. I learn that Ignatius's words are real: when consolation has returned, review of earlier desolation prepares me to notice and respond to it more quickly in the future.

"To Be Is to Be Loved"

This from the examen prayer at the end of a day:

Driving to the dentist this afternoon, I kept the radio off. I found a joy in just being with you, Lord, in the car. I think of Gabriel Marcel's words, that "to be is to be loved." This comes alive.

As I think of this, I see that I need never be alone. This way of living can be present whenever I am free to focus my thoughts and heart in this way. Brother Lawrence [*The Practice of the Presence of God*] is right. This is the way to live. It is the truth.

This was a blessed experience of spiritual consolation—while driving to the dentist! By reviewing it in the examen prayer, I saw more clearly its gift and its applicability to the whole of life. One such experience, obviously, did not mean that this was already a constant practice. But reviewing this consolation while still experiencing it did help me take in strength against the lie of desolation when we feel "as if separated from our Creator and Lord" (rule 4).

In rule 11, Ignatius will address spiritual consolation and spiritual desolation for a final time. We turn now to that rule.

Chapter 11

Portrait of the Mature Person of Discernment

This feeling of fervor does not always come when one desires it, nor does it last at length. It comes and goes as He wills who gives it. And therefore whoever has it, let him be humble and thank God.

—Walter Hilton

After a set of rules (5–9) for the person in spiritual desolation, and a rule (10) for the person in spiritual consolation, Ignatius now gives us a rule that brings both together. Rule 11 is the final rule of these fourteen in which Ignatius speaks of spiritual consolation and spiritual desolation. In it, Ignatius paints the portrait of the mature person of discernment, one who responds wisely to both spiritual consolation and spiritual desolation: "The eleventh: let one who is consoled seek to humble himself and lower himself as much as he can, thinking of how little he is capable in the time of desolation without such grace or consolation. On the contrary, let one who is in desolation think that he can do much with God's sufficient grace to resist all his enemies, taking strength in his Creator and Lord."

The first half of this rule recalls rule 9, God's third reason for allowing spiritual desolation, to help us avoid "some pride or vainglory, attributing to ourselves the devotion or other parts of the spiritual consolation." Here Ignatius encourages the person in spiritual consolation to "seek to humble himself and lower himself as much as he can."[1] In the second half of the rule, Ignatius urges one in desolation to "think that he can do much with God's sufficient grace to resist all his enemies." *Humble* in *consolation* and *trusting* in *desolation*: this is the mature person of discernment, faithfully progressing toward God through the alternations of consolation and desolation.

Once more Ignatius calls us to the reflective spiritual life: "let one who is consoled seek to humble himself and lower himself as much as he can, *thinking*" and "let one who is in desolation *think*."[2] Ignatius indicates in both cases the specific thoughts that will help us remain humble and trusting respectively.

Little and Much

One in spiritual consolation is to "seek to humble himself and lower himself as much as he can."[3] Ignatius proposes this effort with a certain vigor: "seek," "humble himself," "lower himself," "as much as he can." In time of spiritual consolation, when all seems easy, we may experience lively desires to serve the Lord in ways that, in reality, are unwise and unsustainable. To pursue these desires would overtax our energies and lead, inevitably, to some form of spiritual collapse with its ensuing discouragement.

To protect us from this pitfall, Ignatius encourages us to strive actively to remain humble in time of consolation. Ever practical, he also supplies the concrete means for such striving: "*thinking* of how *little* he is capable *in the time of desolation* without such grace or consolation."

When I present rule 11, at this point I ask the following question, again without seeking a verbal reply: "How many of us would be happy to have projected now on the screen before us a video of how we handled our last time of spiritual desolation?" I pause for a moment, and then add: "There would probably be a few refrigerators, remote controls, and smartphones in that video." At this point, many smile, recognizing the reality of this description. I also add that I do not exempt myself from this description!

If, in the warmth of spiritual consolation, we consciously think of how we struggled in preceding times of desolation, we will find it easier to remain wisely humble in the joy of the present consolation. We will receive the gift and avoid the pitfall.

The one in spiritual *desolation* is also called to think, in this case, "that *he can do much* with God's sufficient grace to resist all his enemies, taking strength in his Creator and Lord." The danger in time of desolation is discouragement, and its remedy is once again a *thought*. We are to reflect, call to mind, consider, that we can do *much* in this time of desolation to resist *all* our enemies, because God's grace is always *sufficient* to do so. This thought will assist us to *take strength* in our Creator and Lord, and so to resist and reject the desolation.

Little and *much*: in times of spiritual consolation, we are to think of how little we can do without this grace; in times of spiritual desolation, we are to think of how much we can do with God's ever-sufficient grace. Such thoughts root us in the truth and assist us to respond rightly to both spiritual experiences.

Carol is a young adult who has just made a weekend retreat. The weekend was filled with grace. The talks spoke to her heart, and her personal times of prayer were blessed with a joyful sense of God's love and closeness. Sharing the days with the others also encouraged her in her life of faith. Carol now finds herself desiring to grow in her spiritual life. She considers the suggestion of the speaker that she dedicate time to prayer daily. If she rises an hour earlier in the morning before work, she will have such time. Carol also considers attending daily Mass at a nearby church on her lunch hour. She knows that young adults gather each Monday evening in her parish and contemplates joining this group, with its various social and service activities. The speaker mentioned the value of spiritual reading, and Carol is intrigued by the thought of beginning this practice.

"Let one who is consoled seek to humble herself and lower herself as much as she can, thinking of how little she is capable in the time of desolation without such grace or consolation." The first part of Ignatius's rule 11 will help Carol benefit from a time of spiritual consolation and also avoid the pitfall of overextending herself in an unsustainable way. Should such strained efforts collapse, discouragement and, at times, serious spiritual harm may result.

Carol begins dedicating twenty minutes to prayer with Scripture in the morning and attends daily Mass when she is able. She loves the spiritual newness she experiences and finds her faith growing. She is more joyful and ready to serve others.

Recently, however, she has begun to feel that joy less. Work is difficult these days, and the recurrence of physical problems weighs on Carol. Prayer has been dry, and she has struggled to remain the twenty minutes or to attend daily Mass.

One evening, Carol returns to her apartment after work. It is a cold and gray autumn day. She is alone. She feels tired and a little discouraged from work. Her physical ailments also cause some discomfort.

Carol wonders how long she can sustain this new spiritual journey. Certainly, things do not seem to be going well. She does not feel God's closeness and wonders about the value of her prayer. All her efforts since the retreat appear to have changed little in her life. This whole spiritual path seems too difficult, and Carol feels that she is too weak to continue. It might be best just to give up.

"On the contrary, let one who is in desolation think that she can do much with God's sufficient grace to resist all her enemies, taking strength in her Creator and Lord." Now Carol very much needs the second half of rule 11. If this evening, in her time of spiritual desolation, Carol thinks, calls to mind, that she can do much to resist all her enemies and so takes new strength in her Creator and Lord, she will negotiate this desolation safely and pursue her spiritual journey without harm.

Testimonies in the Tradition

I present the following in chronological order. St. Gregory the Great, commenting on Sirach 11:25 ("On the day of prosperity do not forget affliction, and on the day of affliction do not forget prosperity"), writes, "For if a man receives God's gifts, but forgets his affliction, he can fall through his own excessive joy. On the other hand, when a man is bruised by the scourges, but is not at all consoled by the thought of the blessings he has been fortunate to receive, he is completely cast down." Gregory concludes, "Thus both attitudes must be united so that the one may be supported by the other: the memory of the gift can temper the pain of the affliction, and the foreboding and fear of the affliction can modify the joy of the gift."[4] "Thus both attitudes must be united so that the one may be supported by the other": this is exactly the dynamic of rule 11 in regard to spiritual consolation and spiritual desolation.

Walter Hilton, in *The Scale of Perfection*, speaks of those whom the Lord visits with fervor, and continues, "But this feeling of fervor does not always come when one desires it, nor does it last at length. It comes and goes as He wills who gives it. And therefore whoever has it, let him be humble and thank God. . . . And when it withdraws, be not daunted or troubled, but stand in faith and be hopeful, with patient abiding until it comes again. This is a little taste of the sweetness in the love of God, of which David says thus in the Psalter, 'Taste and see how good is the Lord.'"[5] When fervor is present, "let him be humble and thank God"; when it withdraws, let him "be not daunted or troubled, but stand in faith and be hopeful." Hilton's text perfectly exemplifies the dynamic of rule 11.

In his classic *The Imitation of Christ*, Thomas à Kempis writes, "When, therefore, spiritual consolation is given by God, receive it with thanksgiving and recognize it as the gift of God. Do not rejoice excessively nor vainly presume, but be more humble because of the gift, more cautious and more wary in all your actions, because that hour will pass, and temptation will follow." On the other hand, à Kempis continues, "When that consolation has been taken away, do not immediately despair, but with humility and patience wait for the heavenly visitation, because God is powerful to give back greater grace and consolation. This is not new, nor is it strange to those who know the way of God, for in the great saints and in the ancient prophets there was often this manner of alternation."[6] Humility in consolation and patience when consolation is withdrawn: again, the pattern of rule 11 is present.

The three texts just cited predate Ignatius in the tradition. A final illustration derives from his Jesuit companion, St. Pierre Favre: "Sometimes we happen to take notice of benefits and favors that possibly come and can come to us; sometimes the opposite happens: we take notice of evils that only possibly threaten us. In the first state, we must beware of being overelated; in the second, let us not be overmuch cast down."

Pierre refers this, first, to the good spirit: "Our good spirit knows how to make use of each of these two times as a remedy for the other: abundance to counter scarcity, scarcity to counter abundance." "Abundance to counter scarcity, scarcity to counter abundance": such is the dynamic of rule 11. Yet the enemy, Pierre affirms, will attempt the contrary: "But the wicked spirit strives to turn each to our harm: abundance to pride and presumption, scarcity to faintheartedness and the discouragement of a good soul."[7] Rule 11 is precisely our safeguard against this tactic of the enemy.

Rule 11: Some Examples

Two concrete examples follow. They illustrate for me Ignatius's call to be humble in consolation and trusting in desolation.

"As I Write, I Sense My Hope Rising"

This experience occurred when I was a writer in residence at the college in Toronto. A few days remained before moving to the parish near my mother, who was alone at the time, where I would spend some weeks helping her and writing as I was able. These were, therefore, days of ending one stay and preparing for the next. While still at the college, I was pressing to finish the chapter of the book I was then writing. At the same time, I was in conversation regarding an invitation to teach in a program of spiritual training. The invitation was welcome, but the conversation regarding the details proved difficult. I had recently received an email concerning these details that I found discouraging. I began to think that the position would not work.

This day, as at other times, I sat before the Lord and wrote what I was thinking and feeling:

> Lord, these ups and downs are amazing. I was "down" when I received the email from the reader of this book I am writing. He commented on the latest chapter, and his message questioned the approach I am taking. It left me discouraged and uncertain of how to proceed.
>
> Then, after talking with three other readers, that doubt was resolved. I was "up" when I got the favorable feedback, and when my hosts at the college asked me to give them a talk on this book I am writing. The talk was well received. I also felt the warmth of a genuine welcome by my hosts. I was encouraged, too, by a more positive email regarding the faculty position.
>
> And now my heart is heavy again this morning. These rules for discernment really help. It helps during the "down" times to know that they will pass (rule 8), and it is good, when "up," to be grateful and, warmly and with hope, to prepare for the returning "down" time (rule 10). I begin, in these days, to see the balance of rule 11, almost day by day: to be humbly grateful in consolation and trusting in desolation. I see it all the more these

days because of the writing life with its long periods of silence and solitude.

So often I have called to you, Lord, during the "down" times (rule 6), and you always answer. I discover after the fact, often enough, that you have already answered. As I write, I sense my hope rising that you will resolve all this, too.

Lord, you do not promise to take away the down times, the desolation; that is, that we will not have to go through them, but you do promise to see us safely through them, without harm, even with growth. Even as I feel the burden today, this thought helps me.

On days like these, as so often in life, I am grateful to Ignatius for the wisdom of his rules. Without them, such times would be much more confusing and discouraging; with them, I find a path to freedom.

"I Know This Desolation May Be Gone in an Hour"

At the beginning of the day, several years later, when about to start a new book:

Rising with desolation. My voice wore out yesterday, and I had to stop trying to use it when saying evening prayer with the community and at supper. This was the first time this has happened in a long time, and so I felt worry and discouragement. I know the enemy enters this vulnerable space: "Everything will go badly, you won't be able to do any more public speaking, you'll be marginalized"—all the old tapes.

In the discouragement, I feel a weakening of energy for this new book, and this, too, worries me. Lord, now

I have to write it. I wrote the title page yesterday. It's been six years since I've written on this topic.

I know that this "rising-in-the-morning" feeling may be gone in an hour or by midmorning (rule 8). Lord, be with me.

I know, too, that this feeling that the new book will be flat, that I'll have nothing to say, is of the enemy, that "defeated-before-I-start" feeling. I choose to trust in you, Lord. I ask you to let me receive the writing as a gift of grace.

I think also that the concern about the physical issue may be the space into which the enemy attempts to bring this discouragement, this feeling of lack of energy for the writing, of having to make myself do it.

A few hours later, at eleven that morning:

Great insight into this new book and how to write it. Consolation, gratitude. Then the gift of next Sunday's homily, the content and how to present it. I wonder now if the darkest desolation is not, if I do not give into it, a sign of the greatest grace soon to come.

As I reread these notes, once again I see how much Ignatius's wisdom helps me. To be aware of these ups and downs; to have some sense of the enemy's tactics; to know, even in the desolation, that it will pass, that God hears our prayers of petition for help; to trust that consolation will return much sooner than the desolation tells me—even by eleven that morning—with the answer to the discouragement and confusion: all of this helped set this captive free. Humble in consolation and trusting in desolation: rule 11 gives me a road map for these alternations, and I am grateful.

Chapter 12

When the Enemy Weakens and Loses Heart

> *So I cried out, Come on now, all of you. I am the servant of our Lord, and I should like to see what you can do against me.*
>
> —St. Teresa of Avila

In his final three rules, Ignatius turns from the enemy's desolations to his temptations (rule 12), deceits (rule 13), and attacks (rule 14). In general, Ignatius focuses on the other garden-variety tactic of the enemy, his deceptive suggestions or *temptations*. Temptations and spiritual desolation are the two basic tactics of the enemy that we all experience: deceptive suggestions ("Why don't you let your prayer go till later?" "You can let yourself see that ... it doesn't have to get too far out of hand.") and the discouraging lies of spiritual desolation. Often these two tactics will be found together (see rules 4 and 7).

Having equipped us to reject spiritual desolation in the preceding rules, Ignatius now focuses on this second tactic of the enemy. His goal is unchanged: to help us be aware of, understand, and take action—in this case, to reject the enemy's temptations. For this purpose, in rules 12–14, Ignatius highlights three qualities of the enemy's temptations to help us identify them in our experience, reject them, and so remain unharmed by them.

In each rule, Ignatius first proposes a metaphor and then from it highlights the quality of the enemy that he wishes us to see. This is good pedagogy! Because these metaphors describe the action of the enemy, we should expect that they will feel wrong to us, that something will grate on us as we read them. In fact, they describe the action of the "enemy *of human nature*," the expanded title Ignatius gives to the enemy in these three final rules. There is about these metaphors an unnatural, antihuman quality. When we read them, we instinctively say, "This is not what God intended." And we are right.

The metaphor of rule 12 presents the unhappy situation of a man and woman fighting with each other; in rule 13, that of a man attempting to seduce, rather than sincerely love, a woman; and in rule 14, that of a leader of a band of thieves who seeks only to pillage and rob. Each situation is antihuman, and each illustrates well a tactic of "the enemy of human nature."

Rule 12: Metaphor and Application

Ignatius writes, "The twelfth: the enemy acts like a woman in being weak when faced with strength and strong when faced with weakness. For, as it is proper to a woman, when she is fighting with some man, to lose heart and to flee when the man confronts her firmly, and, on the contrary, if the man begins to flee, losing heart, the anger, vengeance, and ferocity of the woman grow greatly and know no bounds."

In my earlier book, I discussed Ignatius's metaphor of the woman fighting with a man and the uneasiness it may awaken in our culture today.[1] I will note once more that Ignatius does not compare the enemy simply to a woman but to "*a woman when she is fighting with some man.*" The metaphor portrays, therefore, "an unnatural situation: one that does not describe the true nature of either woman or man, created by God not to battle with each other but to share life in love and mutual service."[2] Consequently, if the metaphor grates on us as we read it, we are understanding it correctly: it describes a situation utterly contrary to God's intention for women and men as they relate to each other. This unnatural quality must be present in a metaphor that illustrates the action of "the enemy of human nature."

The enemy is *weak when faced with strength* and *strong when faced with weakness*: this is what Ignatius wants us to see in rule 12. In the antihuman metaphor given, everything depends on the man's initial response: if the man *begins* to flee . . .

Ignatius now applies the metaphor: "In the same way, it is proper to the enemy to weaken and lose heart, fleeing and ceasing his temptations when the person who is exercising himself in spiritual things confronts the temptations of the enemy firmly, doing what is diametrically opposed to them; and, on the contrary, if the person who is exercising himself begins to be afraid and lose heart in suffering the temptations, there is no beast so fierce on the face of the earth as the enemy of human nature in following out his damnable intention with such growing malice."

The enemy is weak when faced with strength. If, when the temptations first present themselves, the person "confronts the temptations of the enemy *firmly*, doing what is *diametrically opposed* to them" (enemy: "You can let yourself see that. It need not get too far out of hand"; person: "No, I will not even pick up the smartphone"), the enemy's weakness is revealed. He *loses heart, flees,* and *ceases his temptations.* We may note that the enemy is not weak compared to us: as an angelic being, he belongs a higher order of being than we. The enemy, however, is weak compared to the power of Christ's grace in us (Lk 11:21–22), if we open ourselves to that grace.

When I present the rules, I invite participants to note this remarkable language, that in a given circumstance—if we are willing, with God's grace, to stand firm when the temptation first presents itself—the enemy *flees,* the enemy *loses heart,* and the enemy *ceases his temptations.* Have we ever thought of the enemy in this light, as fleeing, losing heart, and abandoning a given effort to tempt us? Ignatius wants to deflate the enemy's false assumption of insuperable power and wants us to know that he can be undone. Simply to perceive this gives great hope when resisting temptation.

The enemy is strong when faced with weakness. If, when temptation first presents itself, *we begin to be afraid* and *lose heart* in suffering the temptation (enemy: "You can let yourself see that. It need not get too far out of hand"; person: "Yes, maybe I could . . . I don't feel like working right now. I've looked at that before, and it hasn't always gotten out of hand . . . "), the enemy's temptation will grow in strength. Then, Ignatius says, employing a further metaphor, "there is no beast so fierce on the face of the earth as the enemy of human nature in following out his damnable intention with such growing malice." In this case, the person is very likely to succumb to the temptation. Whether, therefore, the temptation will simply cease or whether it will grow in strength, even great strength, depends on how we respond to the temptation *when it first begins.*

"Weak When Faced with Strength"

In Scripture, we read, "Resist the devil, and he will flee from you" (Jas 4:7).[3] This is precisely Ignatius's point in rule 12: with trust in God's grace and with courage, *resist* and he will *flee*.

Witnesses to this truth abound in the tradition. St. Athanasius, in his classic *Life of St. Anthony*, describes Anthony's victories over temptation and then refers his words to the enemy: "You, then, are much to be despised, for you are black of mind, and like a powerless child. From now on, you cause me no anxiety, *for the Lord is my helper, and I shall look upon my enemies* [Ps 117:7]. Hearing these words, the black one immediately fled, cowering at the words and afraid even to approach the man."[4]

St. Thomas More's son-in-law, William Roper, recounts Thomas's words on this subject. Adopting a different metaphor, he closely parallels Ignatius's rule 12. Thomas urged his wife and children, William writes, to bear trials patiently, in imitation of Jesus. William continues:

> So would he in like case teach them to withstand the devil and his temptations, valiantly saying, "Whosoever will mark the devil and his temptations, shall find him therein much like to an ape. For as an ape not well looked to will be busy and bold to do shrewd turns, and contrariwise being spied will suddenly leap back and adventure no farther: so the devil, seeing a man idle, slothful, and without resistance ready to receive his temptations, waxes so hardy that he will not fail still to continue with him, until to his purpose he hath brought him: but on the other side, if he see a man with diligence present to prevent and withstand his temptations, he waxes so weary, that in conclusion he forsakes him."[5]

Teresa of Avila comments, "'Well now,' I went on, 'if this Lord is powerful, as I see he is, and know he is, and if the devils are his slaves (and of that there can be no doubt, for it is an article of the faith), what harm can they do me, who am a servant of this Lord and King?'"[6] In personal spiritual notes, the Venerable Bruno Lanteri writes, "Scorn the demon, lose completely any fear of him, treat him with authority, since we assail him in the name of Jesus Christ, our captain and king."[7]

Ignatius's rule 12 leads to a spiritual stance of courage and confidence. Toner aptly summarizes this attitude as that of one "who has conquered fear in himself without growing careless or rash." His words summarize well the attitude Ignatius inculcates in rule 12: spiritual awareness, attention, and care, but without anxiety or fear. This is a person, Toner continues, "who knows the divine power available to him and is confident of overcoming the enemy by that power."[8] Rule 12 teaches that we will overcome the enemy most readily if we resist his temptations *in their very beginning*.

Stop the Snowball at the Top of the Mountain

I return now to an image that I used in the earlier book and regularly employ in presenting rule 12. Here is a high mountain covered with snow. And here, at the very peak, a snowball is just getting started. You can put out a finger and stop it. Let the same snowball roll halfway down the mountain, gaining mass and speed, and it will run you over.

When is it easiest to reject the enemy's temptation to pick up the smartphone in a way that is "low and earthly" (rule 4)? When is it easiest to avoid the temptation to relinquish prayer? When is it easiest to resist the temptation to

anger against a family member? When is it easiest to overcome the temptation to speak badly of another? In every case,
the answer is the same: *right at the very beginning*, when the
temptation first presents itself—when the snowball is just
getting started at the peak of the mountain. It is easiest to
resist the temptations just mentioned if we never even touch
the screen of the smartphone for a first time, if we immediately dismiss the first suggestion to delay prayer, if we quickly
reject the first angry thoughts against the family member, and
if we never allow the first negative word to pass our lips.

I always welcome the opportunity to present rule 12: it
can save us an enormous amount of suffering in the spiritual
life. *If the snowball never gets started*, no exhausting struggle against overwhelming temptation will be needed. When
we resist temptation in the very beginning, "doing what is
diametrically opposed to it," two things happen: the power
of that temptation is undone, and we close the door to the
further struggle that would likely follow had we not resisted
in the very beginning.[9]

Rule 5 tells us that when we are in spiritual desolation we
should never change a spiritual proposal chosen before that
desolation began. Rule 12, if we follow its wisdom, will make
rule 5 easier to observe. If we resist the temptation to make a
change *in the very beginning*, before it can snowball, we will
much less likely succumb and make such changes.

In Thomas à Kempis's *The Imitation of Christ*, we read,
"Someone has said: 'Stand firm in the beginning, or remedies
will be provided too late.' For first the simple thought comes to
the mind, then a strong imagination, afterward pleasure, and
distorted stirrings, and consent. Thus the evil enemy, a little
at a time, gains complete entry, because he was not resisted in
the beginning. And the longer a man delays his resistance, the

weaker he becomes each day, and the enemy stronger against him."[10] *Resist in the beginning*, and none of the subsequent sorrow will ever occur. Such is the gift of rule 12.

Standing Firm in the Beginning: Testimonies from the Tradition

Ignatius's call to stand firm in the very beginning of temptation echoes scriptural teaching and our entire tradition. I present the following in chronological order.

Strong before weakness and weak before strength: biblically, this is the difference in the responses to the tempter of Eve and of Jesus. When the tempter approaches Eve (Gn 3), he does so with a question, "Did God really say . . . ?" Eve listens and replies, the tempter in turn answers her . . . and a process of temptation is under way.[11] The process continues, Eve sees "that the tree was good for food and pleasing to the eyes," and eventually yields to the temptations, with the unhappy consequences that follow.

The tempter approaches Jesus in the desert (Mt 4), "If you are the Son of God, command that these stones become loaves of bread." Jesus's response is immediate, based on the Word of God, and definitive, "It is written, 'One does not live by bread alone, but by every word that comes forth from the mouth of God.'" And the temptation is over. Jesus responds in a similar immediate and decisive fashion to the subsequent temptations, and the tempter is vanquished and departs from him.

The difference between Eve's and Jesus's responses to the enemy is precisely that which Ignatius wishes to highlight in rule 12. Our call is to respond like Jesus, confronting "the enemy firmly, doing what is diametrically opposed to him."

Evagrius, a desert father from the fourth century, names the "eight principal thoughts" with which the enemy assails the spiritual person: thoughts of gluttony, fornication, love of money, sadness, anger, listlessness, vainglory, and pride.[12] The urging of Evagrius's teaching is that the spiritual person resist these suggestions of the enemy *while they are still thoughts* and before they become actions.[13]

In his classic Rule, St. Benedict supplies seventy-two "Instruments of Good Works."[14] The fiftieth of these is this: "As soon as wrongful thoughts come into your heart, dash them against Christ, and disclose them to your spiritual father."[15] *As soon as*: this is pure rule 12. And the figure is striking. We can imagine a piece of pottery, ugly and misshapen, because it represents the temptations of the enemy, hurled against a solid mass of stone and so utterly shattered that it can never be restored. This, Benedict says, is to be our response as soon as the enemy's temptations present themselves: bring them immediately to Christ that they may be destroyed. The final phrase, "and disclose them to your spiritual father," anticipates Ignatius's rule 13.

In *The Imitation of Christ*, we read:

The beginning of all temptations to evil is inconstancy of soul, and little trust in God. For as a ship that has no rudder is driven here and there by the waves, so the careless man who is slow of resolve is tempted in many ways. Fire reveals the quality of iron, and temptation that of the just man. Often we do not know what strength we have, but temptation shows what we are. We must watch, therefore, above all for the beginning of temptation, because then the enemy is more easily overcome, if he is not allowed even to enter the door of the mind, but is met outside the threshold as soon as he knocks.[16]

Once again the counsel: "We must watch *above all* for *the beginning of temptation*, because then the enemy is more easily overcome."

On the final day of a discernment, when Ignatius has now found clarity, he terminates the process. In great consolation, he writes, "I considered everything concluded, with no further seeking, or Masses, or consolation of any kind, but that this day would see the end. Finished."[17] Ignatius then goes to his midday meal, and the following occurs: "After the stroke of one, as I sat down to eat, and for a good space, the tempter did nothing, but he sought to have me make some sign of hesitating, and answering at once, without any disturbance, rather as in the event of victory, 'Down, where you belong!' I felt a confirmation with tears and every security concerning all that had been determined."[18] When the tempter assails the clarity of Ignatius's discernment, he responds *at once*, decisively, and the temptation is undone.

St. Alphonsus de Liguori, in *The Practice of the Love of Jesus Christ*, writes, "As soon as we become aware of some thought that has an evil look about it, we must immediately dismiss it, close the door, so to speak, in its face, and deny it entrance into the mind, without stopping to decipher what it says or what it seeks to do. We must shake off such wicked suggestions as we shake off sparks of fire when they land upon us."[19] The image is apt: as quickly as we would dislodge a spark that alights upon us, so quickly should we dismiss the enemy's temptations when they first appear.

Céline, the sister of St. Thérèse of Lisieux, refers similar words of the saint, "You must practice the little virtues. This is sometimes difficult, but God never refuses the first grace—courage for self-conquest; and if the soul corresponds to that grace, she at once finds herself in God's sunlight. The praise given to Judith has always struck me: 'You have done manfully, and your heart has been strengthened' [Jdt 15:11]. In the onset we must act with courage. By this means, the heart gains strength, and victory follows victory."[20] *In the onset we must act with courage.* If we do, "victory follows victory." Thérèse is fully confident that "God never refuses that first grace."

A wonderful priest, whom I knew in his final years, one day shared the following: "When I am tempted to delay my prayer—let's say that I planned to pray at 5:00 p.m.—I start my prayer five minutes earlier. And when I do this, there is always some sweetness in the prayer, something that speaks to me and moves me." When people tell him of temptations just beginning—for example, angry thoughts—one spiritual director says to them, "Don't get on that bus!" A nice image! He also shares this: "If I'm walking along a path and step slightly off the path, if I see it right away, it's a short and easy step back on to the path. But if I don't see it right away and keep walking, it gets harder and harder to get back on the path."

At various points in this book, I have used the examples of Philip and Laura who encounter discouraging struggles of some kind, become vulnerable to spiritual desolation, and later reach a point in the day when they must struggle with desolation: Philip alone in his room at 10:00 p.m., poised between the Bible and the smartphone, and Laura alone in her apartment in late afternoon, poised between the Bible and the remote control. Both need to employ the wisdom of Ignatius's rules 5–11. If they do, they will navigate the desolation without harm.

What if, however, *that morning* Philip and Laura become aware that they are *just beginning* to enter spiritual desolation with its associated temptations? And what if they strive *immediately*, already that morning, to reject the desolation, employing the means of seeking God's help, recalling God's faithful love that will see them through this discouraging time without harm, examining how this began, and the like? Then the 10:00 p.m. and late-afternoon struggles with spiritual desolation will never even happen! The snowball has been stopped at the peak of the mountain. This is why I can say so confidently that rule 12, if we put it into practice, will save us much struggle and suffering in the spiritual life.

Rule 12: Some Examples

In my own daily living, I have come to appreciate rule 12 increasingly as the years pass. I find myself applying it more often now, grateful that it helps me stop discouraging, angry, troubled, or worried thoughts when they first begin. Sometimes the thoughts return and I need to repeat the process! But always this rule helps me.

"Call Out to Jesus Quickly"

This was another time of struggling with physical issues and with the consequent anxiety. As we spoke, Ed said the following:

> The enemy will tempt you to look to the future, to take the struggle of the present and predict the future, to get you thinking about this. That draws you into aloneness. His goal is to disturb your peace and draw you out of communion with the Lord. This is a tactic of the enemy:

it's going to get worse. . . . And the goal is to draw you away from Jesus.

To go against this, call out to Jesus quickly, invite him quickly to be with you: Jesus, this is hard for me. Be with me, help me. Then this very struggle draws you deeper into union with the Lord.

Things may not change right away, but turn right to him and the burden will get lighter.

In time of temptation, "Call out to Jesus quickly, invite him quickly to be with you." Ed's advice applied rule 12 to this specific temptation regarding the future. It proved a blessing in the measure I was able to apply it.

"I Felt Spiritual Strength Come"

One evening, I was to give the final talk in a series I had presented over several weeks. That morning, I wrote the following:

> I am experiencing a subtle desolation: "The talks thus far have gone well, but this one tonight will not be as effective. You've become complacent, and so this will not be as blessed. And you don't really have very much to say . . . ."
>
> In the prayer, I imaged Jesus as sitting before me.[21] I felt spiritual strength come as I asked his help for tonight. I felt an increase of hope, trust, consolation, and a sense that I am spiritually ready, that it will be rich tonight. This increased when I asked Mary for her help.
>
> Desolation was claiming power over the future in a quiet, subtle way, and I did not see it until now.

Prayer that morning was blessed, a time of perceiving more clearly the desolation and the its related temptation—to lose hope, a little at least, that God would accompany that evening's talk with his grace. Turning to Jesus in prayer that morning lifted both the desolation and the temptation. The talk went well, and the next morning I wrote, "Simple joy and gratitude for the way this teaching concluded." This time, too, by God's grace, the snowball was stopped at the peak of the mountain.

Chapter 13

"His Manifest Deceits
Have Been Revealed"

*I see now that the tactic of the enemy is
to try to get us to keep things in, not to
talk about them, because once you do,
Christ can come in.*
—Words of a Retreat Director

When I present rule 13 to groups, I repeat and then expand a statement made earlier when discussing rule 5. I express it this way: "When we examined rule 5, I begged of us never to forget rule 5, saying that it would get us safely through almost any darkness. Now I will complete that statement. I beg of us never to forget *rules 5 and 13 together*. Together, these two rules will guide us safely through any darkness we may face in the spiritual life: Do not make changes in the darkness of desolation (rule 5), and speak with a wise and competent spiritual person (rule 13). If we do these two things, we will come safely through any darkness the enemy may bring."

The Text of the Rule

Like rule 12, rule 13 consists of metaphor and application. The metaphor is the following: "The thirteenth: likewise he conducts himself as a false lover in wishing to remain secret and not be revealed. For a dissolute man who, speaking with evil intention, makes dishonorable advances to a daughter of a good father or to a wife of a good husband, wishes his words and persuasions to be secret, and the contrary displeases him very much, when the daughter reveals to her father or the wife to her husband his false words and depraved intention, because he easily perceives that he will not be able to succeed with the undertaking begun."

Like a false lover. The enemy's pleasures are *apparent* (rule 1), his reasons *false* (rule 2), and his "love" is *false* (rule 13), intent only on seducing and using the victim.[1] The enemy is ever the liar.

Because so much in these rules arose from Ignatius's own experience, I have often wondered whether this metaphor, too, may not have arisen from personal experience. Polanco attests of Ignatius that before his conversion, "although very much attached to the faith, he did not live in keeping with his belief or guard himself from sins; he was particularly careless about gambling, affairs with women, brawls, and the use of arms."[2] In his autobiography, Ignatius states simply that before his conversion "he was a man given over to vanities of the world."[3] Might not urging a woman to maintain silence about his advances have been among those "vanities"?

The enemy "wishes to *remain secret* and *not be revealed.*" Ignatius highlights the enemy's urging to secrecy when he brings his temptations. The metaphor is clear: in the moment itself that the "daughter of a good father or wife of a good husband" speaks to her father or husband about the false lover's seductions, those seductions will immediately be nullified. The false lover, therefore, insistently urges the daughter or wife to remain silent about "his words and persuasions," so that those persuasions may proceed. Only the woman's silence can render his "depraved intention" attainable.

Ignatius then applies the metaphor: "In the same way, when the enemy of human nature brings his wiles and persuasions to the just soul, he wishes and desires that they be received and kept in secret; but when one reveals them to one's good confessor or to another spiritual person, who knows his deceits and malicious designs, it weighs on him very much, because he perceives that he will not be able to succeed with the malicious undertaking he has begun, since his manifest deceits have been revealed."

When dedicated people find themselves burdened by the enemy's "wiles and persuasions," the enemy "wishes and desires" that these burdens "be received and kept *in secret*."[4] If such is the enemy's tactic, what is to be our response?

Ignatius urges those so burdened *to reveal* these wiles and persuasions, and carefully specifies the appropriate persons to whom they might reveal them: to *one's good confessor* or to *another spiritual person*, who *knows his deceits and malicious designs*. When they do this, "it weighs on him [the enemy] very much" because "he perceives *that he will not be able to succeed* with the malicious undertaking he has begun." When, like the upright woman who speaks with her father or husband, these persons reveal the enemy's wiles and persuasions to their good confessor or to another knowledgeable spiritual person, those wiles and persuasions will be completely undone.

What Does the Enemy Wish Us to Keep Hidden?

Ignatius speaks in rule 13 of the enemy's *wiles and persuasions*.[5] Here, perhaps more than anywhere else in these rules,

I need to approach the human heart with great reverence and sensitivity. I know that rule 13 can touch deep places within us.

What does Ignatius mean by the enemy's "wiles and persuasions"? These might include troubling temptations, doubts, fears, and spiritual burdens of various kinds brought by the enemy. They might involve something from our past about which we have never spoken and which weighs spiritually upon us. They might focus on something in our life at present about which we have never spoken and which likewise weighs upon us. They may center on that "something" that always surfaces in our hearts and burdens us when we feel the approach of God's love and desire to return that love.

Then, if we were to put our experience into words, we would say something like this: "Lord, I would feel so free to receive your love and to love you in return were it not for . . . " And there it is: the thing about which we have never spoken, the hidden experience, memory, fear, burden, doubt, or pain that holds us back and causes much suffering. The enemy's urging will be, "You can't talk about this. You can talk about anything else, but not about this . . . " because as long as we do not speak, the burden will remain—precisely the enemy's purpose.

As I noted in my earlier book, Ignatius speaks in rule 13 of *spiritual* burdens.[6] It would be a terrible misapplication of rule 13 were one, in its name, to press persons who bear deep pools of *nonspiritual*, emotional pain, to reveal these completely and at once—though it tear apart their hearts— to a good confessor or to another spiritually knowledgeable person. Such might be, for example, persons who have experienced profound emotional trauma.

These persons are *nonspiritual* captives who do need to be *set nonspiritually free*. These persons, too, will benefit greatly through speaking with an appropriate person. In this case, however, the appropriate person is a professionally trained and competent psychologist or counselor. Such psychologists and counselors will never demand in a first meeting that the person reveal everything. They will allow a relationship of trust to develop that will permit the person, over time, to speak about the emotional pain and so progress toward freedom. If, in addition to this nonspiritual help, the person also employs spiritual means, liberation will proceed all the more solidly: the eagle flies with two wings (see above, Prologue).

Having said this, dedicated persons may indeed find themselves *spiritually* burdened by the enemy's temptations, doubts, fears, and the like. Though it may require courage, they *can* speak about these with the appropriate spiritual person. If, by God's grace and with that courage, they do so, these *spiritual* captives will be *spiritually set free*. Such is the liberation to which Ignatius invites us in rule 13.

With Whom Should We Speak?

Who may that appropriate person be? Ignatius presents two profiles: *one's good confessor* or *another spiritual person*. What renders this confessor *good* and the other person *spiritual* is, as Ignatius immediately specifies, that they are knowledgeable: "who *knows* his [the enemy's] deceits and malicious designs." The confessor and the other person may be devout, and that is a very good thing. But devotion alone does not qualify them to be recipients of the sharing Ignatius intends. They must be *knowledgeable*: they must possess a solid understanding of and practical familiarity with the enemy's "deceits and malicious designs"—the ways in which the enemy seeks to burden the hearts of dedicated people—so that when they receive this sharing, they will understand well what they hear. As a result, they will know well how to assist these persons toward spiritual freedom.

The first profile is *one's good confessor*: a priest whom we know through the sacrament of confession (*confessor*), whom we know to be knowledgeable (*good*), and whom we know to be such by personal experience (*one's*). Ignatius's description suggests that we have approached that priest in the sacrament of confession sufficiently to recognize him as this kind of confessor. Such priests are a great blessing to their people. In his own life, Ignatius conferred with "good confessors" in times of struggle and doubt.[7]

The second profile is *another spiritual person*. This might be a priest, religious man or woman, or layperson. Again, what qualifies these persons as *spiritual* is that they are knowledgeable. Most often, this will presume some formal training in spiritual direction and also experience of accompanying others on the spiritual journey. Such persons, too, are a great blessing in the Church.

I will note, in addition, that in a rule found in Ignatius's *Spiritual Exercises*, he does not name "the one who gives the Exercises"—his language for the retreat director[8]—as the person with whom we would speak about the enemy's burdens. Such is the more remarkable in that retreatants meet daily with "the one who gives the Exercises" to share their spiritual experience. This omission may be a further indication that Ignatius intended these rules to serve beyond the formal retreat and in daily life.

Setting Captives Free

One of the happiest experiences in my ministry over the years has been to witness people set free when, at times with great courage, they speak of their spiritual burdens. In spiritual direction, retreats, and the sacrament of confession, a space is created in which people can speak, and *you see before your eyes* captives set free. At times, tears express the release of heart and the new freedom.

Years ago, I used to give parish missions. I would come to a parish for four or five days, give various talks, and be available for confessions or simply to talk. At times, people would share burdens carried for decades—thirty, forty, or more years. I loved this part of the mission, and it often made me think of Ignatius's rule 13: I saw new freedom born in human hearts as they spoke.

May I reverently ask: Are there spiritual burdens in our hearts that might find release through speaking with a wise and competent spiritual person?

The Imagined Scenario

The enemy's urging to secrecy will always involve an imagined scenario, and that scenario will always be painful. We do not generally express the imagined scenario explicitly in words, but it is there. I suggest here some ways in which we may experience this scenario.

When persons feel the enemy's burdens, and when there is a wise and competent spiritual person with whom they could speak, they may find thoughts like these arise:

• "I could speak with him or her, but he/she is too busy." Comment: Always let that person make this decision. You need not hesitate for this reason to approach him or her. Spiritual guides will take responsibility for their own time and will let you know whether or not they are too busy to meet now.

- "I wish I could speak with him or her, but I am too busy."
  Comment: If this is an especially pressured week or two,
  I can grant that this may be so. But if three, four, or six
  months have passed, and you are still too busy, then you
  need to begin to think in terms of rule 13: there is an enemy
  who does not wish you to speak.

- "If I talk about this, he/she will laugh at me." Comment:
  This may be the most painful imagined scenario of all. Do
  not let this stop you. If the person you approach is truly the
  good confessor or spiritual person Ignatius describes, this
  person will not laugh but rather reverence the deep place
  in your heart that seeks healing.

- "If I talk about this, he/she will never understand me."
  Comment: Again, if this person is truly the good confessor
  or spiritual person whom Ignatius intends, this person will
  understand. When you have identified such a person, do
  not let this imagined scenario prevent you from speaking.

- "If I talk about this, he/she will be kind about it, but will
  never respect me in the same way again." Comment: The
  same as the preceding. Genuinely competent guides will
  love and reverence your courage in speaking about this
  burden. Their respect for you will increase.

- "If I talk about this, he/she will gently reply, 'If that is part
  of your life and that is who you are, then we can no longer
  work together.'" Comment: The same as the preceding.

- "What's the point of talking about this? There is nothing
  anyone can say that will change things." Comment: This
  imagined scenario says that "no words of any spiritual person can help in my situation." This is obviously not true,
  as experience repeatedly shows. But even if the spiritual

person were to say little, the simple act *of putting the burden into words* in that setting will already powerfully begin healing. Never let this thought stop you from speaking.[9]

The imagined scenario will always be painful and embarrassing; the real scenario will bring joy, release of heart, and new energy to love and serve the Lord—it will *set captives free*. The distance between the two scenarios lays bare the enemy's desire to "remain secret and not be revealed" and the power in breaking the spiritual silence.

"It Is Not Good to Be Alone"

At the origin, God said, "It is not good for the man to be alone" (Gn 2:18).[10] The creation of the woman and the mutual belonging of the man and the woman follow. This principle—that it is not good for us to be alone—applies broadly to human experience.

It applies also to the spiritual life and it underlies Ignatius's rule 13: it is not good for us to be alone on the spiritual journey, and, certainly, it is not good for us to be alone in living the discerning life.

Recent pontiffs have reiterated this classic teaching of our tradition. Benedict XVI writes that "to advance toward the Lord, we always have need of a guide, of a dialogue. We cannot do it with just with our own reflections. And finding this guide is part of the ecclesial nature of our faith."[11] Striking words! To advance toward the Lord—I am sure that this is what all who read these pages desire: to advance, to grow toward the Lord, to live our vocations more fully, to progress in holiness—to do this, we always have need of a guide. The language could not be clearer.

We may also know by experience the truth of Benedict's words that "we cannot do it just with our own reflections." If we have tried to advance toward the Lord just with our own reflections, we know how exposed we are to doubt, confusion, and desolation, with the consequent loss of spiritual energy. We always have need of *some form of dialogue* in the spiritual—and so in the discerning—life. In his writing, Pope Francis has also emphasized what he calls "Personal Accompaniment in Processes of Growth."[12]

Forms of Spiritual Accompaniment

What concrete shape might such accompaniment take? I offer here an overview of various forms it might assume. Dedicated persons will find the form or mixtures of forms that, in their circumstances, best meet their needs.

Spiritual Direction

Benedict XVI also affirmed the following: "As she has never failed to do, again today the Church continues to recommend the practice of spiritual direction, not only to all those who wish to follow the Lord up close but to every Christian who wishes to live responsibly his baptism, that is, the new life in Christ. Everyone, in fact, and in a particular way all those who have received the divine call to a closer following, needs to be supported personally by a sure guide in doctrine and expert in the things of God. A guide can help defend oneself from facile subjectivist interpretations, making available his own supply of knowledge and experiences in following Jesus."[13] Rooted in the Church's age-old tradition, Benedict strongly encourages classic spiritual direction.

Such direction generally involves a monthly meeting of an hour with the director. Directees share their spiritual experience and are helped, through the director's accompaniment, to follow the Lord's leading and to avoid the enemy's tactics.

When I present rule 13, the question always arises, "How do I find a spiritual director? I have tried and have not succeeded. Those I know seem so busy." Yes, the demand for spiritual directors is high, and, yes, it can be difficult to find "a good confessor or another spiritual person" who is both knowledgeable in the enemy's tactics and also available.

One author suggests the following: Begin by praying, asking the Holy Spirit's help to find the right director. Then identify the possibilities in your area, considering the directors—priests, religious, and laypersons—whom you know personally. Likewise, ask the advice of others who know the directors in the area and whose judgment you trust. When you have identified the best possibilities, contact a few of these, and ask for a single meeting. You might say, for example, "I desire to grow in the spiritual life and have some decisions to make. I would be glad of guidance on how to proceed. Could I meet with you?" If the first meeting is helpful, you may later ask for a second. Once you sense which of these directors seems most helpful, you can then ask for regular direction.[14]

Of the difficulties we may encounter in finding a director, another author writes:

> We believe, nonetheless, that . . . at times it is not possible, at least not immediately, to find the ideal person. In such cases, we must continue trying until we find this person . . . since the act itself of manifesting our temptations weakens their grip and renders them more intelligible to the one who so manifests them. . . . We

should never cease to search for such a person and to ask the Lord that he grant us to find a good confessor or a spiritual person who "knows the deceits and malicious designs (of the bad spirit)," remembering the promise of the Lord: "Ask and it will be given to you; seek and you will find. . . . For everyone who asks, receives, and the one who seeks, finds" (Mt 7:7).[15]

Might God be calling you to seek spiritual direction? Could this make a difference in your spiritual life and help you live the discerning life?

The Sacrament of Reconciliation

We have noted that Ignatius names "one's good confessor" as an option for the sharing that sets us free. If finding a spiritual director may, at times, require much effort, the same is not true of the sacrament of reconciliation. In general, this is available to all.

The sacrament of reconciliation is primarily centered on forgiveness, a grace that brings healing and renewed energy in the spiritual life. From the further perspective of rule 13, if we find a good confessor whom we can approach regularly, we will no longer be alone in the spiritual life. The encounter of confession may be brief, but even that brief sharing and the briefly given advice of the confessor can assist us greatly.

I become increasingly grateful for this sacrament as time passes. For some years now, after confession, I write the words of counsel given by the confessor. Often this is just a few sentences. The writing helps me remember his words and the encouragement and light they offer me.

The counsel of one confessor stays with me to the present. That particular confession took place during the worst of my vocal struggles and in a time of repeated surgeries. Because of vocal limitations, I was forced to cancel almost all of my active ministry. The confessor urged me to look beyond the physical limitations to the ministerial opportunities that my situation afforded: further writing, communication of spiritual teaching through the Internet, and the like. His words were bracing in a spiritually healthy way. They helped lift the desolation into which I had slipped. He was for me, that day, the "good confessor" of whom Ignatius writes.

What place does the sacrament of reconciliation have in our spiritual lives? What place might it have?

Retreats

Retreats provide a further opportunity for spiritual sharing. If, for example, we make an annual retreat, during it we might meet with the retreat director and speak of any spiritual burdens we may be experiencing. A weekend retreat may allow one or two such meetings. A longer Ignatian retreat of three, five, or eight days, when possible, will allow for daily meetings with a director during that time. Retreats may also be made in daily life, without leaving our homes and tasks, and with regular guidance by a director during the weeks or months of the retreat.[16]

Should we be carrying any spiritual burdens, the quiet, recollection, and prayer of such retreats often help us perceive them more clearly than in the bustle of daily life. This clarity and the meeting or meetings with the retreat director to discuss such issues may bless the entire year to follow. Over the years, I have experienced this often, and I am grateful for these retreats and the meetings of direction during them.

If we struggle to find a spiritual director—and even if we have a director—annual retreats richly provide, as Benedict

XVI writes, a "form of dialogue" that may serve efficaciously to dispel the enemy's burdens. Can we consider this option?

Spiritual Friends

On a different level, one that no longer involves formal spiritual direction, friends in the Lord may provide yet another "form of dialogue." Such friends do not attempt to offer spiritual direction to each other, but simply accompany each other as friends. This accompaniment also can help lift the enemy's burdens.

I mentioned above that when I was provincial, after periods of extensive international travel, I sometimes spent three or four days in a retreat house to recover my energy. This was not entirely wise, since I was too alone during those days, and in a time of tiredness. On one such occasion, the nonspiritual desolation gave place to a dark spiritual desolation. Prayer, even in the retreat house, grew difficult, and things generally appeared bleak.

Some time earlier, I had arranged to have dinner with a priest-friend, and the date fell during my days at the retreat house. As we shared the meal, I told him what I was experiencing. He listened, and then said one sentence in reply. He did not attempt to be a director but spoke simply as a friend: "It sounds like you're in desolation." His words broke the desolation. With his help, I understood (title statement to the rules: be aware, *understand*, take action) what I was experiencing, and that set me free to resist it. The remainder of my stay at the retreat house was no longer desolate.

A woman told me that, for years, she and a group of her friends would meet on Saturdays for breakfast. They enjoyed being together, but they also gathered to share their spiritual experiences. After the meal, each would share what she wished, and each found encouragement in the others. This, too, is a "form of dialogue" that can help lift burdens and provide strength on the spiritual journey.

Today, means for such sharing among spiritual friends have multiplied. Where personal presence may be difficult, phone conversations, whether one-on-one or in multiperson conference calls, or video meetings through Skype, FaceTime, and similar digital resources, render conversation across geographical distances more possible than ever before. These means may help us accompany each other as spiritual friends.

Groups

In parishes and other institutions in the Church, groups are available. These may focus on formation in the faith, on active service, on growth in prayer, discernment, and the like. In such groups, we meet others who share our interest in the spiritual life. These groups provide an excellent "form of dialogue" that helps move us from spiritual aloneness to spiritual communion. They are an option well worth our consideration.

Married Couples

Marriage provides a unique form of dialogue, found only in this vocation. Where possible, husband and wife may accompany each other as spouses on the spiritual journey. The Church describes this as *conjugal spirituality*, in which each assists the other to grow in the life of faith. Again, this is not spiritual direction but a loving accompaniment that strengthens both.

Various couples have told me that they pray Ignatius's examen prayer together each evening, and have done so for years.[17] Together they review the spiritual experience of the day. This prayer often leads to a sharing that strengthens their mutual bond and provides an opportunity to speak about any burdens, nonspiritual or spiritual, they may be experiencing.

In terms of rule 13, this "form of dialogue" and others like it that spouses may adopt also help husbands and wives break the spiritual silence and find new energy to resist the enemy's burdens.

These forms of dialogue, especially if adopted in combination, aid us in resisting the enemy who "wishes to remain secret and not be revealed." I believe that whether or not we are spiritually accompanied will determine, in the long run, whether or not we will sustain the discerning life. *It is not good to be alone.* Finding ways to be accompanied is a primary need for the discerning life in general and specifically in regard to rule 13. Do we have them?

Rule 13: Some Examples

I offer the following examples of rule 13 in practice. This rule has been and remains a great blessing in my life.

"Once You Do, Christ Can Come In"

Some years ago, I spoke with a young priest who had just finished leading a retreat for young adults. This was a new initiative for him, and it had gone very well, with a large group. He was tired but very happy about the retreat.

He described the final group sharing on Sunday morning after the talks, the prayer, the time for confessions, and the celebration of Masses that had filled the weekend. The sharing was deep, on the level of the heart. The young adults spoke of their searching and their struggles. As they spoke, they felt a deep connection with each other and a new sense of peace and hope, with an overcoming of isolation and loneliness.

Then the priest mused aloud about the experience: "I see now that the tactic of the enemy is to try to get us to keep things in. Don't say it. Don't talk about it. Because once you do, Christ can come into this, and everything changes. The tempter's game is up." *Once you do, Christ can come in, and everything changes.* As I listened, I heard Ignatius's rule 13. *This* is the enemy's constant urging: *Don't say it. Don't talk about it.* Once the spiritual silence is broken, "the tempter's game is up."

"Just Leaving a Message"

This was another experience of that vulnerable time after a trip. I had traveled to teach these rules for discernment to a group of spiritual directors. The trip had included occasional struggles with desolation, but had, above all, been a happy and consoled time.

Now I was home, feeling worn, a little ill, and too alone. I found myself drifting toward novels and food, struggling to pray. Earlier that year, I had asked an older priest, a fine spiritual director, if I could call him at such times. He had agreed. I did call, and he was out. I left a message on his answering machine—and found that just leaving that message left me feeling much better. I began doing simple tasks, responding to emails from friends, and went out to do an errand.

That gesture of reaching out to speak in a time of spiritual burden changed everything. Even before the priest replied— as he did when he returned—the spiritual silence was broken, and the burden lifted.

"I Don't Need to Talk about That"

This next experience has repeated many times, and I notice it now more quickly than in the past. As mentioned, I find that keeping a journal helps me in the spiritual life. In the weeks between meetings with my director, as I write, I note different things that I sense I will need to talk about in the next meeting. By each, I place a small symbol. That symbol reminds me that I intend to speak of that item in direction.

Shortly before the meeting, I review the items marked with the symbol. At times, I find myself looking at one of these and saying to myself, "No, I don't need to talk about that." When I am spiritually aware, I catch myself at this point and ask, "Well, why is it that you don't need to talk about that? You obviously thought that you did just a few days or weeks ago." Then, often with a certain sinking of my heart, I realize that I *do* need to speak about "that." This speaking may require a little courage—and very often, "that" becomes the most fruitful part of the meeting of spiritual direction.

There is a reason why the enemy wishes us to keep things secret. There is likewise great fruit in revealing his burdens to a wise and competent spiritual person.[18]

"You Knew that You Were Not Alone"

On the third day of a retreat, I had spent an hour of prayer by the lake on the grounds of the retreat center. It was a cool fall day with a breeze blowing, the sky filled with rows of clouds. Around me was the beauty of the foliage and before me the water, stirred by the wind. I loved being there for the prayer, simply absorbing my surroundings and letting my thoughts move freely toward the Lord.

Later, a doubt arose: Was this really prayer? Was I regressing? Would it not have been better to have a specific focus for the prayer, perhaps a passage from Scripture? In that hour, I felt no desire to do so and found my heart at peace in the beauty of the setting, just letting the prayer unfold freely. Should, however, the prayer have been more focused and so more truly prayer? The question introduced an uncertainty and a little worry into the day. I felt this all the more since I had experienced this same uncertainty about prayer during the preceding year.

That evening, I brought this experience and this question to the conversation with my retreat director. The director replied, "Yes, that was real prayer. It was where the Lord was leading you. When you feel drawn this way, continue with confidence. The question arises because this is new and does not feel like prayer as you were familiar with it. But you knew that you were not alone, that it was a time of 'being with.'"

The director continued, "This is the enemy's trap. He turns the newness in prayer around and tells you that you are going backward, heading to ruin. The uncertainty the newness brings is the space in which he acts. He takes growth and presents it as destruction." I found myself replying spontaneously, "That's diabolical!" I know Ignatius would agree.

After this conversation, the uncertainty and worry resolved. As so often is true, speaking with a competent spiritual person revealed the enemy's "manifest deceits." In a quiet but blessed way, I was a captive set free.

"Now I Feel Lighter and Happier"

Some years ago, my provincial asked me to interrupt the Ignatian writing I had been doing to write a biography of our founder, the Venerable Bruno Lanteri.[19] I understood the need for this biography and was willing to write it. At the same time, after years of working with Ignatian spirituality, I found it hard to shift to a very different topic and genre of writing. The biography also proved the most difficult task I have ever undertaken.

As I did the research for the biography, one year quickly became two, and still the research remained far from complete. For many reasons, including cultural, historical, and linguistic differences, the work proved highly demanding.

I had no clear sense of when I would even begin to write and no clarity on how long that would take. I worried that this book would require many years, and I saw my return to Ignatian writing fade into the distant future, if I returned to it at all. After so many years away from Ignatian spiritual writing, would the creative spark still be there?

This was the human (nonspiritual) vulnerability into which the enemy brought spiritual burdens as well. I had no doubt that God willed me to write the biography as the request came from my religious superior. In fact, this was a project I had hoped to undertake ever since, years earlier, I had written my doctoral thesis on the life and spirituality of Venerable Bruno. But the work was laborious and slow . . . and the future of the writing uncertain.

I brought this concern to my next meeting of direction with Ed. I shared the thought that weighed on my heart: "My fear is that my creative writing is over. The biography will take years and exhaust my energy for writing. When I try to resume after this, the quality of the writing will be lessened. My best writing is over . . . "

Ed replied, "The enemy, when he brings desolation, claims power over the future, 'Your creative writing is over.' His aim is to discourage you in your mission. Name the fears: 'I'm never going to be able to . . . ,' 'It's just going to get worse . . . ' Acknowledge the fears. There is no shame in experiencing them. This is how the enemy assaults you, entering through the vulnerability. No! If God wants you to write a book like the earlier books, he will give you what you need. He will do it. It will be *easier* than in the past, because he will be doing it in you. Go to the Lord, and talk to him about it. Receive from his heart what he wants to give you."

After that conversation, I wrote, "Desolation claims power over the future. I didn't see that this was happening in regard to the writing, and I needed Ed to point it out to me. I knew that the biography was God's will, but I didn't see the enemy's trap, 'This will go very slowly, on and on for years . . . You'll do it poorly, just to get it done . . . It will mean, in practice, the end of your writing.' This was like an open window through which the heat in the room was leaking out. Now, after talking, I feel lighter and happier."

I finished the biography in five years, happy with the way it was written, and then resumed my former writing. I am grateful for Ignatius's rule 13 and his counsel to speak with the right person about the spiritual burdens we experience.

Chapter 14

Freedom Where We Feel Least Free

*All of the virtues grow through the
practice of any one of them.*
—St. John of the Cross

For many years, I saw rule 14 as a final piece, after the high point of rule 13. The listeners and I, having explored thirteen rules, were all aware that this was the last. During those years, I tended to present it more briefly, with the end in view.

I now believe that the opposite may be true, and that in rule 14, as it were, Ignatius saves the best for last. Now when I present rule 14, I begin by saying, "It may be that as we've gone through these rules, some have found themselves thinking something like this: 'Ignatius's rules are good, and I see how they will help in my life. But . . . there is this one difficult area of my life—this issue, this struggle, this aspect, this burden—that will not change. I may do better in other areas, and Ignatius's wisdom will help, but in this area I am still going to keep failing. Yes, I may progress a little in this area, but basically things will remain the same, and I will continue to carry this burden.'"

In rule 14, Ignatius wants to bring hope *right there*, in that place where we feel most hopeless. This is the final piece in the rules, and they would remain incomplete without it.

240

The Text of the Rule

As with rules 12 and 13, Ignatius presents a metaphor and its application. First, the metaphor: "The fourteenth: likewise he [the enemy] conducts himself as a leader, intent upon conquering and robbing what he desires. For, just as a captain and leader of an army in the field, pitching his camp and exploring the fortifications and defenses of a stronghold, attacks it at the weakest point . . . " Again the unnatural, antihuman quality is evident. This leader is intent only upon "conquering and robbing" according to "what he desires," that is, his lust for possession. He is not a noble leader fighting a just battle in defense of the common good, but an astute and grasping thief, seeking only to sack and pillage.

To that end, he sets up camp and then carefully explores the defenses of the stronghold (*castillo*). With razor-sharp perception, he locates the weakest point in the walls. To a less practiced eye, that point might appear as strong as the rest of the defenses. This leader, however, notes that in that place the stonework, for example, is weakened and will quickly collapse under assault. Shortly thereafter, the attack begins *at that precise point*. Of what value to the inhabitants are walls of stone ten feet thick, if in one place the masonry is in disrepair and crumbling? The defenses are only as strong as the weakest point.

The application follows: "In the same way the enemy of human nature, roving about, looks in turn at all our theological, cardinal, and moral virtues; and where he finds us weakest and most in need for our eternal salvation, there he attacks us and attempts to take us."

Like the leader of thieves, the enemy of human nature examines the spiritual fortress he wishes to take: "all our *theological, cardinal,* and *moral virtues.*" He examines the strength of our faith, our hope and trust in God, and our love for God and for others in God (*theological virtues*); he explores our practical wisdom in choosing good means toward good ends, our uprightness in our dealings with others, our courage in difficult situations, and our wise moderation in the enjoyment of the blessings of this world (prudence, justice, fortitude, temperance: the *cardinal virtues*); he reviews our worship of God, our life of prayer and devotion, our adherence to God's will, our purity of heart, our gentleness toward others, our humble recognition of who we are in relation to God, and the like (virtues of religion, devotion, obedience, chastity, gentleness, humility, and the other *moral virtues*).[1]

In Ignatius's language, this indicates that the enemy examines the whole of our spiritual lives—what gives us strength in God and what weakens us, what gives us courage and what makes us afraid, what gives us confidence in God's love and what causes us to doubt that love, what helps us grow spiritually and what inclines us to regress—and "where he finds us *weakest* and *most in need* for our eternal salvation, *there* he attacks us and attempts to take us."[2] *There*, where we are *weakest* and *most in need*, he attacks us and attempts to take us: such is the enemy's tactic.

Throughout the rules, and the *Spiritual Exercises* in general, Ignatius consistently avoids superfluous words. This style is evident in the text of rule 14, which is shorter than that of rules 12 and 13.

In rule 12, Ignatius explicitly describes *both responses* to the enemy's tactic, firm or weak. In rule 13, he describes explicitly *only the first response*: the person speaks with a good confessor or another spiritual person and finds freedom. The second possible response—the person does not speak and the enemy's burdens persist—remains implicit, though clear. In rule 14, Ignatius describes explicitly *neither response*—the person does not strengthen the weak point and succumbs to the enemy, the person does strengthen the weak point and so overcomes the enemy. Both remain implicit though, again, clear.[3]

In these three rules, we find, as one author describes it, a pattern of "progressively incomplete redaction."[4] Having established in rule 12 the pattern of two possible responses to a tactic of the enemy, Ignatius feels no need to present explicitly the full pattern in rules 13 and 14. This pattern is already clear from rule 12, and the reader easily applies it to the two rules that follow. So true is this that we hardly notice the progressively incomplete redaction of the rules. With his customary economy of words, Ignatius achieves his purpose.

The Enemy Is Harsh, Christ Is Gentle

"Where he finds us weakest and most in need for our eternal salvation, *there* he attacks us and attempts to take us." *There*, where we feel weakest, where we are held captive and see little hope of change, right *there* Ignatius wishes to bring clarity, hope, and freedom. Rule 14 calls captives to freedom on a deep, radical level of the heart.

This next point is key, and I emphasize it when I present rule 14: *There is no shame in having a weakest point*. We all do. From our upbringing, temperament, and the varied experiences of our lives, all of us are somewhere most vulnerable to the enemy's burdens. This is simply what it means to live in a fallen, redeemed, and loved world. There is no shame in this. What does matter is to *know* that weakest point and to *strengthen* it. Such is the invitation of rule 14, and such is the path to freedom right *there*.

I have often seen how the enemy will attack us in what is closest to our hearts and matters most to us. A woman loves her vocation to marriage and motherhood or to religious life, and seeks to live it well. The enemy says to her, "Look at you. You're not much of a spouse. You're not a very good mother." Or "You aren't an authentic nun." A couple who deeply desire children are unable to have them or at this point experience tensions in their marriage, and the enemy says, "It's your fault. You'll always fail at being a husband, a wife. You'll always be a disappointment to your spouse." A man loves purity and sincerely strives to live it (Mt 5:8). When his humanity makes itself felt, the enemy says, "See how you struggle and fail. You'll never live the way you want to live. Look at who you are. Don't think you'll ever be close to God."

I write this last paragraph with great reverence, because I know how painful these and similar tactics of the enemy can be. Good people may feel them, and such burdens of the enemy may persist, even for years. Rule 14 tells us that *right there*, where we feel most vulnerable to the enemy's burdens, captives can be set free.

In this most vulnerable place, the enemy— the accuser, the liar—is harsh: "Look at you! See who you are. See how you fail. You will never be close to God. You will always live with this pain. You will always carry this burden." And in this most vulnerable place, Christ is gentle: "Come to me, all you who labor and are burdened, and I will give you rest. Take my yoke upon you and learn from me, for I am meek and humble of heart; and you will find rest for yourselves. For my yoke is easy, and my burden light" (Mt 11:28–30).[5] This is the Jesus who will not break a bruised reed or quench a smoldering wick (Mt 12:20). This is the Jesus who came "to bring glad tidings to the poor," "to proclaim liberty to captives," and "to let the oppressed go free" (Lk 4:18).[6]

By revealing the enemy's astute sense of our most vulnerable point and indicating that he will attack us there, Ignatius powerfully invites us to learn what that most vulnerable point is and to strengthen it. The principle of rule 14—that we all have a most vulnerable point and that the enemy will attack there—applies to all; the specific application will be as individual as our individual personalities and histories.

Identifying the Vulnerable Point

I offer now a series of questions that may help us identify that point of greatest vulnerability.[7] They are all variations of the same question. These are questions on which we might reflect and pray and about which we might then speak with "one's good confessor or another spiritual person" (rule 13). This combination of personal reflection and prayer with "some form of dialogue" (Benedict XVI) greatly assists identification of this point and the choice of means to strengthen it.

◆ Is there some situation that frequently discourages you? That frequently strips you of spiritual energy? Comment: The key word here is *frequently*, that is, this same pattern repeats over and over, and always leads you to discouragement, to the stripping of your spiritual energy. You are happy in your relationship with God, and then this happens again . . .

◆ Are there circumstances in which you often become afraid? Comment: When this pattern or these circumstances repeat, you find yourself anxious, worried, afraid in your relationship with God. And this has happened over and over . . .

◆ Are there circumstances in which you frequently feel worn out and spiritually helpless? Comment: When this situation occurs, you feel tired, worn down, as though all your spiritual energy is gone. You feel that you are helpless, that you cannot avoid this, that you will keep failing in this, that it will always weigh on your freedom to receive and return God's love . . .

◆ Does one thing seem to diminish most your energy to love and serve others? Comment: You are praying, growing in the life of the sacraments, serving God and others with more generosity . . . and then this happens again. You sit in your room feeling that you cannot go on with these efforts . . .

◆ Is there something that habitually disheartens you in prayer? Comment: This same thing repeats, and you grow uneasy when you seek to meet God in prayer. You find yourself saying, "I really want to pray, but when I do, this thing always comes to mind and makes it hard for me to be with God . . . "

◆ Is there something that causes you to doubt God's love for you? Comment: This touches a deep place in the heart. You try to live your spiritual life faithfully, but always, because of this one thing, you find yourself doubting that God can really love you . . . Again, I write with great reverence.

◆ Is there a *repeating pattern* of these experiences? Comment: If you experience burdens like these just mentioned, and if you find that *this one pattern especially* keeps repeating, that it *more than anything else* leads you to discouragement, then you have found the point of vulnerability. This is the first step toward freedom.

Rule 14 applies to one, key area of our spiritual lives the ancient adage, "Know thyself." In that magnificent opening of her *Dialogue*, Catherine of Siena writes, "A soul rises up, restless with tremendous desire for God's honor and the salvation of souls. She has for some time exercised herself in virtue and has become accustomed to dwelling in the cell of self-knowledge in order to know better God's goodness toward her, since upon knowledge follows love. And loving, she seeks to pursue truth and clothe herself in it."[8] She has dwelt in the "cell of self-knowledge," and so she "rises up, restless with tremendous desire for God's honor and the salvation of souls." To dwell in the cell of self-knowledge is the beginning of liberation. The one who does this *rises up* with rich spiritual energy to love and to serve. Such is the dynamic of rule 14.

How Do We Strengthen the Vulnerable Point?

Once we have identified the vulnerable point, how do we proceed? I will review some spiritual and nonspiritual means that may help.

Prayer

"Ask and it will be given to you. . . . For everyone who asks, receives" (Mt 7:7–8).[9] Prayer is the first and most powerful way to strengthen the vulnerable point. It is the most powerful because prayer disposes our hearts to receive the love and grace of God right *there* where we most need that love. In the Mass, the Liturgy of the Hours, quiet prayer before the Blessed Sacrament, *lectio divina*, Ignatian meditation and contemplation, the Rosary, or simple prayer from the heart, we ask God's grace to strengthen the vulnerable point. I once heard a speaker say that if we really understood the power of prayer, we would never rise from our knees. This was one way to describe the richness, the fruit, and the growth that flow from the gift that we call prayer.[10] Such prayer is the first channel of grace for strengthening the vulnerable point (Phil 4:13).

Some Form of Dialogue

All that we said about this when discussing rule 13 applies: spiritual direction, a "good confessor," retreats, friends in the Lord, groups, or a spouse. If nonspiritual wounds underlie the spiritually vulnerable point, conversation with a counselor may also help. It is not good for us to be alone: this is true in a special way of our efforts to strengthen the vulnerable point. Some form of dialogue will greatly bless and help sustain this effort. As we have seen, Ignatius always presumes accompaniment in the discerning life.

The Examen Prayer

In rule 6, we saw Ignatius call the person in desolation to "much examination." Jesuit author William Broderick comments, "If we take rules 6 and 14 together, what Ignatius seems to be saying is that a thorough self-knowledge is essential if we are to cope successfully with desolation and the attacks of the enemy. Prayer and reliance on God by themselves are not sufficient. Ignatius did not neglect ordinary human means. A thorough self-knowledge would count as such a means. By reflecting on ourselves, on our previous successes and failures, on the circumstances in which we succeeded and the circumstances in which we failed, we can build up an accurate picture of our personality. There is a pattern to our past and present behavior, a pattern in the way we react to people and events."[11] The daily examen prayer raises this "ordinary human means," this search for "a thorough self-knowledge" to the level of our relationship with the God who loves us, the level of faith and grace.

I find that when we identify our vulnerable point (rule 14), the "much examination" to which Ignatius calls us in spiritual desolation (rule 6) grows easier. This vulnerable point may often be the opening for the enemy's spiritual desolations. To know this vulnerable point and how it influences our spiritual lives helps us to pinpoint more clearly the origin and development of a given spiritual desolation. Such clarity greatly aids our effort to resist and reject the desolation.

Concretely, rule 14 invites us to pray the daily examen prayer. In this prayer, we stop for perhaps eight to ten minutes to review the spiritual experience of the day. We note God's gifts, ask his help to understand our spiritual experience of the day, review that experience, ask forgiveness as we need it, and plan for the next day with the Lord. This daily review can help us identify the vulnerable point, see how it operates in our daily lives, and choose the best means to strengthen it.[12] Because self-knowledge is central to strengthening the vulnerable point, the examen prayer will greatly assist this effort.

A further component of Ignatian prayer may apply specifically to rule 14. In addition to the general examen of the day just described, Ignatius also speaks of the particular examen (*SpirEx* 24–31).[13] In this examen, Ignatius invites us to identify our spiritually weakest point, "that particular sin or defect, which we wish to correct and amend" (*SpirEx* 24). Upon rising in the morning, we renew our readiness to pursue growth in this area. At midday, we briefly review our progress, and do this once again in the evening. Ignatius also proposes a simple form of journaling to assess our progress over time. In this way, we intentionally seek to strengthen that specific weak point. What if, having found that weak point, we were to apply to it this daily particular examen?

When I first perceived the link between the particular examen and rule 14, it shed a new light on the particular examen. I understood this examen, respected its wisdom, and made efforts to practice it, but did not feel greatly attracted to it. When I saw this examen in the light of discernment and as a means for strengthening the vulnerable point, it grew more welcome. I found my interest in it awakened in a new way.

Learning

When the point of greatest vulnerability has been found, we may then pursue deeper learning with respect to it: how this vulnerability arose, how it developed, and the best means to strengthen it. Such knowledge is of great value in this effort.

A woman's parents, for example, divorced when she was eight years old. Her world was shattered when the family split. She continued with school, graduated from college, and now holds a responsible job. She would like to marry but finds it difficult to believe in lifelong commitments. Spiritually, she struggles to trust God and easily grows anxious in her relationship with God. When anxious, her resolutions to love God, pray, and serve others falter. This pattern repeats over and over . . . and she finds herself weary on the spiritual journey.

If this woman learns more about the effects of divorce on children, she may understand her experience more clearly. This might involve psychological (nonspiritual) accompaniment with a good counselor. Conversations with such a counselor may aid her nonspiritual (psychological) growth and help her grasp the emotional roots of her spiritual vulnerability. The patient process of nonspiritual healing will also shed light on that spiritually vulnerable point. She will find it easier to trust God, her spiritual life will grow less tense, and the discouraging pattern will occur less often. As her freedom from nonspiritual captivity grows, she will likewise grow in spiritual freedom.

Pertinent reading on both the nonspiritual and spiritual levels may reinforce this growth. Reading, for example, about the effects of divorce on children will help. Prayerful reading of scriptural texts that express God's love and fidelity, and of classic and recent works on confidence in God, will further assist this growth. Relevant podcasts, videos, and the wide variety of digital resources may also strengthen this process.

A saying has it that we are condemned to repeat what we do not know. As we grow in understanding, we progress toward freedom.

"Lord, in Your Mercy, Give Me the Gift of Prayer"

On June 7, 1925, a man walking through the streets of Dublin on his way to Sunday Mass collapsed and died.[14] At the hospital, he was identified as Matt Talbot, a sixty-nine-year-old worker in a timber yard. The instruments of penance found on his body first alerted viewers to his remarkable spiritual journey. Many attended his funeral on June 11, and six years later his cause of canonization was introduced. In 1975, Pope Paul VI declared him venerable, an official witness to his heroic virtue.

When Matt was twelve, he abandoned the little education he had received, equivalent to the first and a part of the second grade. He began work as a messenger boy for a firm of wine merchants and by the following year was a complete alcoholic. For the next fifteen years, he lived an alcoholic's life, spending his wages at the pubs and then begging, pawning, doing whatever he could to obtain the alcohol his body craved.

The moment of grace arrived when Matt was twenty-eight. One day, when he had no money, he stood outside the pub as his "friends" entered, hoping that someone would invite him in for a drink. None did, either because they did not care or because they pitied what he had become. He went home to his mother and told her that he was going to take the pledge, a promise to abstain from alcohol. She told him not to take it unless he meant it. Matt took the pledge for three months, then six, then for life. From that day, he never touched a drop of alcohol.

But it was a bitter struggle. Matt knew that he was too weak to be on the streets where the pubs awaited. He also knew that he needed a place where he would find strength. Matt began attending Mass in the early morning before work; when work finished, he returned again to church. He stayed for several Masses on Sundays. And this man, desperate for God's help, attempted to pray, while every cell in his body cried out for alcohol. Again and again he made this prayer: "Lord, in your mercy, give me the gift of prayer." Slowly prayer grew less painful. Gradually, it became easier and then began to draw him; finally it transformed him.

Matt sought the help of a priest who guided him in his efforts. This laborer in a timber yard, who had so little education, began reading spiritual books. Slowly, painstakingly, he read the Bible, the *Confessions* of St. Augustine, the writings of St. Francis de Sales, and others. During their lunch break one day, a fellow worker saw Matt reading the *Apologia pro Vita Sua* of John Henry Newman. When his companion asked if Matt found that reading difficult, Matt simply replied that the Lord helped him.

Matt knew that he could not hope to deny his body alcohol if he allowed it all else it desired. So he began a life of strict penance. He simplified his food. He observed the fasts of the Church and more. He slept on a wooden plank with a block of wood for a pillow. And he adopted the instruments of bodily penance that were found on him at his death.

His fellow workers knew Matt as a quiet man and good worker, ready to help others. His full story was discovered only after his death, and it remains an inspiration for thousands.[15]

This was a man who knew his weakest point. He built his whole spiritual life on strengthening that weakest point, *and it made him a saint.*

This is the hope and the gift of rule 14. Our individual points of greatest vulnerability may be, like Matt's, evident and dramatic. They may be more hidden, known only to us who experience their effects in our lives. To identify them and to strengthen them releases great energy and fosters great growth on the spiritual journey.

Rule 14: Some Examples

A final time, I offer personal examples from my journals. Such experiences teach me how rule 14 assists me on the spiritual journey.

"This Vulnerable Place in Your Heart"

At one point, a rich ministerial opportunity had arisen. After prayer and reflection, I concluded that it promised much fruit and that I should pursue it. As best I could see, this seemed of the Lord. My religious superior agreed and authorized conversations toward pursuing this option. The parties involved met, and all moved forward well.

Then . . . week after week, month after month, nothing happened. I grew angry—very angry. I found myself churning inside and saying interiorly, "If they can't get together and make this happen, then I won't help either. If they won't act, neither will I. I just won't do this new ministry. I have my work, and I'm busy enough already." At times, I felt this anger intensely.

Thank God for a wise and competent spiritual guide! I am grateful that these thoughts remained just thoughts and that I never expressed them to anyone before I met with Ed. When we spoke, I shared what I was feeling, and he said this:

> Yes, objectively things are moving slowly, and could have been done more quickly. But the intensity with which you feel this, and the anger, arise from your specific vulnerability, that sense in you that "I am alone. I can't count on others to notice and to help. I have to work hard to make things happen, because otherwise they won't." When you find yourself in a situation that touches this vulnerable space, you become angry—more angry than the situation merits. Those involved in these conversations have good will and want this to go forward. It is simply a time of great busyness for them.
>
> Bring this vulnerable place in your heart to the Lord. Let him love you right there. It may be that through this he is seeking deeper communion with you in that vulnerable place.
>
> Note the feel of the enemy in this, the diminishing of the joy you felt in this prospect, the worm of doubt, the hard "I won't," trying to stop you from a greater good.

You are not alone. You don't have to make it happen.
Let the Lord be with you in this place in your heart.

Ed's words helped me see my vulnerable point at work in what I was feeling and thinking—my angry feelings and angry thoughts about what, from various perspectives, was a reasonable delay. The persons involved were occupied with other matters at the time, and in fact, because of commitments already taken, I could not have begun this new ministry for some time yet. A few months later, everything resolved, and the new ministry began.

This was a learning experience for me, one of my clearest of rule 14. With Ed's help, I understood that much of my reaction arose not from the objective situation but from my vulnerability. This was priceless clarity. Without it, I might have sabotaged a fruitful path in ministry; with it, not only was the new opportunity preserved but I was also more ready to perceive this vulnerability at work in future situations.

"Come to Me, Let Me Do It"

This next occurred during a retreat. That day I met with the director and spoke about how I understood this weakest point. I shared my sense that, for me, it was this feeling that I am alone, isolated, and that I have to make things happen because otherwise no one else will. I described all the effort this involves and the tiredness I often feel after working hard—at times, too hard—on the project at hand.

The retreat director replied:

The truth is, "Come to me, all you who labor and are burdened, and I will give you rest" (Mt 11:28).[16]

The pattern is the activity that comes from the feeling of isolation, the burden, that you have to do it yourself, and that it has to be perfect. You absorbed this sense without fault, but it is a false perception. The truth is: Come to me, let me do it. That's the shift. You aren't alone. I'm here with you. I will do it with you, if you let me.

This is the doxology, "*Through* him, *with* him, *in* him." This is a way of life.

Let him reveal his love for you, let yourself experience it. When you are before the Blessed Sacrament, you know that you are not alone. That's the truth. Ask the Lord to draw you deeper, to bring healing.

The journey is inward, like deep-sea diving, to hear the still, small voice of his love.

This conversation, too, fostered clarity and hope.

"Ask the Lord to Carry It All"

At times, I experience this vulnerability, with the push to work too hard, when preparing for retreats and seminars. I love the communication of spiritual teaching, but the preparation could often feel burdensome—on the plane traveling to the event, early in the morning before the first talk, during the lunch hour, and so on. Only gradually, and with Ed's help, did I come to see my vulnerability at work in this: "*I* have to make it happen. No one else will. It has to be perfect, no matter how hard and tiring this preparation is." At times, the hours of preparation felt brutal—that was the word I used interiorly.

Ed said the following:

Do the preparation with the Lord—the beginning, middle, and end. When it's brutal, hard, turn to the Lord, and ask him to do it for you.

Before, you carried 100 percent of the effort: you had to do it, and it had to be perfect. Now you carry 45 percent. Ask the Lord to carry it all.

Prepare for this attack of the enemy now, before you have to teach again. Like the people in Ignatius's castle in rule 14, strengthen the weak point in the walls before the enemy even comes.

I have tried to do this since, and it makes a great difference. My love for the teaching remains, and I continue to prepare. What has changed is the way I prepare. The heaviness and sense of isolation have lessened. The preparation is no longer "brutal," and I no longer grow so tired.

Like the preceding rules, rule 14 is a great gift for the spiritual journey. It offers a final and decisive step toward freedom.

Conclusion

Setting Captives Free

*A tiny little Spaniard, a bit lame, with
joyful eyes*
—Description of St. Ignatius by a Witness

The writing of this book has proven a blessing in ways I could
not have foreseen. What the examen prayer is to the day—a
review of its spiritual experience with a view to following
God's leading more closely and avoiding the enemy's lies more
firmly in the future—writing this book has been for the thirty-
five years that I have worked with Ignatius's rules. Reviewing the hundreds of small sheets of paper I mentioned in the
introduction, each with its own insight, question, or reflection regarding the rules, and rereading the journals quoted in
this book, has renewed my awareness of the patterns of grace
(good spirit) and of discouraging lies (enemy) in my life. I find
myself newly conscious of both as I continue to experience
them. I hope this increased awareness will not fade!

Years ago, novelist Mary Roberts Rinehart wrote a little
book titled *Writing Is Work*.[1] The title is vivid, and she is
right: writing *is* work, most often very hard work. Much
work, and much reflection, has gone into the writing of
this book—gathering material over the years, recording my
experiences in journals, and then the assembling, sifting, and
writing of all of this into the present book. As Robert Frost

expressively notes, "No tears in the writer, no tears in the reader."[2]

Yet, in a way specific to this book, I have found the writing more a joy than a labor. To have the opportunity to share what I have learned and experienced regarding the rules since writing *The Discernment of Spirits*, and what, because of time constraints, I never have time to share when presenting the rules, has been welcome. I hope that readers have found it of value and that it has served to deepen their awareness of their own spiritual experiences.

One man, when we explored the rules, commented thoughtfully, "Ignatius is a realist." Yes, Ignatius is a realist. In his rules, he simply describes what we all experience. In them, he adds nothing to the spiritual life; he only—only!—helps us understand at last what we have long experienced and did not know how to name or understand. I believe that this is why people respond so warmly to these rules when they are well explained: Ignatius *reveals them to themselves*. What they have long experienced—the joy of spiritual consolation, the discouragement of spiritual desolation, and the enemy's various "wiles and persuasions"—now, finally, they understand. With that understanding comes freedom to respond in new ways, now with awareness of this experience, the ability to understand it, and the spiritual tools to take appropriate action.

Luis Gonçalves da Câmara, SJ, a companion of Ignatius, writes, "I remember one thing, that is, how many times I have noticed how the Father [Ignatius], in his whole way of proceeding, observes all the rules of the Exercises exactly, such that he seems first to have planted them in his soul, and from the acts of his soul, to have drawn those rules."[3] For Ignatius, these rules were a way of life. He invites us also to make them a way of life.

I have always thought it a special grace, intended by the
Holy Spirit and perhaps—I would say even probably—consciously intended by Ignatius, that the language of the rules
applies so readily to daily life. In a few places, the rules
explicitly refer to their original setting in the Spiritual Exercises: "And these rules are more proper for the first week [of
the Exercises]" (title statement); "we are tepid, slothful, or
negligent in our spiritual exercises" (rule 9); "the person who
is exercising himself in spiritual things" (rule 13).[4] In general, however, the language applies equally to daily life. Some
rules, in fact, appear explicitly to presume life outside the
Spiritual Exercises: "persons going from mortal sin to mortal
sin" (rule 1); "when one reveals them to one's good confessor
or to another spiritual person" (rule 13).

Certainly, when I present these rules to groups, all immediately feel that Ignatius is addressing them in their daily
lives. There, in everyday living, with all its spiritual ebb and
flow, and in the often unseen decisions that form the tapes-
try of our relationship with God, Ignatius wishes to bring
awareness, understanding, and the tools necessary to act. He
desires, as we have said so often, to set captives free to love
and serve the Lord.

When I conclude the presentation of the rules, I know
that at this point the participants appreciate the wisdom of
the rules and see the hope they bring. At the same time,
some, perhaps many, wonder how well they will be able
to apply them. And so I ask, "When Ignatius's eyes were
opened, how much were they opened?" Because we have
quoted this phrase so often in the presentation, all immediately reply, "A little." Then I add, "That 'little' was all God
needed to transform his life." That "little" opening of our
eyes, that imperfect but sincere effort we make to live with

new spiritual awareness: that is all God needs to transform our lives as well.

At this point, I quote a line from G. K. Chesterton. He takes the saying, "If a thing is worth doing, it is worth doing well," and reverses it: "If a thing is worth doing, it is worth doing badly."[5] Chesterton is right. If the best we can do is to live the discerning life imperfectly, with occasional lapses of awareness, struggles to understand, and failures to take the appropriate action—this will be true for all of us, including the author—*this daily effort is worth doing*. God's grace will unite with it, and we will rejoice to see the spiritual newness that enters our lives.

Ignatius wrote of himself, "For my part, I am convinced that I am nothing but obstacle, both before and after, and I find this a source of greater satisfaction and spiritual consolation in our Lord because I can thus attribute nothing to myself that has any appearance of good."[6] "Nothing but obstacle," and "I find this a source of greater satisfaction and spiritual consolation in our Lord," because he thus depends more fully on the One who loves him. We can do the same. Is it any wonder that Ignatius was described by one set free through his guidance as "a tiny little Spaniard, a bit lame, with joyful eyes"?[7]

In his commentary on the opening verse of Psalm 27, the bishop John the Serene (a lovely name) writes, "We should then in the fullest sense not only with our voice but also with our very soul cry out, *The Lord is my light and my salvation; whom shall I fear?* If he enlightens and saves me, whom shall I fear? Even though the dark shadows of evil suggestions crowd about, *the Lord is my light*. They can approach, but cannot prevail; they can lay siege to our hearts, but cannot conquer them. . . . *The Lord is my light*. For he is our strength; he gives himself to us and we give ourselves to him."[8]

When I present the rules, I conclude by quoting the last verse of John 16, verse 33. These are the final words of Jesus to his disciples before he goes to his passion. John 17 gives us his priestly prayer to the Father, and in John 18, the passion begins.

Jesus knows that his disciples' hearts are heavy. They do not fully understand all that he has said at the Last Supper, but they do know that, in some form, trials and separation from him lie ahead. And so Jesus says to them, "In the world you have tribulation"—and we do. He then continues, *"But be of good cheer, I have overcome the world."* [9]

This is the spirit in which we live the discerning life, with hope and, on a deep level, with confidence. Christ has overcome, and in him, the door to freedom opens for us as well. May that hope bless us daily on the spiritual journey.

Notes

In most cases, after a first full reference is given, a short reference—author or editor, short title, page number(s)—will be used for subsequent notes. The following short references will also be used:

Autobiography—This is found in Manuel Ruiz Jurado, SJ, ed., *San Ignacio de Loyola: Obras* (Madrid: Biblioteca de Autores Cristianos, 2013).

MHSI, vol. 76—This refers to material found in Ignacio Iparraguirre, SJ, ed., *Directoria Exercitiorum Spiritualium* (1540–1599) (Rome: Monumenta Historica Societatis Iesu, 1955).

MHSI, vol. 100—This refers to material found in José Calveras, SJ, and Candido de Dalmases, SJ, eds., *Sancti Ignatii de Loyola Exercitia Spiritualia* (Rome: Monumenta Historica Societatis Iesu, 1969).

Obras—This refers to material found in Ruiz Jurado, *San Ignacio de Loyola* as noted above.

Introduction

1. Timothy Gallagher, OMV, *The Discernment of Spirits: An Ignatian Guide to Everyday Living* (New York: Crossroad, 2005).

2. This book also allows me to share the insights I must omit for lack of time when teaching the rules.

3. Dorothy Day, *The Long Loneliness* (San Francisco: Harper & Row, 1952), 10.

4.   "The general rule . . . is to use *people* for large round numbers, and to use *persons* for small and precise numbers." James Kilpatrick, *The Writer's Art* (Kansas City: Andrews McMeel, 1988), 212. Since, however, Ignatius uses "persons" (*personas*) in his rules, I will likewise use "persons" rather than "people" in my commentary on his text.

Text of the Rules

Author's translation in *The Discernment of Spirits: An Ignatian Guide for Everyday Life* (New York: Crossroad, 2005), 7–10. In his *Spiritual Exercises*, Ignatius provides two sets of rules for the discernment of spirits. The fourteen rules given here are those of the first set—the topic of this book. For the second set, see Timothy Gallagher, OMV, *Spiritual Consolation: An Ignatian Guide for the Greater Discernment of Spirits* (New York: Crossroad, 2007). The numbers in parentheses are standard usage for citing paragraphs from the *Spiritual Exercises*. Thus, "(313)" indicates paragraph 313 in the *Spiritual Exercises*. Elsewhere in this book, these paragraphs will be given together with the abbreviation "*SpirEx*."

Prologue: Be Aware, Understand, Take Action

1.   *Autobiography*, para.1, in Manuel Ruiz Jurado, SJ, ed., *San Ignacio de Loyola: Obras* (Madrid: Biblioteca de Autores Cristianos, 2013), 28. Author's translation, as are the subsequent quotations from this text. If Ignatius was born in 1491, as is generally accepted, then his conversion took place at the age of thirty rather than twenty-six. See *Obras*, lxv–lxvii. See also James Broderick, SJ, *St. Ignatius of Loyola: The Pilgrim Years* (New York: Farrar, Straus and Cudahy, 1956), 25, n.1.

2.   José Ignacio Tellechea Idígoras, *Ignatius of Loyola: The Pilgrim Saint*, trans. Cornelius Buckley, SJ (Chicago: Loyola University Press, 1994), 69.

3.   Tellechea Idígoras, *Ignatius*, 70.

4. Tellechea Idígoras, *Ignatius*, 85–86. The biographer writes, "May Saint Ignatius . . . pardon us if we suspect that this desire for revenge, which was so tenacious and relentless, and that this will to murder, which was so determined and well planned, makes sense only in the context of a love affair, of an external triangle in which the woman this time was not an ethereal, inaccessible Dulcinea, the lady of his thoughts" (p. 86).

5. Tellechea Idígoras, *Ignatius*, 83.

6. "If we take Ignatius's words in their obvious sense, it was French and not Navarrese or Guipuzcoan soldiers who bore him on their shoulders to Loyola." Pedro de Leturia, SJ, trans. Aloysius Owen, SJ, *Iñigo de Loyola* (Syracuse, NY: Le Moyne College Press, 1949), 73.

7. *Obras*, 29; *Autobiography*, para. 2.

8. Quoted in Candido de Dalmases, SJ, *Ignatius of Loyola, Founder of the Jesuits: His Life and Work* (St. Louis, MO: Institute of Jesuit Sources, 1985), 42.

9. I discuss what follows systematically in *The Discernment of Spirits*, 11–15.

10. *Obras*, 30; *Autobiography*, para. 6.

11. *Obras*, 31, n. 7.

12. Pedro de Leturia, in his study of Ignatius during these years, suggests this identification: *Iñigo de Loyola*, 37, 59–60, 79–80. If, Candido de Dalmases writes, the woman was not an imagined person—a hypothesis de Dalmases considers probable—but truly existed, "the probabilities are greater that she was the sister of Charles V, Catalina [Catherine], whom Iñigo could have seen in Valladolid or Tordesillas." *Ignatius of Loyola*, 44. When I read Ignatius's autobiographical account, I find it hard to believe that the woman was only imaginary and not real. *Obras*, 30–31, n. 7, names Catherine as one of three principal hypotheses.

13. *Obras*, 31; *Autobiography*, para. 7.

14.   Ignacio Iparraguirre, SJ, *Historia de la práctica de los Ejercicios Espirituales de San Ignacio* (Rome: Institutum Historicum Societatis Jesu, 1946), I, 44.

15.   Iparraguirre, *Historia*, 1:44.

16.   *Obras*, 31; *Autobiography*, para. 7. More literally, the translation would read, "What would it be, if I did this that St. Francis did, and this that St. Dominic did?"

17.   *Obras*, 31; *Autobiography*, para. 7.

18.   *Obras*, 31, *Autobiography*, para. 8. The use of the third person in the *Autobiography* derives from the fact that it was written by Luis Gonçalves da Câmara, to whom Ignatius recounted these events.

19.   I have explored these three steps in *The Discernment of Spirits*, 16–25.

20.   In the *Autobiography*, referring to Ignatius's conversion experience on his convalescent bed, da Câmara comments, "This was the first experience he had of the things of God. Later, when he formed the Exercises, it was from here that he began to find light for what regarded the diversity of spirits." *Obras*, 31.

21.   See *SpirEx* 9. Author's translation from the original Spanish *Autograph*. All subsequent quotations from the *Spiritual Exercises*, unless noted otherwise, are also translated by the author. The *Autograph* is found in various publications and most authoritatively in MHSI, vol. 100, 141–417.

22.   See Gallagher, *Discernment*, 197, n. 12. We will return to this question in chapter 5.

23.   When Ignatius's eyes were opened, they were opened "a little." He did not become aware of, understand, and act in response to all his interior spiritual experience, but only to one thread within it: his different affective responses to two sets of thoughts regarding how he might live. That "little" was all God needed to transform entirely his life.

24.   In the *Confessions*, 10:27, Augustine turns to God and, considering his years of wandering, writes, "*Intus eras, et ego*

foris": "You were within, and I was without." See Gallagher, *Discernment*, 17–18.

25. Ian Kerr, ed., *John Henry Newman: Selected Sermons* (New York: Paulist Press, 1994), 82.

26. From her essay, "Reflections on the Right Use of School Studies with a View to the Love of God," in *Waiting for God* (New York: HarperCollins, 2001), 61–62.

27 Recorded conferences for Trappist novices in the 1960s. Merton uses "thoughts" here in the sense of Evagrius and Cassian: the different movements of the heart with their related thoughts.

28 For a number of these factors, see Jules Toner, SJ, *A Commentary on Saint Ignatius' Rules for the Discernment of Spirits* (St. Louis, MO: Institute of Jesuit Sources, 1982), 41–42, and Gallagher, *Discernment*, 18–20.

29. See Gallagher, *Discernment*, 19–20.

30. Blaise Pascal, *Pensées*, ed. Ch.-Marc des Granges (Paris: Éditions Garnier Frères, 1964), no. 139. Author's translation.

31. *Pensées*, no. 139. Emphasis added.

32. See Peter Kreeft, *Christianity for Modern Pagans: Pascal's Pensées* (San Francisco: Ignatius Press, 1993), 167.

33. See Simone Weil's lovely essay, "Reflections on the Right Use of School Studies with a View to the Love of God," which makes this point as it applies to the years of schooling. *Waiting for God*, 57–65.

34. The examen prayer develops the capacity for awareness of daily spiritual experience. See Timothy Gallagher, OMV, *The Examen Prayer: Ignatian Wisdom for Our Lives Today* (New York: Crossroad, 2006).

35. Revised Standard Version Catholic Edition (RSVCE), as also the title to this section, taken from the same verse.

36. For Ignatius's understanding of God as continually giving out of love, see Gallagher, *Examen*, 57–60.

37. See Gallagher, *Examen*, 58.

38. "Pastoral Constitution on the Church in the Modern World," *Gaudium et spes*, 22, in Austin Flannery, OP, ed., *Vatican Council II: The Conciliar and Post Conciliar Documents* (Boston: St. Paul Editions, 1980), 922.

39. Karl Stern, *The Pillar of Fire* (New York: Harcourt, Brace, & Co., 1951), 228.

Chapter 1 Sensual Delights and a Stinging Conscience

1. Gallagher, *Discernment*, 7. Emphasis added.

2. In rule 4, "all the contrary of the first rule" is changed to "all the contrary of the third rule"; and in rule 8, "as is said in the fourth rule" becomes "as is said in the sixth rule." Both changes accommodate the later addition of the two new rules— the present rules 1 and 2—at the beginning of the series. See MHSI, vol. 100, 376, 380.

3. See Daniel Gil, SJ, *Discernimiento según San Ignacio. Exposición y comentario práctico de las dos series de reglas de discernimiento de espíritus contenidas en el libro de los Ejercicios Espirituales de San Ignacio de Loyola (EE 313–336)* (Rome: Centrum Ignatianum Spiritualitatis, 1983), 142; Miguel Angel Fiorito, SJ, *Discernimiento y lucha: Comentario de las reglas de discernir de la primera semana del libro de los Ejercicios Espirituales de San Ignacio de Loyola* (Buenos Aires: Ediciones Diego de Torres, 1985), 138–39; Manuel Ruiz Jurado, *El discernimiento espiritual: Teología. Historia. Práctica* (Madrid: Biblioteca de Autores Cristianos, 1994), 224 n. 75; Santiago Arzubialde, SJ, *Ejercicios espirituales de S. Ignacio: Historia y análisis* (Bilbao, Spain: Mensajero, Sal Terrae, 2009), 706–7.

4. See Ruiz Jurado, *El discernimiento espiritual*, 224 n. 75.

5. I will examine the meaning of "enemy" below in this chapter. By it, I understand the *evil one* (personal angelic being), the *legacy of original sin* (concupiscence), and *harmful influences around us* in the world.

6. The term "good spirit" indicates "above all, *God* in his direct action in the human heart. For Ignatius, 'good spirit' also signifies the *angels*, who, by God's design, serve as instruments of his love for his children. The term expresses as well God's working in us through the gift of *grace* implanted in us at baptism: sanctifying grace, the theological, cardinal, and moral virtues, the gifts of the Holy Spirit, and individual charisms. 'Good spirit' includes the manifold *influences for good* that surround us in the world and in the communion of the saints." Gallagher, *Discernment*, 35. I have discussed the terms "enemy" and "good spirit" fully in the same work, pp. 32–35.

7. See the entirety of Francis Thompson's lovely poem "The Hound of Heaven," which describes precisely this troubling action of the good spirit in one far from God. For this poem, see http://www.bartleby.com/236/239.html.

8. See Gallagher, *Discernment*, 192–93 n. 6.

9. See also *SpirEx* 33, 35, 36, 37, 41, 52, 165, 349, 370.

10. These are pride, envy, anger, lust, sloth, gluttony, and avarice. Our tradition understands the capital sins not as sins committed by the person (actual sins) but as tendencies we experience, even after baptism, as a legacy of original sin and which must be resisted lest they move us to actual sin.

11. See also *SpirEx* 18, 244.

12. Gil (*Discernimiento*, 56, 97–98) and Thomas Green, SJ (*Weeds Among the Wheat. Discernment: Where Prayer & Action Meet* [Notre Dame, IN: Ave Maria Press, 1984], 100–101), see "mortal sin" in rule 1 as grave sin; Toner (*Commentary*, 50–51) and Fiorito (*Discernimiento y lucha*, 40–41) adopt the broader interpretation described. In "La primera regla de discernir de S. Ignacio, ¿a qué personas se refiere...?" *Stromata* 33 (1977): 341–60, Gil argues for the first interpretation and Fiorito for the second.

13. Toner utilizes the terms "progressing" and "regressing" Christians in *Commentary*, 50–51.

14. Toner, *Commentary*, 71.

15. "The expression 'leading them to imagine sensual delights and pleasures' signifies: fostering carnal images of impure pleasures, sensual delights, and worldly vanities. These are those representations of a principally sensual nature that a man experiences more sharply when he is far from God." Arzubialde, *Ejercicios*, 711, n. 14.

16. The persons Ignatius intends in both rules, Gil writes, appear to be "extreme cases": "La primera regla de discernir de S. Ignacio, ¿a qué personas se refiere...?" *Stromata* 33 (1977): 341. We may also note that when Ignatius uses "mortal sin" in the sense of capital sin, he clarifies this by supplying the adjective "seven" (*SpirEx* 238, 244, 245). When he speaks of "mortal sins" in *SpirEx* 18, Ignatius refers the reader to *SpirEx* 238; when he does so in 242, it is clear from 238 that he intends "mortal sins" in the sense of capital sins. In rule 1, Ignatius does not use the adjective "seven" but simply speaks of "mortal sin," as he generally does in when using the phrase in the sense of grave sin.

17. On this point, Johann Roothaan, SJ, comments: "Let us note, however, that our holy father [St. Ignatius] refers to two extremes, that is, to the sinner who is *completely lost* ["exemplum peccatoris *perditissimi*"] in the first rule, and to the *fervent* penitent ["*ferventis* poenitentis"] or just person in the second." Roothaan concludes, "Thus, when a person is *tepid*, great discretion is needed in applying these rules." *Exercitia spiritualia S. P. Ignatii de Loyola: Versio litteralis* (Ratisbonae, Romae, Neo Eboraci et Cincinnati: Ex Typis Friderici Pustet, 1911), 296–97, n. 2. Author's translation. Leo Bakker cites this passage in *Libertad y experiencia: Historia de la redacción de las reglas de discreción de espíritus en Ignacio de Loyola* (Bilbao, Spain: Mensajero, 1970), 66, n. 17.

18. Is permitting spiritual desolation the only way God works in progressing Christians who may slip in some aspect of their spiritual lives? If my read of rule 9 is correct—that this is the place, rather than rule 1, where Ignatius deals with lesser regressions—then Ignatius simply does not answer this question, as he does not answer many others we might raise.

19.   In my earlier translation, I adopted "through their rational power of moral judgment" from Toner, *Commentary*, 23. See Gallagher, *Discernment*, 193 n. 9.

20.   Servais Pinckaers, OP, *The Sources of Christian Ethics* (Washington, DC: Catholic University of America Press, 1995), 384.

21.   Joseph Ratzinger, "Conscience and Truth," a talk presented at the 10th Workshop for Bishops, February, 1991, Dallas, Texas: www.peped.org/philosophicalinvestigations/article-conscience -and-truth-pope-benedict-on-conscience.

22.   M. W. Hollenbach, "Synderesis," in the *New Catholic Encyclopedia*, www.encyclopedia.com/religion/encyclopedias -almanacs-transcripts-and-maps/synderesis. St. Thomas Aquinas explains, "As 'being' is the first thing that falls under the apprehension simply, so 'good' is the first thing that falls under the apprehension of the practical reason, which is directed to action: since every agent acts for an end under the aspect of good. Consequently the first principle of practical reason is one founded on the notion of good, that is to say, that 'good is that which all things seek after.' Hence this is the first precept of law, that 'good is to be done and pursued, and evil is to be avoided.'" *Summa Theologica*, q. 94, a. 2: http://www.ccel.org/ccel/aquinas /summa.FS_Q94_A2.html.

23.   See the preceding note.

24.   "As a natural or innate habit, synderesis is possessed in equal degree by all men. Just as human nature is equally shared by all, so the principles attained by synderesis are self-evident to all. Nevertheless, one man may have greater insight into their meaning than another, if he has greater capacity of intellect; this in turn will depend upon the state of refinement of his internal and external sense powers." M. W. Hollenbach, "Synderesis," www.encyclopedia.com/religion/encyclopedias-almanacs -transcripts-and-maps/synderesis.

25.   In the second set of rules (*SpirEx* 328–336), Ignatius also speaks of "the bad spirit" (*SpirEx* 333, 336) and "the bad angel" (*SpirEx* 331, 332, 335). In *SpirEx* 6–10, where Ignatius

explains the different uses of the two sets of rules, he employs both the word "enemy" (once) and the phrase "enemy of human nature" (twice), without using the phrase "bad spirit."

26. Ignatius to Sister Teresa Rejadell, 18 June 1536, in William Young, SJ, ed. and trans., *Letters of Saint Ignatius of Loyola* (Chicago: Loyola University Press, 1959), 18–24.

27. See Gallagher, *Discernment*, 33.

28. Among many others, for example, John of the Cross speaks of the soul's "three enemies—devil, world, and flesh." E. Allison Peers, trans., *Dark Night of the Soul* (Garden City, NY: Image, 1959), 1. 13. 11., p. 86.

29. C. S. Lewis writes, "There are two equal and opposite errors into which our race can fall about the devils. One is to disbelieve in their existence. The other is to believe, and to feel an excessive and unhealthy interest in them." *The Screwtape Letters* and *Screwtape Proposes a Toast* (New York: Harper-One, 2012), xlvii.

30. On "good spirit," see Gallagher, *Discernment*, 35. The term includes God, who works directly in the human heart, and all influences that are from God and that, if we receive them, lead toward him: the good angels, the supernatural organism imparted to us in baptism (indwelling of the Trinity, sanctifying grace, the supernatural virtues, the gifts of the Holy Spirit, individual charisms), and influences for good around us in the world.

31. Antonio Denis, SJ, *Commentarii in Exercitia Spiritualia S. P. N. Ignatii* (Malines, Belgium: L. & A. Godenne, 1893), 4:206. Author's translation.

32. Denis, *Commentarii*, 206–7. We may note that Ignatius's description of the enemy's tactic of "proposing apparent pleasures . . . leading them to imagine sensual delights and pleasures" is not a general commentary on human sexuality but only a description of how the *enemy* works in *one specific spiritual situation*, that of persons "going from mortal sin to mortal sin."

33. Denis obviously assumes that "mortal sin" here signifies grave sin.

34. Blaise Pascal, *Pensées*, 199, no. 498. Author's translation. Much of the fiction of Flannery O'Connor is an illustration of this stinging and biting action of the good spirit in those who have distanced themselves from God.

35. Hal M. Helms, ed., *The Confessions of St. Augustine* (Brewster, MA: Paraclete Press, 2010), 131.

36. Thomas Merton, *The Seven Storey Mountain* (New York: Harcourt, 1998), 123.

37. Merton, *Seven Storey Mountain*, 123.

38. Alessandro Manzoni, *The Betrothed: I promessi sposi*, trans. Archibald Colquhoun (New York: E. P. Dutton & Co., 1961), 304.

39. Manzoni, *The Betrothed*, 343.

40. Noel Morales, "Our God Is an Awesome God," in Patricia Proctor, OSC, *101 Inspirational Stories of the Priesthood* (Poor Clare Sisters, 2005), 30. The subsequent quotations are from this page.

Chapter 2 Placing and Removing Obstacles

1. Ignatius to Sister Teresa Rejadell, 18 June 1536, in Young, *Letters*, 21. Emphasis added.

2. *Autobiography*, para. 22. Author's translation.

3. Ignatius to Sister Teresa Rejadell. See Gallagher, *Discernment*, 40.

4. R. S. Pine-Coffin, trans., *Saint Augustine: Confessions* (Harmondsworth, UK: Penguin Books, 1961), 8. 11, pp. 175–76. See Gallagher, *Discernment*, 29.

5. Leo Tolstoy, *Resurrection*, trans. Rosemary Edmonds (London: Penguin, 1966), 141. See Gallagher, *Discernment*, 194, n. 6.

6. RSVCE.

7. E. Allison Peers, trans., *Ascent of Mount Carmel* (Garden City, NY: Image Books, 1958), I.12.6, p. 152.

8. *dándole ánimo y fuerzas* (*SpirEx* 7); *dar ánimo y fuerzas* (*SpirEx* 315).

9. Pine-Coffin, *Saint Augustine: Confessions*, 8.11, p. 176.

10. The following are the concluding words of this lovely message: "The Lord replied, my precious, precious child, I love you and I would never leave you! During your times of trial and suffering when you see only one set of footprints, it was then that I carried you." See www.wowzone.com/fprints.htm.

11. William Kernan, *My Road to Certainty* (New York: D. McKay Co., 1953), 63.

12. The examen is an Ignatian prayer in which persons review their spiritual experience of the day. See Timothy Gallagher, *The Examen Prayer: Ignatian Wisdom for Our Lives Today* (New York: Crossroad, 2006).

Chapter 3 When the Soul Is Inflamed with Love

1. Rules 6, 9, and 14. Otherwise Ignatius writes in the third person singular. In rule 3, Ignatius employs language similar to that of his Principle and Foundation (*SpirEx* 23): "its Creator and Lord," "created thing," "on the face of the earth," "the Creator," "his service and praise," "salvation of one's soul," "its Creator and Lord."

2. Ignatius to Sister Teresa Rejadell, 18 June 1536, in Young, *Letters*, 21.

3. Sampaio writes, "In order that a consolation be spiritual in the sense Ignatius intends there must be a *growth in the theological virtues in the person*." Alfredo Sampaio, SJ, *Los tiempos de elección en los directorios de ejercicios* (Bilbao, Spain: Mensajero/Sal Terrae, 2004), 120. Emphasis in the original. On the link between spiritual consolation and the theological virtues, see also p. 117 in the same work, and Ruiz Jurado, *El discernimiento espiritual*, 227–28, cited in Sampaio, 117.

4. See Gallagher, *Discernment*, 48–51. Paul VI, in *Gaudete in Domino* (*On Christian Joy*), 1975, calls these "the many human joys" that God has built into creation: http://w2.vatican.

va/content/paul-vi/en/apost_exhortations/documents/hf_p-vi_
exh_19750509_gaudete-in-domino.html.

5. See, for example, Toner, *Commentary*, 115–21.

6. Dorothy Day, *From Union Square to Rome* (Silver Spring, MD: Preservation of the Faith Press, 1942), 26–27.

7. See Gallagher, *Discernment*, 51.

8. See Gallagher, *Discernment*, 49–51, for a detailed example in St. Thérèse of this nonspiritual-spiritual sequence. A further note: the fact that, in God's providence, this sequence—healthy nonspiritual consolation as the space into which God infuses the grace of spiritual consolation—may readily occur indicates that a certain amount of healthy nonspiritual consolation is a blessing not only for our humanity on the natural level but also for the spiritual life.

9. *Catechism of the Catholic Church*, para. 2000 (Liguori, MO: Liguori Publications, n.d.), 484. Emphasis in the original. "Habitual grace" is otherwise known as "sanctifying grace."

10. Adolphe Tanquerey, *The Spiritual Life: A Treatise on Ascetical and Mystical Theology* (Rockford, IL: TAN, 2000), 66.

11. Joseph de Guibert, SJ, *The Theology of the Spiritual Life* (New York: Sheed & Ward, 1953), 111. "Actual grace derives its name from the Latin *actualis* (*ad actum*), for it is granted by God for the performance of salutary acts and is present and disappears with the action itself." See www.newadvent.org/cathen/06689x.htm.

12. Ruiz Jurado, *El discernimiento espiritual*, 228. Emphasis in the original.

13. *Official Directory of 1599*, in Martin Palmer, SJ, trans. and ed., *On Giving the Spiritual Exercises: The Early Jesuit Manuscript Directories and the Official Directory of 1599* (St. Louis, MO: Institute of Jesuit Sources, 1996), 330. Reginald Garrigou-Lagrange, OP, describes different forms of actual grace: "a light or interior illumination," "a grace of inspiration and attraction," a grace "that acts on the will and leads one to

love and to action," and "a grace of strength." *The Three Ages of the Interior Life* (San Bernardino, CA: CreateSpace Independent Publishing Platform, 2017), 1:90.

14. Sampaio, *Los tiempos*, 116, n. 61.

15. Quoted with author's permission.

16. Gil, *Discernimiento*, 127.

17. Spiritual consolation may be expressed physically in other ways as well. On one occasion, Ignatius recounts that "there came to him a great consolation and spiritual strength with such great joy that he began to shout as he walked through the fields and to speak with God." *Autobiography*, para. 79. Author's translation.

18. Pius of Pietrelcina to his spiritual director, in Gerardo di Flumeri, OFM.Cap., ed., *Letters: Correspondence with His Spiritual Directors* (San Giovanni Rotondo, Italy: Our Lady of Grace Capuchin Friary, 1984), 1:267. Emphasis added. St. Francis de Sales affirms that "the sadness of true contrition . . . is a sadness that in the height of its bitterness always produces the sweetness of incomparable consolation." Quoted in Garrigou-Lagrange, *Interior Life*, vol. 1:405.

19. A "provincial" in a religious congregation is the canonical superior of a geographical region of the congregation called a "province." In my case, this was the United States province of the Oblates of the Virgin Mary.

20. Ignatius describes this experience of spiritual consolation at greater length than any of the others. It may be that, in some measure, this reflects the prominent place that tears of spiritual consolation played in Ignatius's own life. See his *Spiritual Diary*, where tears recur frequently: *Obras*, 269–364, and Joseph Munitiz, SJ, and Philip Endean, SJ, trans., *Saint Ignatius of Loyola: Personal Writings* (London: Penguin Books, 1996), 65–109. See also Mary Purcell, *The First Jesuit* (Garden City, NY: Image, 1965), 187.

21. Gil, *Discernimiento*, 128.

22. Verse from New American Bible, Revised Edition (NABRE).

23. "This is an increase in the level ordinarily experienced and perceived by the person, who perceives this in his examens as something of note." Gil, *Discernimiento*, 129.

24. *Autograph Directory*: "gaudium spirituale" (no. 11) and "alegría espiritual" (no. 18). MHSI, vol. 76, 72, 76. The *Autograph Directory* is a brief set of notes that Ignatius composed for those who give the Spiritual Exercises. In his description of consolation, Polanco gives both adjectives together: "interius gaudium spirituale" ("interior spiritual joy"). MHSI, vol. 76, 311.

25. Evelyn Waugh, *Monsignor Ronald Knox* (Boston: Little, Brown and Company, 1959), 169–70. Emphasis added, except for "seen."

26. *Lectio divina* is a Latin term that "means 'divine reading', and describes a way of reading the Scriptures whereby we gradually let go of our own agenda and open ourselves to what God wants to say to us." See http://ocarm.org/en/content/lectio /what-lectio-divina, where a more complete description is also available.

27. *Autograph Directory*, 11, 18, in MHSI, vol. 76, 72, 76.

28. MHSI, vol. 76, 703. This *Directory* was promulgated in 1599, forty-three years after Ignatius's death. For further nuances in other directories, see Sampaio, *Los tiempos*, 109–11.

29. NABRE.

Chapter 4 Darkness of Soul

1. On the difference between spiritual and nonspiritual desolation, see Brigitte-Violaine Aufauvre, "Depression and Spiritual Desolation," *The Way* 42 (2003): 47–56.

2. *Life*, 11. 16. Translation in Augustin Poulain, SJ, *The Graces of Interior Prayer* (London: Routledge & Kegan Paul Limited, 1950), 140.

3. Ignatius makes this abundantly clear in his classic letter to Sister Teresa Rejadell, 18 June 1536. See Young, *Letters*,

21–22. In this letter, Ignatius teaches that *God gives* spiritual *consolation* and *permits* the *enemy* to bring spiritual *desolation*. God permits this for reasons of a love Ignatius will describe in rule 9. See also Gallagher, *Discernment*, 67.

4. Poulain, *Interior Prayer*, 201.

5. Thomas Dubay, SM, *The Fire Within* (San Francisco: Ignatius Press, 1989), 160–61.

6. For an excellent and detailed discussion of this difference, see Toner, *Commentary*, 271–82.

7. Brian Kolodiejchuk, MC, ed., *Mother Teresa: Come Be My Light* (New York: Image, 2007), 214.

8. Quoted in Kolodiejchuk, *Mother Teresa*, 382, n. 16.

9. Kolodiejchuk, the postulator of her cause of canonization, comments, "By all indications this was the case with Mother Teresa. With Father Neuner's help, she began to understand that her trial was a part of her mission, indeed an opportunity for greater charity, and thus she began to love her darkness." *Mother Teresa*, 382, n.16.

10. Flannery O'Connor to "A" (not further identified), 6 September 1955, in Sally Fitzgerald, ed., *The Habit of Being: Letters of Flannery O'Connor* (New York: Farrar, Straus and Giroux, 1988), 100.

11. Gerald May, *The Dark Night of the Soul: A Psychiatrist Explores the Connection Between Darkness and Spiritual Growth* (New York: HarperOne, 2004), 161, 176.

12. Marco R. della Cava, "Gibson personalizes 'Passion of the Christ,'" *USA TODAY*, February 20, 2004, p. 2A.

13. John Paul II to Father Felipe Sainz de Baranda, Apostolic Letter, *Master in the Faith*, December 14, 1990, no. 14. www.totus2us.com/vocation/saints/st-john-of-the-cross/jpii-apostolic-letter-master-in-faith/.

14. Published in the original languages in Ignacio Iparraguirre, SJ, ed., *Directoria Exercitiorum Spiritualium (1540–1599)* (Rome: Monumenta Historica Societatis Iesu, 1955), and in translation in Martin Palmer, SJ, *On Giving the Spiritual*

Exercises: The Early Jesuits Manuscript Directories and the Official Directory of 1599 (St. Louis, MO: Institute of Jesuit Sources, 1996).

15. MHSI, vol. 76, 72, para. [12].

16. *sequedad contra lágrimas.*

17. *ariditas*, MHSI, vol. 76, 311, para. 81.

18. *siccitas*, MHSI, vol. 76, 400, para. 85

19. *ariditas*, MHSI, vol. 76, 703, para. [193].

20. *siccitas affectus*, MHSI, vol. 76, 457, para. [76].

21. In these first three forms of dryness, I am following Thomas Green, SJ, in *Drinking from a Dry Well* (Notre Dame, IN: Ave Maria Press, 1991), 29–32. Green also includes John of the Cross's dark nights as forms of dryness (pp. 32–45).

22. Teresa of Avila, describing the time before her profound conversion, writes: "I began to return to prayer without, however, removing the occasions of sin. . . . My life was very hard, because in prayer I understood my faults more clearly." *Life*, 7. 17. Author's translation.

23. These forms of dryness, however, may become spaces into which the enemy brings the discouragement of spiritual desolation. As we have said, the enemy willingly works in our vulnerabilities.

24. We may add that spiritual consolation also presents itself as our spiritual identity, and in this case with truth: the good spirit is speaking, strengthening us in our identity as deeply, personally, warmly, and eternally loved sons and daughters of God.

25. Toner, for example, distinguishes between *essential* spiritual consolation (an enduring, underlying feeling of spiritual peace and joy rooted in living faith, hope, and love) and *contingent* spiritual consolation (the occasional intensifications of this essential spiritual consolation that are the subject of Ignatius's rule 3), and affirms that essential spiritual consolation coexists with spiritual desolation. *Commentary*, 90–93. Poulain distinguishes between *substantial* consolation ("consolation of the higher order . . . affecting the higher faculties, the intelligence,

and the will") and *sensible* consolation ("a consolation of the lower order, that which has its beginning in the *senses* or sensible faculties"). He writes, "Sensible desolation is the opposite of sensible consolation. It may co-exist with consolation of a higher kind, just as in the natural order we can feel sufferings in the body and joy in the soul at one and the same time." *Interior Prayer*, 405–6. Gil introduces no further distinctions and firmly states that spiritual consolation and spiritual desolation cannot be experienced together, but are experienced in mutually exclusive times. *Discernimiento*, 138. I share his position as the closest to Ignatius's text and the most usable in practice: that spiritual consolation and spiritual desolation, as Ignatius describes them in rules 3 and 4, are mutually exclusive.

26. "Some ask, on a theoretical level, whether or not it is possible to be *simultaneously in consolation and desolation*. Since they work with an understanding of these that does not sufficiently underscore their mutual contrariety, none can convince them that no, this is not possible. The reciprocal contrariety is not only on the level of conceptual representations but also of contrary *times* or the duration of the one experience and the other: consolation and desolation are mutually exclusive times. Because of this they cannot be simultaneous; but when, as is inevitable, the one follows the other, they relate to each other in such a way that we can recognize in these times a single spiritual experience." Gil, *Discernimiento*, 138. Emphasis in the original.

27. Gallagher, *Discernment*, 63.

28. For the examen prayer, see Gallagher, *The Examen Prayer: Ignatian Wisdom for Our Lives Today*. The examen prayer is a contemporary presentation of the classic examination of conscience that incorporates into it the discernment of spirits.

29. *Autograph Directory*, n. 12, MHSI, vol. 76, 72. Author's translation.

30. Toner, *Commentary*, 151. See Gallagher, *Discernment*, 91.

Chapter 5 In Time of Desolation Never Make a Change

1. Philosophy of Immanuel Kant. For Kant, the categorical imperative is "an objective, rationally necessary, and unconditional principle that we must always follow": https://plato.stanford.edu/entries/kant-moral/. I borrow the term without subscribing to his philosophy.

2. RSVCE, second edition.

3. Tellechea Idígoras, *Ignatius*, 225, 18.

4. See also, for example, Ignatius's *Autobiography*, paras. 26 and 27.

5. On this point, see Gil, *Discernimiento*, 167–68. Ignatius uses this same procedure—discernment by the distinction of times rather than by comparing the merits of different proposals—even more abundantly in the second set of rules. See second rules, rules 2, 3–6, 8, in *SpirEx* 330, 331–334, 336.

6. I discussed this question briefly in *Discernment*, 197, n. 12.

7. Gil, *Discernimiento*, 171. I consider Gil's treatment of this question (pp. 171–73) the best, and I essentially follow it in my own.

8. *como en la consolación nos guía y aconseja más el buen espíritu*. MHSI, vol. 100, 378. I have rendered the text with a contemporary orthography.

9. *dum fruitur quis consolatione illa, quam diximus, non proprio suo, sed boni spiritus instinctu regitur*. MHSI, vol. 100, 378. Here the "more" disappears, and the contrast is between the counsel of the person's own spirit (*non proprio suo*) and that of the good spirit (*sed boni spiritus instinctu*).

10. *sicut bonus spiritus dirigit nos magis* [later addition to the text] *ac docet in consolatione*. MHSI, vol. 100, 379. See Gil's discussion, *Discernimiento*, 171.

11. "As in consolation the good spirit guides and counsels us, so in desolation . . . " Louis Puhl, SJ, *The Spiritual Exercises*

of St. Ignatius: Based on Studies in the Language of the Auto-graph (Chicago: Loyola University Press, 1951), 143.

12. Toner, *Commentary*, 25, 152. The text on p. 152 reads: "For just as the good spirit leads and counsels us in [spiritual] consolation, so in [spiritual] desolation . . . " Brackets in the original.

13. Gallagher, *Discernment*, 8. See also the translation of rule 5 at the beginning of this book and chapter.

14. Gil, *Discernimiento*, 172.

15. MHSI, vol. 100, 378. Author's translation.

16. This holds true throughout the first set of rules that is the subject of this book. In this first set of rules, Ignatius explores a first (and more common) spiritual situation in which the enemy attempts to harm those who love the Lord through *spiritual desolation*. In his second set of rules, Ignatius explores a later tactic of the enemy, adopted when persons have grown and now love God with great generosity. At this point, the enemy may also bring *spiritual consolation,* but a deceptive spiritual conso-lation, intended to lead the person away from God's will. I have discussed these rules in detail in *Spiritual Consolation: An Igna-tian Guide for the Greater Discernment of Spirits* (New York: Crossroad, 2007).

17. See Gil, *Discernimiento*, 172, from whom I adapt this example.

18. Fiorito opts for this interpretation: *Discernimiento y lucha*, 151–53.

19. J. R. R. Tolkien, *The Fellowship of the Ring,* part 1 of *The Lord of the Rings* (New York: Ballantine Books, 1986), 488.

20. "I should not consider spiritual changes," writes Toner, "until I am again in spiritual consolation or at least in a time of spiritual calm." *Commentary*, 153.

21. Toner, *Commentary*, 155.

Chapter 6 Spiritual Means for a Spiritual Struggle

1. In each case, Ignatius renders this pairing explicit in the text: "the method is contrary to that in the first rule" (rule 2); "I call desolation all the contrary of the third rule" (rule 4); "although in desolation we should not change our first proposals" (rule 6).

2. NABRE.

3. RSVCE.

4. See *Discernment*, 86, where I discuss this.

5. Janet Ruffing, RSM, ed. and trans., *Elisabeth Leseur: Selected Writings* (New York: Paulist Press, 2005), 272.

6. See Gallagher, *Discernment*, 197, n. 2, for different interpretations of Ignatius's elliptic "prayer, meditation" in rule 6.

7. RSVCE.

8. See Timothy Gallagher, *Praying the Liturgy of the Hours: A Personal Journey* (New York: Crossroad, 2014), 43–46.

9. Ruffing, *Elisabeth Leseur*, 140.

10. MHSI, vol. 76, 479, para. [35]. Emphasis added.

11. RSVCE.

12. David Brakke, trans., *Evagrius of Pontus—Talking Back: A Monastic Handbook for Combating Demons* (Collegeville, MN: Liturgical Press, 2009).

13. Brakke, *Evagrius: Talking Back*, 99. From the New Revised Standard Version Bible, as are the subsequent quotations from *Talking Back*.

14. Brakke, *Evagrius, Talking Back*, 116.

15. Brakke, *Evagrius, Talking Back*, 138.

16. RSVCE.

17. "It is important to repeat that Ignatius is speaking of *spiritual* desolation here, as described in the fourth rule. He is not addressing situations of nonspiritual desolation as, for example, intense psychological stress or the various psychological disorders. Such afflictions exceed the limits of discernment of spirits and require other solutions, including professional help."

Gallagher, *Discernment*, 197–98, n. 4. To attempt to examine deep pools of psychological pain without professional help is unwise.

18. See Gallagher, *Examen*, 160–61. One woman says, "Without the examen, I would be just *reacting* and not *responding* throughout the day." *Examen*, 161.

19. Gallagher, *The Examen Prayer: Ignatian Wisdom for Our Lives Today* (New York: Crossroad, 2006).

20. David Townsend, *The Examen Re-Examined* (Rome: Centrum Ignatianum Spiritualitatis, 1987), 54.

21. Francis Bacon, *Of Studies*, www.authorama.com/essays -of-francis-bacon-50.html.

22. See Gallagher, *Examen*, 132–35. "Will all who pray the examen find such spiritual journaling helpful? Once again no single answer can be given. Here too the answer will vary according to the individuals who pray the examen. Certainly, given the experience of so many and given the witness of the tradition, the question is worth our consideration." *Examen*, 134–35.

Chapter 7 When You Think that You Can't, Know that You Can

1. Note the title of the following: Mary Margaret Funk, *Thoughts Matter: The Practice of the Spiritual Life* (New York: Continuum, 1998).

2. See Gil, *Discernimiento*, 188, 219–20.

3. See, for example, http://www.flashcardmachine.com/the-examen.html, http://www.livingchurch.org/suffering-christian -life, and http://sfxcityofgod.org/doc/Discerment_of_Spirits_Part _I.pdf.

4. Achille Gagliardi, SJ, *Sti. Ignatii de discretione spirituum regulae explanatae* (Naples, 1851). The work was published posthumously. Edward Flajole, SJ, in an unpublished manuscript, translated this work into English with an introduction: Achille Gagliardi, SJ, *The Discernment of Spirits: A*

Commentary on the Rules of St. Ignatius of Loyola for the Discernment of Spirits, typescript, 1969.

5. Gagliardi, *Sti. Ignatii*, 74. Author's translation.

6. "Certainly, there are situations of *nonspiritual* desolation that surpass our physical and emotional energies and that we cannot face and should not try to face by dogged resistance alone. If our physical or emotional resources are depleted and we are overly tired or experience depression, the primary need is for wise measures to replenish those resources. Having done so, we will the more effectively face the situation at hand. Ignatius, however, is not speaking here of nonspiritual but specifically of *spiritual* desolation." Gallagher, *Discernment*, 101.

7. W. H. Gardner, ed., *Gerard Manley Hopkins: Poems and Prose* (Harmondsworth, UK: Penguin Books, 1981), 60. Emphasis in the original.

8. NABRE.

Chapter 8 "Let Him Think that He Will Soon Be Consoled"

1. See Gil, *Discernimiento*, 194.

2. "Patience, says St. Thomas, is a virtue attached to the virtue of fortitude, which hinders a man from departing from right reason illumined by faith by yielding to difficulties and to sadness. It makes him bear the evils of life with equanimity of soul, says St. Augustine, without allowing himself to be troubled by vexations." Garrigou-Lagrange, *The Three Ages of the Interior Life* (London: Catholic Way Publishing, 2014), 2:122.

3. Gagliardi, *Sti. Ignatii*, 71. Author's translation.

4. Maisie Ward, *Caryll Houselander: That Divine Eccentric* (Westminster, MD: Christian Classics, 1962), 93. Caryll Houselander (1901–1954) was an English Catholic spiritual writer and poet.

5. Walter Elliot, ed. and trans., *The Sermons and Conferences of John Tauler* (Washington, DC: Apostolic Mission House, 1910), 273.

6. J. R. R. Tolkien, *The Return of the King*, part 3 of *The Lord of the Rings* (New York: Ballantine Books, 1984), 259.

7. In *SpirEx* 7, Ignatius counsels something similar to those who give the Spiritual Exercises. If the retreatant is "desolate and tempted," the director is not to be harsh with him but gentle, "helping him to prepare and dispose himself for the coming consolation."

8. C. S. Lewis, *The Screwtape Letters* (New York: Macmillan Company, 1959), 44.

9. Lewis, *Screwtape Letters*, 44.

10. Ignatius, in fact, expresses concern when one making the Spiritual Exercises does not experience consolations or desolations (*SpirEx* 6).

11. *Autobiography*, para. 21. Author's translation.

12. Madeleine L'Engle, *Two-Part Invention: The Story of a Marriage* (New York: Farrar, Straus and Giroux, 1989), 100.

13. Green, *Weeds Among the Wheat*, 125.

14. We will address this issue—why God permits spiritual desolation—in more detail in the next chapter when we discuss rule 9.

Chapter 9 "It Is Better for You that I Go"

1. Gallagher, *Discernment*, 113–14. Biblical quotation from NABRE. In this, I am following Toner who links John 16:7 with rule 9 in *Commentary*, 183.

2. NABRE.

3. In terms of Aristotle's four kinds of causes—material, formal, efficient, and final—"cause" in rule 9 signifies the final cause (purpose) God intends in allowing the spiritual desolation.

4. Gil, *Discernimiento*, 201.

5. See *Discernment*, 118–19, where I cite this text from Ignatius's *Spiritual Diary*.

6. Ignatius to Don John de Vega, 31 May 1550, in Young, *Letters*, 217.

7. *La segunda, por probarnos para quánto somos, y en quánto nos alargamos en su servicio y alabanza, sin tanto estipendio de consolaciones y crescidas gracias.*

8. John Rotelle, ed., and Edmund Hell, trans., *The Works of St. Augustine—A Translation for the 21st Century: Sermons,* vol. 1 (Hyde Park, NY: New City Press, 1990), sermon 2.

9. *Interior Castle,* 3, 1, 9. Translation in Marcelle Auclair, *Teresa of Avila* (New York: Image Books, 1959), 164.

10. Cited in Sampaio, *Los tiempos,* 116–17, n. 62. Author's translation.

11. Ignatius to Magdalene Angelica Domenech, 12 January 1554, in Young, *Letters,* 318–19.

12. Commentary on Psalm 60, in *The Liturgy of the Hours* (New York: Catholic Book Publishing Co., 1976), 2:87.

13. Cited in St. Alphonsus de Liguori, *The Practice of the Love of Jesus Christ* (Barnhart, MO: Liguori, 1999), 46. Reference given as *Life,* chapter 11. Alphonsus has either mistaken the place in Teresa's writings or he (or his source) may be loosely citing *Life* 11. 5 *(¡Y bienaventurados trabajos, que aun acá en la vida tan sobradamente se pagan!)* or 11. 11 *(He visto claro que no deja Dios* [any one of these trials] *sin gran premio, aun en esta vida.).*

14. Edmond Murphy, SJ, and Martin Palmer, SJ, trans., *The Spiritual Writings of Pierre Favre* (St. Louis, MO: Institute of Jesuit Sources, 1996), 12.

15. John Wickham, SJ, counsels spiritual directors, "Teach the pray-er to take the desolate condition as *a time of trial and testing* when it is necessary to resist and struggle against the powers of evil. It is important to accept this summons to spiritual warfare and not to run away from it." *Prayer Companions' Handbook* (Montreal: Ignatian Centre Publications, 1991), 85. Thomas Green, SJ, comments on rule 9, the second reason, "Ignatius . . . says that the Lord also permits desolation in order to test our love. I think the point of this 'testing' is to purify, the way steel is tested by fire. Committed souls learn to love much

more deeply in the hard times. In the marriage ceremony the spouses promise fidelity 'for better or worse.' In the better, they learn the joy of loving; but in the worse, in desolation, they learn to love unselfishly. I think it is in that sense that our love is tested in the 'worse' of desolation, like steel by fire. All the impurities of selfishness, timidity, and so on are burned out of it, and our love becomes very strong." *A Vacation with the Lord* (Notre Dame, IN: Ave Maria Press, 1986), 91.

16. Ignatius employs the adjective "spiritual" three times in the text of rule 9 when referring to consolation.

17. Rules 1, 5, 6, 8, 10, and 11.

18. See Gallagher, *Discernment*, 122.

19. MHSI, vol. 100, 382.

20. I owe this summary of rule 9 to Father Scott Traynor.

Chapter 10 "One Who Is in Consolation"

1. In *The Dark Night*, 1, 6. See Kieran Kavanaugh, OCD, and Otilio Rodriguez, OCD, trans., *The Collected Works of Saint John of the Cross* (Washington, DC: ICS Publications, 1991), 371–73.

2. Ignatius to Francis Borgia, 20 September 1548, in Young, *Letters*, 181.

3. Ignatius to Francis Borgia, 20 September 1548, in Young, *Letters*, 181.

4. Gagliardi comments, "Ignatius does not say that when consolations come we are to reject them; on the contrary, he supposes that they are to be retained and accepted, since they are sent by God and can accomplish many good things. We need such help in as much as we are powerless and weak." *Sti. Ignatii*, 63. Of the dynamic of rule 10, Gil writes, "Without surrendering the consolation—since, in this case, to discern is to receive it—the one consoled looks to the future, to *this* future that will be the contrary of the present experience." *Discernimiento*, 216. Author's translations.

5. Poulain, *Interior Prayer*, 405–6.

6. Gallagher, *Discernment,* 128.

7. Marion Habig, ed., *St. Francis of Assisi: Writings and Early Biographies* (Quincy, IL: Franciscan Press, 1991), Major Life, 2, p. 706.

8. Gagliardi, *Sti. Ignatii,* 65. Author's translation.

9. Gallagher, *Discernment,* 133–36.

Chapter 11 Portrait of the Mature Person of Discernment

1. Toner notes, "Besides enlightening us on how to prepare for desolation which will come, Rule I:11 [rule 11], when read in coherence with rule I:9 [rule 9] on God's reasons for permitting spiritual desolation, is advising us about how to eliminate the third of those reasons. In so doing, it goes beyond preparing us for desolation to preventing the desolation that would come if it were needed for that reason." *Commentary,* 196.

2. One Catholic psychologist described this as "bringing reason to emotion."

3. *humiliarse y bajarse* ("humble himself and lower himself"), another of Ignatius's doublets. The doublet calls one in consolation to remain humble, poor in spirit (Mt 5:3; 11:25), grateful, and receptive, without self-satisfaction or pride on account of the gift given. For a similar doublet, see *SpirEx* 165: *así me* baje *y así me* humille ("I so lower and humble myself"). When the angel Gabriel comes to Mary, Ignatius writes, "She humbles herself [*humillándose*] and gives thanks to the Divine Majesty" (*SpirEx* 108). Gil comments, "There is no question of rejecting the consolation! On the contrary, since it is a *good* spiritual movement, it is to be received as a messenger of the Lord's will. There is only a question of containing our own thoughts of pride and vanity that can grow warm and make themselves felt in the warmth of the devotion." *Discernimiento,* 218. Author's translation, emphasis in the original.

4. St. Gregory the Great, *Moral Reflections on Job,* quoted in *The Liturgy of the Hours,* 3, 265.

5. Walter Hilton, *The Scale of Perfection*, book 1, chapter 6. See http://d.lib.rochester.edu/teams/text/bestul-hilton-the-scale-of -perfection-book-i. Author's translation from the fourteenth-century English. Walter Hilton was a fourteenth-century English Augustinian whose best-known work is *The Scale of Perfection*.

6. Thomas à Kempis, *The Imitation of Christ*, book 2, chapter 9, 4. See http://www.thelatinlibrary.com/kempis /kempis2.shtml. Author's translation.

7. Murphy and Palmer, *Pierre Favre*, 297.

Chapter 12 When the Enemy Weakens and Loses Heart

1. Gallagher, *Discernment*, 150–52.

2. Gallagher, *Discernment*, 151.

3. NABRE.

4. Robert Gregg, trans., *Athanasius: The Life of Antony and the Letter to Marcellinus* (Mahwah, NJ: Paulist Press, 1980), 35.

5. http://law2.umkc.edu/faculty/projects/ftrials/more /morebiography.html. I have removed the archaic "eth" from several words.

6. E. Allison Peers, trans. and ed., *The Life of Teresa of Avila* (New York: Image, 1960), 242.

7. Timothy Gallagher, OMV, ed., *Un'esperienza dello Spirito: Pio Bruno Lanteri. Il suo carisma nelle sue parole* (Cuneo, Italy: AGA, 1989), 70. Author's translation. Venerable Bruno (1759–1830) founded my religious community, the Oblates of the Virgin Mary. This page is from notes written shortly before priestly ordination. For the life of Venerable Bruno, see Timothy Gallagher, *Begin Again: The Life and Spiritual Legacy of Bruno Lanteri* (New York: Crossroad, 2013).

8. Toner, *Commentary*, 198–99.

9. If there is a snowball effect to the enemy's temptations, I believe there is also a spiral of grace when we take even small

steps to reject these temptations. Such small acts of courage open the path to greater steps of grace.

10. Book 1, chapter 13, 5: http://www.thelatinlibrary.com /kempis/kempis2.shtml. Author's translation.

11. These and the following quotations are from the NABRE.

12. Brakke, *Evagrius: Talking Back*, 4.

13. Evagrius writes, "For a monastic man is one who has departed from the sin that consists of deeds and action, while a monastic intellect is one who has departed from the sin that arises from the thoughts that are in our intellect and who at the time of prayer sees the light of the Holy Trinity." Brakke, *Evagrius: Talking Back*, 51.

14. *The Holy Rule of Our Most Holy Father Saint Benedict* (St. Meinrad, IN: Grail Publications, 1956), 13–16.

15. https://christdesert.org/prayer/rule-of-st-benedict /chapter-4-the-tools-for-good-works/.

16. Book 1, chapter 13, 5: http://www.thelatinlibrary.com /kempis/kempis2.shtml. Author's translation.

17. Simon Decloux, SJ, *The Spiritual Diary of St. Ignatius Loyola: Text and Commentary* (Rome: Centrum Ignatianum Spiritualitatis, 1990), 52.

18. Decloux, *Spiritual Diary*, 52.

19. de Liguori, *Pratica*, chapter 17, 9: http://www. sanpiodapietrelcina.org/pratica/capitolo17.htm. Author's translation.

20. http://www.ccel.org/ccel/therese/autobio.xxi.html.

21. See Ignatius's "see the persons, hear the words, and observe the actions" (*SpirEx* 106–108) in imaginative contemplation.

Chapter 13 "His Manifest Deceits Have Been Revealed"

1. *placeres aparentes* (rule 1), *falsas razones* (rule 2), and *vano enamorado* (rule 13).

2. Quoted in Candido de Dalmases, SJ, *Ignatius of Loyola, Founder of the Jesuits: His Life and Work* (St. Louis, MO: Institute of Jesuit Sources, 1985), 33. Juan Alfonso de Polanco, SJ, (1517–1576) was Ignatius's secretary from 1547 until Ignatius's death in 1556. See also Broderick, *Pilgrim Years*, 43–45.

3. Joseph O'Callaghan, trans., *The Autobiography of St. Ignatius Loyola with Related Documents* (New York: Harper Torchbooks, 1974), 21.

4. Ignatius's use of doublets is once again evident.

5. *el enemigo . . . trae sus* astucias y suasiones. Ignatius employs similar language in *SpirEx 7*: *las* astucias *del enemigo de natura humana*. Author's emphasis in both quotations.

6. Gallagher, *Discernment*, 163.

7. See Tellechea Idígoras, *Ignatius,* 186–87, 192–93, 198, 227, 435. Ignatius's reference to a confessor in the context of discernment of spirits, also suggests that this sacrament and the sharing it allows may be of great assistance in living the discerning life.

8. *SpirEx* 6, 7, 8, 9, and throughout the *Spiritual Exercises*.

9. When St. Thérèse of Lisieux, the evening before her vows, shared the burden of her heart with her novice mistress, she wrote that "my doubts left me completely *as soon as I finished speaking*." Emphasis added. Thérèse appears to say that her doubts left her as soon she shared her burden and even before the novice mistress said anything in reply, such that the act itself of sharing the burden openly with her competent spiritual person already resolved the difficulty. See Gallagher, *Discernment*, 166.

10. NABRE.

11. General Audience, 16 September 2009, http://w2.vatican.va/content/benedict-xvi/it/audiences/2009/documents/hf_ben-xvi_aud_20090916.html. Author's translation, with some wording from other English translations.

12. Apostolic Exhortation, *Evangelii Gaudium*, nos. 169–173: http://w2.vatican.va/content/francesco/en/apost_exhortations/documents/papa-francesco_esortazione-ap_20131124_evangelii-gaudium.html.

13. https://zenit.org/articlespapal-address-to-the-teresianum/.

14. Brett Brannen, *To Save a Thousand Souls: A Guide to Discerning a Vocation to Diocesan Priesthood* (Valdosta, GA: Vianney Vocations, 2009), 126–28. I have applied Father Brannen's advice more widely and not only to those discerning diocesan priesthood.

15. Fiorito, *Discernimiento*, 234–35. See Gallagher, *Discernment*, 203–4, n. 5.

16. This is the Nineteenth Annotation Retreat (*SpirEx* 19), also termed the Exercises in Daily Life. If one makes the full Spiritual Exercises in this fashion, the process normally involves several months with weekly meetings of direction.

17. See Gallagher, *Examen*, 38, 162.

18. One spiritual director says it in this way: "Do you want your meeting of spiritual direction to be really, really, really fruitful? Then talk about the thing you don't want to talk about."

19. Gallagher, *Begin Again: The Life and Spiritual Legacy of Bruno Lanteri* (New York: Crossroad, 2013).

Chapter 14 Freedom Where We Feel Least Free

1. See Gallagher, *Discernment*, 204, n. 3, and Gil, *Discernimiento*, 255.

2. Antonio Denis, SJ, writes, "*He* [the enemy] *examines every side*: he cannot see the soul itself and its thoughts; only God can enter and go out of the soul: therefore only God *can see the heart*. But from sins committed at an earlier time, or from the whole of our actions, this most subtle spirit, taught by great

experience, easily grasps which are the stronger and which the weaker parts of the soul." *Commentarii*, 282. Author's translation, emphasis in the original.

3. See Gil, *Discernimiento*, 223–24, and Gallagher, *Discernment*, 204, n. 4, which follows Gil.

4. Gil, *Discernimiento*, 223.

5. NABRE.

6. NABRE.

7. See Gallagher, *Discernment*, 182.

8. Suzanne Noffke, OP, trans., *Catherine of Siena: The Dialogue* (New York: Paulist Press, 1980), 25.

9. NABRE.

10. See the *Catechism of the Catholic Church*, 2558.

11. William Broderick, SJ, "First Week: Rules for Discernment" *The Way Supplement*, 48 (1983): 36–37. I would add that this examen is more than an "ordinary human means" alone; it is the examen *prayer*, involving human effort, yes, but fruitful as God's gift of grace, as is all prayer.

12. As mentioned earlier, I have described this prayer in *The Examen Prayer: Ignatian Wisdom for Our Lives Today*. See also http://www.discerninghearts.com/catholic-podcasts/?s=a+daily +prayer+of+discernment.

13. See George Aschenbrenner, SJ, "Consciousness Examen," *Review for Religious* 31 (1972): 18–19, and Gallagher, *Examen*, 180, n. 7.

14. For the life of Matt Talbot, see, among others, Joseph Glynn, *The Life of Matt Talbot* (Dublin: Catholic Truth Society, 1942); Albert Dolan, O.Carm., *We Knew Matt Talbot: Visits with His Relatives and Friends* (Englewood, NJ: Carmelite Press, 1948); Eddie Doherty, *Matt Talbot* (Milwaukee, WI: Bruce Publishing Company, 1953); Mary Purcell, *Matt Talbot and His Times* (Chicago: Franciscan Herald Press, 1977); Susan Wallace, FSP, *Matt Talbot: His Struggle, His Victory over Alcoholism* (Boston: Pauline Book & Media, 1992).

15. Among other websites, see http://www.matttalbot.ie/ and www.retreathouse.org/matt.html.

16. NABRE.

Conclusion

1. Mary Roberts Rinehart, *Writing Is Work* (Boston: Writer, Inc., 1939).

2. Interview with Richard Poirier, https://www.theparisreview.org/interviews/4678/robert-frost-the-art-of-poetry-no-2-robert-frost.

3. Benigno Hernández Montes, SJ, ed. and trans., *Recuerdos ignacianos: Memorial de Luis Gonçalves da Câmara* (Bilbao, Spain: Mensajero, Sal Terrae, 1991), 163. Author's translation.

4. These quotations from rules 9 and 13 easily transfer to our spiritual practices ("exercises") in daily life.

5. G. K. Chesterton, *The Paradoxes of Mr. Pond* (New York: Dodd, Mead & Company, 1937), 63.

6. Ignatius to Francis Borgia, end of 1545, in Young, *Letters*, 84.

7. Alexander Eaglestone and Joseph Munitiz, SJ, eds. and trans., *Remembering Iñigo: Glimpses of the Life of Saint Ignatius of Loyola. The Memoriale of Luís Gonçalves da Câmara* (Leominster, St. Louis, MO: Gracewing Publishing/The Institute of Jesuit Sources, 2004), 109.

8. In *The Liturgy of the Hours* (New York: Catholic Book Publishing Co., 1975), 3, 130. Emphasis in the original.

9. RSVCE. Emphasis added.

Index of Names

About the Author

Father Timothy M. Gallagher, O.M.V. (frtimothygallagher.org), was ordained in 1979 as a member of the Oblates of the Virgin Mary, a religious community dedicated to retreats and spiritual formation according to the Spiritual Exercises of Saint Ignatius. He obtained his doctorate in 1983 from the Gregorian University. He has taught (St. John's Seminary, Brighton, MA; Our Lady of Grace Seminary Residence, Boston, MA), assisted in formation work for twelve years, and served two terms as provincial in his own community. He has dedicated many years to an extensive ministry of retreats, spiritual direction, and teaching about the spiritual life. Fr. Gallagher is the author of nine books (Crossroad) on the spiritual teaching of Saint Ignatius of Loyola and the life of Venerable Bruno Lanteri, founder of the Oblates of the Virgin Mary. He currently holds the St. Ignatius Chair for Spiritual Formation at St. John Vianney Theological Seminary in Denver.

About the Publisher

The Crossroad Publishing Company publishes CROSSROAD and
HERDER & HERDER books. We offer a 200-year global family
tradition of books on spiritual living and religious thought. We
promote reading as a time-tested discipline for focus and understanding. We help authors shape, clarify, write, and effectively
promote their ideas. We select, edit, and distribute books. Our
expertise and passion is to provide wholesome spiritual nourish-
ment for heart, mind, and soul through the written word.

Complete List of Titles by
Timothy Gallagher, O.M.V.

Praying the Liturgy of the Hours
A Personal Journey
Paperback, 112 pages, ISBN 978-0-8245-2032-8
Also available in eBook format

Begin Again
The Life and Spiritual Legacy of Bruno Lanteri
Paperback, 358 pages, ISBN 978-0-8245-2579-8
Also available in eBook format

The Discernment of Spirits
An Ignatian Guide for Everyday Living
Paperback, 232 pages, ISBN 978-0-8245-2291-9
Also available in eBook format, audio CD, &
audio digital download

A Reader's Guide
The Discernment of Spirits
An Ignatian Guide for Everyday Living
Paperback, 104 pages, ISBN 978-0-8245-4985-5

Spiritual Consolation
An Ignatian Guide for Greater Discernment of Spirits
Paperback, 192 pages, ISBN 978-0-8245-2429-6
Also available in eBook format

The Crossroad Publishing Company

The Examen Prayer
Ignatian Wisdom for Our Lives Today
Paperback, 192 pages, ISBN 978-0-8245-2367-1
Also available in eBook format, audio CD, &
audio digital download

Discerning the Will of God
An Ignatian Guide to Christian Decision Making
Paperback, 172 pages, ISBN 978-0-8245-2489-0
Also available in eBook format, audio CD, &
audio digital download

A Handbook for Spiritual Directors
An Ignatian Guide for Accompanying Discernment of God's Will
Paperback, 144 pages, ISBN 978-0-8245-2171-4
Also available in eBook format

Meditation and Contemplation
An Ignatian Guide to Praying with Scripture
Paperback, 112 pages, ISBN 978-08245-2488-3
Also available in eBook format

An Ignatian Introduction to Prayer
Spiritual Reflections According to the Spiritual Exercises
Paperback, 96 pages, 978-0-8245-2487-6
Also available in eBook format

Support your local bookstore or order directly from the publisher
at www. crossroadpublishing.com
To request a catalog or inquire about quantity orders, e-mail
sales@ crossroadpublishing.com

The Crossroad Publishing Company